with lots of love to my

Daddy

on his birthday

Rachel Clare

xxx

# A HAWK AMONG SPARROWS

*

# A HAWK AMONG SPARROWS

## A Biography of Austin Farrer

*

*Philip Curtis*

First published in Great Britain 1985
SPCK
Holy Trinity Church
Marylebone Road
London NW1 4DU

**British Library Cataloguing in Publication Data**

Curtis, Philip
    A hawk among sparrows: a biography of Austin Farrer.
    1. Farrer, Austin
    I. Title
    230′. 092′4    BS501.F3
ISBN 0-281-04151-2

### Acknowledgements

Thanks are due to the following for permission to quote from copyright sources of Austin Farrer's work:
The trustees of the Farrer estate for extracts from *Faith and Speculation*, *Finite and Infinite* and *The Glass of Vision*.
*Saving Belief* © 1964 by Austin Farrer, extracts reprinted by permission of Hodder & Stoughton Limited.

Printed in Great Britain by
the Alden Press, Oxford.

# Contents

*

# Preface

*

When the trustees of the Farrer estate asked me to undertake a biography of Austin Farrer, I was surprised, honoured and conscious of my inadequacy. I was only able to attempt it by the help of some hundreds of correspondents who allowed me to draw on their knowledge with unfailing generosity. Miss Eleanor Farrer and the trustees allowed me access to the Farrer papers in the Bodleian Library at Oxford, so that I could read the letters which he wrote to his parents over thirty years, letters which threw much light on the growth of his thought and raised occasional problems about their chronological order. His sisters Eleanor and Joyce, and his brother-in-law, the late Arthur Newton, gave me generous help with details of his childhood and his family life. St Paul's School, the bursar of Balliol College, and Cuddesdon College gave me the names of his surviving contemporaries, many of whom answered my inquiries.

There are some debts which should be expressly acknowledged. Mr James Woolcock and the late Professor H. A. Hodges contributed much to the understanding of his Balliol years. Mr W. Pickles of Leeds gave me a vivid picture of Dewsbury in the thirties, as did those who answered my appeal in the *Yorkshire Post* for details of Farrer's years in Yorkshire.

For information about his years at St Edmund Hall I relied with gratitude on Dr A. B. Emden, and on his pupils of those years; in particular I owe much to the Reverend Gordon Phillips for his letters and for allowing me to use his unpublished Gresham Lectures. As for the years at Trinity my helpers were so many and so kind that it is invidious to mention names; yet I must acknowledge the help given by the Fellows who knew him and, among his pupils, Dr Michael Goulder and Mr Stephen Willink. Dr Goulder also helped my faltering steps by undertaking the chapter on Farrer's biblical work. For the later years at Trinity and for Keble I was greatly helped by Martyn Skinner

vii

who with great generosity wrote to me at length and made Farrer's letters to him available. For Keble I was greatly helped by Dr D. F. Shaw and by many of his pupils. Dr Edward Henderson, Professor Ray Hart and Professor Julian Hartt among others gave generously of their time in illuminating his visits to America.

My greatest debts however are to the Honourable Penelope Piercy and Canon Cheslyn Jones who for seven years have encouraged me, helped with their criticism and refused to let me go until they had a book they thought adequate. I am most grateful to them for all they did for me and taught me. I could only wish for their sake, and for the sake of the great and good man who taught me that I had done better. If my work encourages others to read him, that will be a happy reward.

Finally, as I have so often promised them, my gratitude to the young gentlemen of Yorkshire who for many years listened to me talk about Farrer, asked when the book would be published, promised to buy it, and forced me to take necessary exercise from time to time, those indeed, quibuscum Curas Ambulando Solvimus.

PHILIP CURTIS

# CHAPTER 1

## 'The Child is Father to the Man'

*

An Anglican bishop once remarked, 'I feared in his youth that Farrer would go the same way as Ronnie Knox, and end in mere cleverness.' Despite some injustice in his comment, there was a remarkable parallel in the lives and careers of these two men. The preface to Knox's *magnum opus*, *Enthusiasm*, reveals a sympathetic understanding of heresies which the younger Knox would have delighted to expose. The closing chapters of Waugh's biography of Knox show him drawing ever nearer to goodness in the difficult years after he left Oxford. Farrer, like Knox, was a scholar of Balliol and Fellow of Trinity, and, again like Knox, changed his religious allegiance; Knox an Anglican submitting to the Roman obedience, Farrer born a Baptist and becoming an Anglican. In Knox's case the change was followed by a life-long alienation from his father, E. A. Knox, Bishop of Manchester and a staunch evangelical. Though Farrer's father was grieved by his son's departure, their love never changed and they continued on the most affectionate terms. Farrer also, like Knox, was schooled by the trials of his later life to goodness, indeed to something near to sanctity.

A happy relationship with his father and mother laid down the lines on which Austin Farrer was to develop. Even as an undergraduate he found himself remarkable in being on good terms with his parents. His father, Augustus John Daniel Farrer, was born in Hampstead in 1872, one of the ten children of the Reverend William Farrer, who was for forty years secretary of New College, the Congregational theological college in London. William had married Hannah Maria Biddle, the daughter of a prosperous London lace merchant. At the time of their marriage William Farrer was forty-five and Hannah twenty-one. She was a woman of acute and unusual intellect who taught her own children until the age of twelve, grounding them in Greek, Latin, French, divinity, mathematics and history. She was one of the foundation members of Heath

1

Street Baptist Church in Hampstead in 1861, a church to which Austin's mother, Evangeline Archer, was later to belong and at which she met Augustus Farrer.

At the age of twelve, Augustus went to the City of London School, then under the rule of the distinguished classical scholar Dr E. A. Abbott. His school work was so promising that he was encouraged to try for Oxford entrance. Augustus felt, however, that he had no right to draw upon the slender resources of so large a family and instead chose University College, London. This was followed by four years, 1894–8, at Regent's Park College, the Baptist theological college then in London, where he won the first prize in the honours division following the examination of the *Senatus Academicus*. Regent's Park College awarded him the Davies Semitic Prize and a New Testament prize.

In 1898 Augustus began his life as a minister at Leamington Road Baptist Church, Blackburn. The following year, on 14 February 1899, he married Evangeline Archer. It was in Blackburn also that he became acquainted with the Marsdens, a family of Blackburn solicitors, the eldest of whom, John Marsden, became Augustus's life-long friend. During the 1920s, when Augustus's son Austin was at Balliol and his daughter Eleanor was at Girton College, Cambridge, the Marsdens gave each of them £100 annually.

At Regent's Park College Augustus had been on friendly terms with Doctor G.P. Gould, who became Principal in 1896. In 1900 he appointed Augustus to teach Church history and the history of religion. Soon afterwards, however, the Free Church colleges in London (Regent's Park, New College, and Hackney) began to work closely together and Farrer, to his great disappointment, had to give up the teaching of church history but continued to teach the history of religion and elementary Hebrew. In 1920 H. Wheeler Robinson became Principal of Regent's Park College and, though Farrer supported him loyally, he did not enjoy the close relationship he had had with Gould. Much later, when the college moved to Oxford and the Farrers were living in Rickmansworth, he put in two or three hours a week helping with the teaching of the New Testament and with the library, before retiring in 1940. He died in February 1954.

In the opinion of those who knew him, Augustus Farrer was

a most capable scholar, widely read, industrious and yet modest, shy and sensitive. Before the 1914–18 War he published one or two papers in the *Transactions of the Baptist Historical Society* and served on the committee of the Society up to 1941. He contributed an essay on the Mediaeval Waldenses and the Early English Baptists to a *Festschrift* for Wheeler Robinson. He also assisted W. F. Whitley in the preparation and editing of *The Doctrine of Grace*, one of the early results of the Lausanne Faith and Order Conference, and translated Lods' contribution to *Record and Revelation* (edited by Wheeler Robinson) from the French original. Some of his papers, which appeared in the *Baptist Quarterly* between 1924 and 1926, seem to have expressed the perplexity he felt when Austin became an Anglican: for example, 'The Place and Use of Scripture in Christian Experience', 'The Present Position of Church and Dissent' and 'Anglo-Catholicism: its Strength and Weakness'.

Augustus Farrer held strongly to the importance of adult baptism, but he was neither an emotional evangelical nor a biblical fundamentalist. He moved in circles which had early come to terms with biblical criticism. R. F. Horton's controversial book, *The Inspiration of the Bible*, which caused a great stir when published in 1888, was accepted in the circles in which the Farrer family moved. William Brock, minister of the Heath Street Baptist Church, with which the Farrers were associated, was certainly no conservative; nor was his successor, Newton Marshall, who was one of the most brilliant Baptist minds of his day. The year after Augustus's appointment as tutor at Regent's Park the distinguished scholar P. T. Forsyth became Principal of Hackney College. Such was the atmosphere, at once evangelical and rational, in which Augustus Farrer lived.

Evangeline Farrer was, like her husband, of Nonconformist stock, the daughter of a master goldsmith and brought up in the same Baptist Church at Hampstead. A lively and intelligent girl, she attended Camden High School, founded as a branch of the North London Collegiate School by the renowned Miss Buss. In five years she was three times top of her form with little effort, but then, with the unselfishness which marked all her life, she came home to look after her five brothers. In her day the devoted and self-effacing woman was admired and, though she was well able to understand her husband, she seldom expressed her opinions. Not long before her death, however, when congratulated on maintaining her own view before her husband, 'Ah,' she said, 'I can do that better now than I used to be able to.'

The Augustus Farrers at first lived at 28 Kempley Road, Hampstead, where their three children were born, Joyce on 31 March 1903, Austin on 11 October 1904, and Eleanor on 5 April 1907. In 1909, finding Hampstead too expensive, they moved to Pinner. The children went first to Oakfield, a Dame school run by an old lady, Miss Florrie Thompson, where, their parents said, they were taught like parrots. They then moved on to Woodrings School at Hatch End, a walk of more than a mile from their home. Just before 1914 the family moved to a rather dull district of terraced houses in 72 Grafton Road, Acton, in search of better schools. Eleanor and Joyce succeeded in entering one of the Haberdashers' schools, and Austin at the age of ten went to the Acton Collegiate School, a day preparatory school of forty to fifty pupils run by a Mr Coules and his formidable daughter. The school specialized in preparing boys for St Paul's School. So in 1917 Austin became one of the 153 foundation scholars at St Paul's. (There were 153 foundation scholars, a number which recalls the 153 fish in the miraculous draught of St John, chapter 21.)

With such parents, it was inevitable that books and the pursuit of learning would play a major part in Austin's life. His early experience of religious practice was to lay the foundation of his Christian life and, perhaps, at the same time, to make it likely that he would eventually change his Church allegiance. At the age of three he was being taken to services at the Heath Street Baptist Church (though mercifully removed before the sermon). After the move to Pinner the family at first attended the local Baptist Church, but, when internal dissension arose in the congregation, they went instead to Sunday services organized in the local Oddfellows Hall. At Acton, the family first attended Haven Green Baptist Church, Ealing, a mile and a half away, because Mr Farrer did not like the nearer Baptist churches. Here again they were unlucky: a split between the minister and his congregation on the grounds that he was too autocratic led to the Farrers' joining another splinter group which hired a cinema for Sunday services. Here various ministers were engaged to conduct evangelistic services; there

4

were religious solos with great popular appeal. Austin certainly disliked all this, and his parents decided to turn in the opposite direction when they left their front door and walked instead to West End Baptist Church, Hammersmith, where the minister was broad-minded and a fluent speaker. This church the Farrers attended until they left Acton.

Austin always hated religious dissension and splinter groups, which he had met among Baptists in his adolescence, and there is little doubt that this helped him on the way to Anglicanism. His mother wrote to him sadly in 1924, when he was contemplating the change, 'I know you have experienced so many splits'; and his father wrote, in a similar tone, 'I know our experience of church life has been unfortunate'. As Baptists the Farrers were in fact isolated; they belonged to the more liberal wing and were not sympathetic to the fundamentalists and followers of Spurgeon. Augustus Farrer's feelings for his colleagues at Regent's Park were cordial and admiring, but his children did not grow up as strict Baptists or among Baptist friends, and they did not go to Baptist Sunday schools.

More helpful, perhaps, was the Sunday afternoon class Mrs Farrer ran for her own children, four cousins and two girl neighbours. They sang hymns, were given simple instruction, and engaged in what would today be called projects. They made scrapbooks of coloured pictures pasted on pink linen; these were sent to a hospital. They were given 'trading pennies'; with these they would buy the materials to make something to sell in order to raise money to make something more expensive to sell and so on. The proceeds went to the Baptist Missionary Society.

The Farrer children had a group of aunts, two married, and the other five unmarried and living together in Hampstead in a house which Austin in a sermon described as the 'Aunt heap'. One of them, Muriel, the most intellectually gifted and experienced in worldly affairs, later became an Anglican and ended her life in the care of the Wantage Community. But the most remarkable of them was Ellen Margaret, born in the middle 1860s, the second child of the family. Though tiny in person, she was endowed with a great capacity for work and an *anima naturaliter Christiana*. At the age of nine she experienced a personal conversion and joined the Baptist Church in Heath Street, Hampstead. She was among the first women to take a medical degree and worked at the Royal Free Hospital for

Women. Nellie, as they called her, became a family heroine not only because of her work in India but also because during her time as a medical student she had a romantic attachment to a male colleague who wished to marry her but, considering herself pledged to the mission field and knowing him to be an agnostic, she refused him. In 1891 she went out to India under the auspices of the Baptist Zenana Mission and established herself with a colleague in Bhiwani on the edge of desert country some miles from Delhi. She lived at first in a native house and found great difficulty in persuading Indian women to trust her. To her earliest patients she was nurse as well as doctor, but her work gradually expanded to the scale of the fifty-bed hospital built in the early years of the century, still known as the Farrer hospital, where her courage, skill and gentleness were long remembered. She also did much for the emancipation of women in India. It was therefore a great occasion for the Farrers when Aunt Nellie came on furlough. She retired when she was seventy. The evidence of his sermons suggests that this aunt (sometimes referred to as Harriet) had a very deep influence on Austin.

When they grew too old for Mrs Farrer's Sunday classes, Joyce and Austin were put to study Stalker's *Life of Christ*, which as adolescents they found far from enjoyable. At this stage, however, Austin was still very close to his mother, a woman of deep faith. When things went wrong she went to her room to pray and emerged with a new and obvious radiance. It was a Christian, a literary and, for lack of wealth, a self-contained home, with much talk about religion and literature. One of Austin's sisters has preserved two characteristic remarks of his precocious childhood which sound very like the Austin of thirty years later. As a small boy, when he tried to understand what it meant to say that God was the Father of the Son, he deduced that this Fatherhood must be different from fatherhood in men (the germ of the future book, *Finite and Infinite*); and he once told his sister that the idea of the Saviour–Friend, put like that, made no personal appeal to him – as later in his Bampton Lectures he was to declare that the Germans might grit their teeth and say 'He speaketh to thee' – but for him it was once easier to say *Deus sive Natura* (not of course that he ever came near to being a Spinozistic pantheist).

All this sounds as if he were a rather priggish, clever little

body. Far from it. He had his moments of determined naughti-
ness, and pursued clarity and exactness with his remarkable
obstinacy. 'Don't spit at me, Hans,' he said at the Dame school
at Pinner to the little German boy sitting next to him. 'Don't tell
tales,' said the Dame. 'Well,' said Austin, 'he blew air and water
at me, and that's spitting.' He played with tin soldiers and
planned his battles with precision and cunning. He also played
with a yacht which his father had made for him, on the Round
Pond at Kensington. Like most small boys he hated to be shown
off in the drawing room at home and having to be polite to his
mother's women friends, and would even whisper, 'I don't
think she's got a nice face' about a visitor. He had a great
passion for getting things right. When in his arguments his
mother reached the end of her patience she would say that he
was not to speak till the kitchen clock had moved half an hour.
He would sit and squirm, his tongue going from cheek to cheek,
and when the time was over he would go on where he had left
off, to his mother's exasperation. She said once that it was
always useless to argue with him, since he could always find a
stronger argument. But he was not happy about such things
and he was relieved when she imposed her authority and told
him he must do as he was told. So in religion perhaps he wanted
a stronger discipline than could be found among Baptists, and
certainly a more formal and ceremonial kind of worship.

But there were not only books and talk. There were also the
summer holidays at the west end of Eastbourne with Beachy
Head in view, or in villages in the Chilterns. Once during their
teens they had a holiday in a house lent by an Anglican
deaconess at Rye. They liked the Vicar of Rye and attended his
services regularly. Mornings by the sea were spent paddling or
bathing. In the afternoon they walked on the Downs and
afterwards their father would read aloud a novel, usually of the
Victorian era, or perhaps Jane Austen or Walter Scott, but
never Thackeray. From Dickens he would choose episodes
connected with a character rather than read a whole book. He
read well, enjoying the humour, so that the family grew up
with a wide acquaintance with Victorian novels. While he read,
Joyce embroidered (all the children were encouraged to use
their hands) and Austin did pen and ink drawings of thatched
cottages. As the children grew older their father took them
sometimes on all-day walks. In his youth he had often walked

forty miles a day, but twenty-five miles was the limit for the children. On the way he would recite Wordsworth or sing German folk songs. He loved the 'Nature' of the Lake poets: 'Nature I loved and next to Nature Art'. In Austin, as he grew, a reversal gradually took place; art and humanity became more important to him than scenery. The only art that never appealed to Austin was music. He did not mind it, he said, before it developed a soul, but emotional and romantic music he disliked.

As a schoolboy at St Paul's Austin's interests began to widen. He persuaded his father to take the family to see *St Joan* when it was first produced, with Sybil Thorndike in the leading role. To spend money in this way was unprecedented; indeed attendance at the theatre was not countenanced in many Nonconformist families. After serious discussion Joyce had been allowed to go with a school party to *A Midsummer Night's Dream*. A kindly uncle had sometimes taken a large party to the pantomime. Conjuring shows and classical concerts were permitted, but until the *St Joan* expedition, modern acting was not. The early interest in Victorian novels continued. Austin later admitted Thomas Hardy to his Pantheon: Hardy was anathema to his father because of his infidelity, but Austin admired the Greek elements in Hardy's doom-laden plots. A love of poetry was to remain with him throughout his life and he would read Spenser aloud avidly in the evenings.

# CHAPTER 2

# The Hidden Years: St Paul's School 1917–23

*

For a boy of Austin Farrer's gifts it would be hard to imagine a better school than St Paul's, 'Founded in Honour of Christ Jesu in Puericia and of his Blessed Mother Mary. For 153 Boys of all Nations and Countries indifferently to be taught free in the same good literature both Laten and Greke' (John Colet, 1509). Since Austin was a day boy living at home, we have no letters to his parents, only the facts of his brilliant academic career and the comments of those who remember him after fifty years or more. References to his schooldays came seldom in his sermons, and for his inner growth we can only guess.

His problems while at school were to be personal rather than academic. He was sometimes confined to bed with nervous stomach trouble and would console himself by reading Green's *History of the English People.* Life was not easy for a clever boy who disliked games. The only forms of physical exercise he really cared for were punting and cross-country running; of the former he became an elegant exponent at Oxford. On one occasion, however, a trace of the old Adam was revealed when Austin hired an organ grinder to play outside one of the form-rooms, ensuring that when the form-master flung up the window, the blind would fall on his neck.

By 1920 he was safely established in the Eighth Form,[1] with his education running on the established classical lines. Divinity was taught by the High Master, A. E. Hillard, who, with Cecil Botting, was to nurture generations of classicists. There was English too, poetry, to be learned for the first period each day. His father at this time suggested to the Surmaster, Wainwright, that for safety's sake Austin should apply to London University, but he was reassured. 'I have had many boys through my hands,' Wainwright said, 'and he is good.' In 1922 Austin was awarded the top classical scholarship at Balliol, at this time almost a Pauline prerogative, but in view of his comparative youth he stayed at school for another year as

9

Captain of the School. He found this task difficult with his natural shyness and his lack of athletic distinction, but carried it off with dignity and was regarded with much affection.

Looking back, Austin remembered little of school life apart from his ambition, fed by the tradition of academic success at St Paul's. The 153 foundation scholars were made up of Junior and Senior Scholars; Junior Scholars had to have their scholarships confirmed before they reached the age of seventeen. Farrer came first in the examination for the Senior Scholarship, a prelude of things to come.

The school day began with Latin prayers in the hall, one prayer for each day of the week, composed by Erasmus for his friend John Colet, Dean of St Paul's and the school's founder. These took place in the hall, a vast room with sun-illuminated tall windows full of the armorials of famous old Paulines. The prayers were led by the Captain of the School. On entry to the school each boy was given a copy of the *Preces*, which contained the prayers, some Latin hymns, Erasmus' *Carmina de puero Iesu* and the Prayer Book Catechism in Latin and Greek. The High Master himself gave a course of instruction on it in a new boy's first term. The little book, beautifully bound in black leather with an engraving of Dean Colet, was usually prized and kept at home.

There were three school periods in the day – but what periods! – and fifteen minutes in the tuck shop. The second period lasted from about 11.15 a.m. to 1.00 p.m. and was followed by lunch in the dining room. Till 3.00 p.m. there were compulsory games – Rugby football in winter, cricket in summer, with boxing, fives, fencing and swimming as alternatives by special permission. Wednesday afternoon was a half day for games – played at school by the élite, and at Wormwood Scrubs, near the prison, by the less expert. The third period of school went on from 3.00 to 4.45 p.m., followed by the final Latin prayers of the day. Then home, unless there were voluntary society meetings, and 'prep', which for a conscientious day boy could take up to three or more hours. At St Paul's, Saturdays were free.

Under Hillard the school remained largely classical, though there were also science, engineering, mathematics and army specialists. There were two groups of Paulines: those who hoped to go to the university, preferably to Oxford or Cambridge (twenty open scholarships a year was a good average) and those who took the London Matriculation or the School Certificate. Art and music were distinctly fringe activities. It was possible for a boy such as Austin, going rapidly up the classical side, to spend three years in the classical Lower, Middle and Upper Eighth, having shed mathematics, French, most of his English and all but ancient history at a reasonable level, and never having done any science. The weekend essays, however, and the learning of English poetry for daily repetition would make this a less narrow education than it sounds.

Austin went to St Paul's in 1917, still under the shadow of the war. Boys passed quickly from the lists of school to the lists of those killed, missing and wounded, but after his first year this shadow was over. The masters who taught him were mostly men long established and included some notable eccentrics: Digby de la Motte, for example, who wore morning dress, a white carnation in his buttonhole and lived in a Mayfair mews. For classics there was the formidable language teaching of Leslie Matthews and of Cecil Botting, for whom Austin had a great regard. The teaching of divinity, at least in the Eighth, was in the hands of the High Master, who taught the New Testament with the aid of Lightfoot's commentaries on the Pauline epistles. The emphasis was on the text, the characteristics of New Testament Greek and on translation, but not on the theological meaning. However, there were confirmation classes, with instruction in the Catechism by one of the clerical members of the staff and a series of talks from the High Master. Confirmation took place in St Paul's Cathedral, preceded by a solemn procession of the OTC. Probably the most enthusiastic expression of Christianity at St Paul's was the 'Pi-squash', somewhat on the lines of the modern Scripture Union, but with its fundamentalist tendency this was not congenial to Austin and he took no part in it.

Home life and school could be kept in separate compartments. A boy might arrive at school in the morning by bus, bicycle or Underground, work agreeably at class work and games, and return home to an entirely separate world. Austin was saved from this by his interest in the debates in the Union Society and by his final elevation to be Head of the School. For him the great advantage of St Paul's (like Balliol afterwards) was that it was a cosmopolitan school; there were Belgian

11

refugees from the Great War, Russians from the Revolution, Jews, Indians, and even a Siamese prince. This must have broadened the perspective of the shy clever boy from a Baptist home in Acton.

As he rose to be Captain of the School Austin was in distinguished company, the middle one of three Paulines who in three successive years won the first Balliol Scholarship (G. G. L. Syers in 1921, A. M. Farrer in 1922, A. D. Farrell in 1923). A 'club' team for which he played included a future Archbishop of West Africa and the future Bishop C. K. Sansbury.

Of Austin's literary abilities one of his contemporaries writes,

His prose and verse compositions put many of us to shame. His knowledge of English literature was remarkable and his essays showed the brilliance of style and erudition that were to mark his later writings, particularly the Bampton lectures and his sermons in college chapel. Not infrequently the form master appealed to Austin if some point arose about which he was not sure and as often as not Austin would provide what was needed.[2]

It is related that when the philosopher J. L. Austin complained that the Latin prose set in a scholarship examination was too difficult, containing such phrases as 'the extra $2\frac{1}{2}$ per cent would have made all the difference', Austin was able to produce an idiomatic rendering off the cuff.

He was then, as he often seemed to be in Oxford later, shy and reserved. He found it no easy task to be Captain of the School, but his friends admired the way in which he rose to the occasion. In virtue of his status as Captain, though he was no athlete, he was promoted to play in the third Rugby XV. He had at least the advantages in Dr Hillard's eyes of being a member of the Classical Eighth, in the days when the Science Eighth was thought to be beyond the pale. But Austin found his High Master aloof and remote. He went about his duties firmly but quietly, rebuking small boys for wearing white socks, reading Latin prayers with distinction, and, as school captains must, taking part in the rough and tumble of school life including games.

He seems to have been admired rather than envied by his friends and contemporaries, who regarded themselves as more run-of-the-mill scholars, for he was a friendly person, without an atom of conceit, and quite unaware that there was anything exceptional in the quickness and clarity of his mind. Something in his make-up is recalled which set him apart – a quality for which neither 'innocence' nor 'transparency' is the right word, since he was not at all lacking in shrewdness or judgement; 'translucent' perhaps expresses it. When he met a Pauline friend in Oxford after nearly forty years he greeted him with the exclamation, 'It's the same man!' This was certainly true of Austin. The man he became was recognizably the boy remembered. The fine intelligence had proved its strength and that indefinable quality of 'translucence' had emerged with the years as sheer goodness in the making. Bishop B. C. Butler wrote in a letter, 'He was one of the few people I have known who seemed totally innocent.'

Though undistinguished in athletics, Austin found his feet debating in the Union Society, membership of which was confined to the Eighth Form, which he reached at the age of fifteen. His development as an orator can be traced in the school magazine, *The Pauline*. On 20 November 1920 on the motion that 'feminism will result in the extinction of chivalry', Mr Farrer, we are told, brought wrinkles to the faces of the light-hearted and by his seriousness appalled even the most irresponsible. A year later he made an excellent impromptu speech on Plato, and in the same year 'the most irresponsible are pallid before the sublime dignity of Mr Farrer'. In October 1921 he became Secretary and received this salutary though somewhat patronizing advice from his predecessor: 'The Secretary to whom the high traditions of the house will be entrusted next year will, with improved delivery and greater command over language, make a very good orator.' The following year he became President and wrote about himself, 'The kindest thing we can say about the President is that he was formerly Secretary – and, after the manner of secretaries, slow, sound and dull.' The following reports seem to come from another hand, both for December 1922:

On the motion that 'the theory of human progress is a dangerous fallacy', the President delivered a short oration which had no point except that it rhymed.

'Is life worth living?' The President replied in the negative in a speech which at least had the merit of being logically connected and an artistic whole. He described all human effort as the attempt to cure the symptoms of human misery instead of cutting out the cause – life itself. The Vice-President told the President to live up to his principles and shoot himself and was not convinced by the latter's reply that he was bravely bearing the woes of life in order to be an apostle of suicide to the nations.

The last report is of February 1923, on the motion that 'socialism is a natural step forward in human progress':

> The President examined the idea of progress, tracing the growth in the abolition of slavery and serfdom, and the spread of democracy. Progress depended on equality, and equality could only come with socialism. Therefore let the nations open their doors to socialism before it was ushered in by revolution.

He had progressed from the seriousness of adolescence to the Chesterton-like ingenuity of the eighteen-year-old. We find the same ingenuity in Austin's own final editorial, neatly describing an OTC manoeuvre:

> *Others apart sit on a hill retired*
> *In thoughts more elevate and reason high*
> *Of evolutions, sections and platoons*
> *And find no end in wandering mazes lost.*[3]

If Austin's chief memories of school were (as he said) of his ambitions, they were gratified. The record shows his achievements in the role of School Captain, President of the Union, editor of *The Pauline* and even as a member of the Athletic Committee. The number of school prizes he carried off at Apposition in 1923 won him congratulations on the management of his breath, which must have been quite exhausted by his journeys to the platform. Also, 'at Apposition the Captain of the School, A. M. Farrer, made a speech which was in the best traditions of his office and consisted principally of an eloquent appeal to the Governors for a boat house. At present the school crew has nowhere to lay its head save a room over a Hammersmith Inn.' At this same Apposition Austin made his last Pauline appearance as Critella in scenes from the *Thesmophoriazusae* of Aristophanes.

Austin's career at St Paul's revealed that he had inherited his father's respect for truth and the marked critical attitude which had induced Wheeler Robinson, when Principal of Regent's

Park College, to submit his books to the elder Farrer for criticism. Austin had laid the foundations of his great learning in the classics and English literature. He was still a Baptist but not a conservative. He had played no part in the evangelical meetings of the Christian Union: thirty years later he was to shepherd similar groups at Trinity College, Oxford, without ever offending the most zealous fundamentalist or abandoning his own very different principles. He was now ready for the university, philosophy, and Anglicanism.

# CHAPTER 3

# Balliol College 1923–7

\*

'Balliolity' said Ingleby to Lord Peter Wimsey[1] 'is a very terrible thing . . .' Certainly Scott and Jowett had set in motion a remarkably successful academic institution and had achieved this by throwing the college scholarships open at a time when most Oxford scholarships were closed to particular schools. The measure of their success is seen in the long period of Balliol's academic predominance, especially in classical studies. The scholars of Balliol had almost a monopoly of the Craven and Ireland scholarships (the most distinguished awards in classics at Oxford). The college record in history, mathematics and chemistry was almost as distinguished. This had of course its disadvantages: the sense of the 'effortless superiority' of the Balliol man could be very irritating. As a classical scholar of the college Farrer did all that could be expected of him: he was placed in the first class in Classical Moderations in 1925, in Literae Humaniores (Greats) in 1927 and in Theology in 1928, as well as collecting a number of university and college awards.

The first five terms of the Oxford classical course concentrated on the extensive reading of Greek and Latin literature (including the whole of Homer and Vergil, Cicero and Demosthenes, as well as special books and compositions in Greek and Latin prose and verse). Farrer was fortunate in having as tutor Cyril Bailey, the expert on Lucretius, then at the height of his powers, himself an old Pauline and always a good friend to his Pauline pupils. The College Fellows were on good terms with their pupils, but, while he was working for Mods, Austin tended to live the life of a recluse. He had a turret room and worked incessantly. A. D. Farrell, his successor as Captain at St Paul's, remembers how in 1924 Austin was so nervous that he had to withdraw from the Ireland and Craven Examination. However, the following year he did take the examination and won a Craven scholarship. Another contemporary remembers him at this time as 'a sort of embodiment of pure intellect, rather an etherial person, most assiduous in his attendance at chapel, friendly in disposition, but not hail fellow well met'.

Austin was not interested in sport as such. We hear of him playing an occasional game of draughts, and he was sometimes persuaded to take exercise. Colin Hardie (later a Fellow of Magdalen) took him to play Rugby fives in the damp court off Merton Street. Austin, surprisingly, often won. There were walks with an Old Pauline friend, Bamforth, scholar of St John's and an ultramontane Anglican, who eventually turned to Rome. Austin's chief relaxation seems to have been punting; his great pleasure was to offer his mother and father a day on the river.

In the 1920s social work, in the Toynbee tradition, was taken up by many Balliol men. Austin went to help at the Balliol Boys' Club, no doubt encouraged by Cyril Bailey. In his first term he wrote vividly to his mother about it:

> The Balliol Boys' Club is in the very worst part of the city. The members are mostly paper-boys and such-like. The club is open every evening and there are games: billiards, shove-halfpenny – with counters of course – draughts and gymnasium. They also play football and do cross-country running and rowing. It is supported by members of the college with their subscriptions, and they go down on different nights to organise games. I played shove-halfpenny with dirty little ragamuffins who played with immense earnestness and the strictest fairness. When the club closed there were prayers to which all came including my atheist friend who had no idea of causing offence by outward nonconformity. It was strange, all to stand there in a small room singing 'Onward Christian Soldiers' without regard for euphony. There was a short reading of the parable of the Good Samaritan with a few emendations, such as 'bandages' for wine. I shall go again. [1][2]

He was rapidly to discover more about human nature, his own and others. He writes again about the Club:

> I go down there and stand about and play various games and just manage to raise an occasional remark. In walks one of the people that I despised at school – a hearty athlete who never probably was above the fourth form. He comes up to a boy, slaps him on the back and begins to talk in a loud voice and the whole room flocks around him to listen. If there is any rioting he stops it with a single look. He

17

comes to take prayers. Some boys snigger and whisper. He looks up and tells them to keep quiet and says further that he has noticed lately that prayers have been said as though they meant nothing, and he wants that altered. He goes on and everyone is quiet and attentive and, instead of gabbling the Pater Noster, say it as if they meant every word. That is my weekly school of humility. I am beginning to believe that it is possible to be over-educated and that altruism has its advantages. [2]

And on another occasion:

Finding the officer in charge unable to be there, I decided that something should be done about prayers. I took them with fear and trembling. They jeered at my reading of the lesson – perhaps I was too jaunty – I will know another time – but were quite good for the rest – the Lord's Prayer, an extempore prayer (which I confess to having written out beforehand) and the benediction. It was the last which was really extempore for me because, in my nervousness, I actually forgot the form of the words and had to invent one. [3]

Most of Austin's friends have commented on his shyness during his first two years at Oxford. He does not seem to have been very sociable, but we hear of talks with H. A. Hodges (later Professor of Philosophy at Reading and a close friend) and with Bamforth, who hoped to convert Austin to his own mode of Anglicanism. These were the 1920s, the years of post-war disillusionment and general cynicism mixed with the hysterical gaiety that was alien to the diligent and clever son of a Baptist family. Austin was never likely to be taken in by the frivolous side of Oxford life in the twenties, so brilliantly satirized by Evelyn Waugh in *Brideshead Revisited*. In 1924 he writes:

I get disgusted and generally fed up with the conversations and discussions of youths up here supposed to be intellectual. They will turn the whole political and religious system inside out in the most airy way, apparently just for the fun of it. They tell me I have been born old. Perhaps they are right. But I cannot help preferring sanity to ingenuity. I was at tea with some people yesterday who were proposing to go and spend the evening listening to and discussing the paper of a Corpus Christi philosopher of the name of Schiller, who, according to their report, regards the whole system of ethics as useless and dangerous lumber which he proposes to scrap and to cure all evils by birth control. They talked of it all in a cold sort of way. I sat and listened. I think it must come of the purely intellectual outlook on things in general which people get up here. That is why I should not like to be a don. I had rather live than think. [4]

And in a later word of withdrawal:

I did not hear the Union debate for the simple reason – and now I am afraid I shall grieve you – that I have purposely let myself lapse from the Society. I came to the conclusion that it was no use to me. I am searching for some club or society into which I can creep, preferably literary. [5]

His mind still preserved the foundations of a Nonconformist upbringing – the solid reading of Dickens and Hardy and a consequent dislike of the books of the twenties. He writes again in 1924:

Talking of broadening the mind, there is a fellow scholar of mine named Kirby who has taken in hand to educate me in modern literature. He denies most emphatically that the old are better and maintains that all really good books have been written since 1910. He lent me one that he holds the best of all, being the precursor of a new movement in literature. More than anything else I have read it convinced me that English literature is really used up and decaying. It was so remarkably like the decadent Latin stuff: a story with no meaning or general flow or unity, but simply a framework for charmingly written episodes, humour and voluptuousness, pervaded by a breath of exquisite yet unhealthy ennui. There is an outward appearance of extreme realism, yet the general feeling of it is perfectly unreal. Anyhow it has nothing to do with my life or the life of the people I know. It is besides very obscene. It filled me with satiety to read it. The author's name is Aldous Huxley.[3] It was not one of his that you read in Cornwall, was it? I do not think it can be, since you described that as passionate and rebellious. This is simply frivolous. [6]

Austin was fortunately not left to brood alone in this pessimism. A fellow Pauline, James Woolcock, an exhibitioner in Natural Science, took him to task for his apparent misanthropy. Austin recounts how

he launched out into a discourse to the effect that we were both guilty of neglecting social duty and being unnecessarily solitary.

Whereupon we swore a solemn league and covenant that we would make frantic efforts to be interested in things that interest other people, would talk at meals and generally behave in a rational manner, which we have made some attempts to do . . . As a matter of fact I had been thinking the same thing myself. It is very pleasant and peaceful to live shut up in one's own mind, associating with a few select friends and by that method one can gain to a sort of philosophical calm. I really do believe when I come to think of it that I have been unconsciously trying to live Horace for several years. [7]

Woolcock's treatment seems to have worked. Not only do we find Austin assisting in the production of a Christmas mime, appearing as an angel and perplexed by the mechanics of the lighting system, but he was later to write of this period:

It was only in the beginning of my second year that I adapted myself and made my way into a circle of college friends. The excitement of that – of making my way and achieving positive social success and being liked by people of better standing who had no particular obligation to notice me – nearly turned my head and I look back on this time as an intoxication of delight. [8]

Austin's apparent unsociability may have owed something to his preoccupation with the question of church membership. Brought up in a Baptist household, he had not yet been baptized. Though as a boy he had attended Baptist services with his family, he had never taken much part in the social activities of his church. Now at Oxford in the heartland of Anglicanism he found Balliol College chapel congenial, the services well ordered and the hymns to his liking, though he did complain of the organist's choice of tunes. The somewhat latitudinarian churchmanship of Balliol would not have appealed to him later when he came to know High Mass at Cowley and St Barnabas. But this was 1923, and soon he was disturbed by the realization that he had no definite membership in any Christian church. The Church of England attracted him, yet he was vexed by the thought of the distress a change of allegiance must cause to his father, a tutor in a well-known dissenting college, and to his mother, a woman of deep religious conviction. He hated the thought of disrupting family worship at home and distressing his two sisters. Some moving letters from his parents reveal something of his state of mind. The crucial months seem to have been from January to May of 1924. Two letters from his mother and father, both written on the same day in January, appear to come in reply to an announcement from Austin that his mind was moving in the direction of Anglicanism and confirmation. His mother writes with great frankness and insight:

I am glad and thankful that the time has come . . . for you to join a Christian church. When you were home at Christmas I could not bear for you to get up, and leave us to stay for the Communion Service without you. I meant after you had gone back to Oxford to write and ask if you would not like to stay to that service with us – although you had not joined any church. Our church at least welcomes anyone who loves Christ in sincerity and truth, whatever are his opinions.

I feel with you a good deal of what I feel you think about the Baptist denomination. I don't like the excitement of some of the services, and the lack of reverence in some of the ministers. I find many people incapable of seeing two sides of a question – but on the other hand, I do not know, as far as I can judge, another body of people who are trying to meet the needs of a sinful community as thoroughly and whole-heartedly as the Baptist Church in foreign missionary work and at home. If you could talk with them you would find many of its more enlightened adherents fully conscious of its blemishes. Here is Mr Marsden, for one, out of office in the Church because the other members cannot rise to his ideal of church work. But he does not leave the church in spite of its defects.

But what do you know of the Baptist Church, you poor boy? It is humiliating indeed to recall that from the time you were a little boy our church life has been spoiled and shadowed by split on split, and owing to your evenings being taken up by homework I have always felt that there was a loss in your religious life. I am afraid I do not care so much whether you join the Baptist Church or the Church of England (God forgive me if I am disloyal to my own church by saying it), but I do care that you join the church where your own soul can best grow and where you will best learn to use to the utmost for the benefit of others the powers that God has given you and where you will best learn to understand the beauty of the character of our Lord. Forgive a poor letter on such an important subject. It is the best my love can find words for and it is a

humiliation that it is not better, but it comes with love from Mother.
[9]

The integrity which was characteristic of the family comes out
in his father's answers to points which Austin must have
raised:

> If I stand for anything it is for the individual's independence of
> thought and judgement in these matters. Had I attempted prosely-
> tism I think it would have proved ultimately vain in your case.
> From quite a small boy you have always shown a disposition to
> think for yourself and not to accept positions of which you were not
> personally convinced, and had I sought prematurely to mould your
> views there would inevitably have come a recoil.

His father was not surprised that Austin found the Anglican
church service congenial. 'The predilections we bring with us
no doubt have much to do with the way the service strikes us.'
As to church government, he saw that Austin did not wish to
insist on his right (as a layman) to share in church government,
'but does not the New Testament doctrine of the priesthood of
all believers commit you to that? It is not a question of what we
want.' There follows a passage of great interest:

> You would not subscribe to the high Anglican doctrine on
> episcopacy with the belief in the apostolic succession, with its
> special charisma transmitted from generation to generation,
> making them and the clergy ordained by them exclusive channels
> of the means of grace. I would agree that church government need
> not be limited to forms which can be found as such in the New
> Testament. But you would not endorse a system of government out
> of keeping with the fundamental truths of the New Testament.
> Your mother and I have no more poignant regret than that our
> family experience of church life has been so unfortunate. But are
> you sure that things are better in the Established Church?

On the legal connection of Church and state Mr Farrer points
out the abuses and persecutions to which it had led. As for
obedience to one's ecclesiastical superiors as a form of Christian
self-denial, his reply is that if the cleric is indeed Christ's
vicegerent, is not a distinction between cleric and layman set up
which the New Testament does not recognize? He continues:
'With you I protest against the view that the Eucharist is a mere

bare commemoration – but there is no priestly miracle. Christ promises us a special grace if we take the sacrament according to His word.'

The letter goes on, taking up Austin point by point:

1. 'Is it not a sin to withstand the truth?' I will not answer in Pilate's words. It is a sin if you are sure that you have it.

2. The Creeds. I object to creeds as such partly because they incorporate such doubtful philosophy, partly because they have been used for persecution, partly because they seem like the scribal habit of laying on men burdens too heavy to bear.

3. Is not infant baptism contrary to the spiritual character of New Testament Christianity?

4. To the doctrine of the apostolic charisma you will not subscribe. Can you join the Church of England without it?

The letter concludes on a more personal note:

I am glad about what you say about our continuing to worship together as one family. You promise to worship with us once on Sundays. But could we bring ourselves to hold you to that promise? As a lonely man, I would miss your sympathy, and how could I speak to you about the things that concern us most without the assurance of your fellow feeling? This grief is *not* an argument. You will do what you are led to believe is right, but hold your hand till we can talk. Your desire to unite yourself with the Church of Christ is an answer to our constant prayer for you, and we rejoice in your devotion to truth. [10]

Whatever his course was to be, his father's blessing came in the end:

My heart leaps to the confidence you utter, that if we are faithful God's love will make a way for us. I know that you will not become a bigot. I have not so learned you. So continue to work without brooding. The question will be settled by conscience and when it declares itself, to that side you will go with your parents' blessing and prayers. God will take care that you do not lapse into indifference. [11]

It was not only his parents who were his concern. Austin wrote also touchingly of his fear that his change of allegiance might prove a stumbling-block to his sisters, especially to Eleanor, the younger sister. After this we have no letters until May 1924 when the decision has been taken and he writes to describe his confirmation:

> It was in the little Latin Chapel of the Cathedral. Woolcock and Bleiben[4] very kindly came and Mr Pickard-Cambridge[5] meant to, but was detained at a meeting. Another man from this college was confirmed at the same time. The Bishop of Oxford[6] was splendid. He did not use the preface prescribed in the book, but one of his own; and after the ceremony he gave his address which he must have made specially for the occasion because it was entirely suited to and dependent upon the peculiar circumstances. He just stood close in front of us where he was after the laying on of hands and gave us a simple exhortation to perseverance, quite short and direct, and then shook hands with us. [12]

We do not know who prepared Austin for confirmation, but it may well have been the Chaplain of Balliol, the Reverend Henry Hensman Gibbon, who began his Balliol career in 1902. He had been at Wycliffe Hall, served as a curate at St George's, Leeds, and then as an army chaplain in the First World War. He is not often mentioned in Balliol letters, but in Evelyn Waugh's biography of Ronald Knox, Gibbon is mentioned as deploring the 'cliques and small clubs' in the college at a time when the Fellows were encouraging the public school men to mix with the 'men from Birmingham'.

Much later in life Austin summed up his Anglican faith in a sermon, 'On Being an Anglican',[7] and here summarized:

> We are not priests in the Church of England but in the Church of God. Did not Christ establish sacraments and an apostolic ministry and a visible company of faithful men? We have our membership of Christ in the Church. There is one Church – its centre is in Heaven. Why, then, do I remain in the Church of England? I dare not dissociate myself from the sacred ministry and I dare not profess belief in the papal errors. We are Anglicans not because of the psalms or the poetry of George Herbert or the cathedral, but because we can obey God here. The Church mediates Christ. To be a loyal churchman is hobbyism or prejudice unless it is the way to be a loyal Christian – to see through the Church to Christ as a man sees through the telescope to the stars.

This nervous trial over, and with the achievement of a good first in Classical Mods in March 1925, Austin's great experience of

1925 was a visit to Greece, made possible by the award of the S. S. Clarke Travelling Exhibition. He found a skilled travelling companion in Basil Gray of New College (later Sir Basil Gray, of the British Museum). This was the one period of his life which was to bring the delights of physical adventure. With his fair skin, Austin suffered terribly from sunburn. He also sprained his ankle walking over the Langala pass in a thunderstorm. The two of them struggled to the next village where they were hospitably entertained by an Albanian couple, although it was Lent in the Greek calendar and there was consequently little to eat. Gray fell ill at Olympia and had to remain there, while Austin went on alone on foot. There were more adventures to come:

> I have made the startling discovery that one man with an excessive pack on his back cannot do a horse-ride of two hours on horrible paths in nine hours. Greece would cure you [he writes to his father] of your affection for paths that wind upwards all the way, when they go up like the side of the Pyramids. It's a bit much, particularly over the boulders with a good torrent in the middle. Firstly I lost my way and threw myself on the compassion of a man ploughing, who wrote me a little note to a man called Stylios Mpithas, whose name I write that you too may honour it. He was the *didaskalos* (schoolmaster) but the sum of his accomplishments were reading, writing and arithmetic. His main occupation was obviously farming. He gave me a share of his meal, half of his two-roomed house and the only proper bed it contained. His wife and mother-in-law and his six children treated me with all possible kindness and great simplicity. After dinner one of the neighbours came in to talk, and they did talk. We all went to bed at half-past-eight and got up at dawn. The whole family turned up to see me shaving and then the schoolmaster shaved himself with my razor and insisted on exchanging with me. He offered me five drachmas. The lady demanded some of my ointment (. . . for sunburn). [13]

He eventually rejoined Gray at Kalamata near the tip of the Peloponnese.

The two years from 1925 to 1927 were to be devoted to the achievement of academic success, the *proxime accessit* to the Hertford in 1925, a Craven scholarship in the winter of the same year, the Jenkyns exhibition and a first in Greats. One external event did attract his attention, the General Strike of

1926, when many undergraduates with great satisfaction abandoned Oxford and their studies to drive buses, work at the docks and try to help in breaking the strike. Austin's reaction is found in a letter to his mother dated 9 May:

> Know in the first place that I am still here, which is a thing not to be taken for granted. Some part of the college is gone down already to do various jobs. Everyone is feverish and excited, unable to work. To sit here seems intolerable and no-one is happy until he has got hold of some work that enables him to feel he is 'in it' some way or another. I met someone in the quad just now smiling all over. 'I've got a job,' he said. 'What sort?' – 'Oh, I don't know, but I'm off tomorrow; I sent someone down to town to look me out any sort of job and he says he's got one for me.' I was on the point of going down to Bristol to unload fruit yesterday but, thank Heaven (for I now see he is right), the Master of his own authority stopped the venture on the grounds that gangs of imported undergraduates at the docks were more likely to provoke violence than to be of any use – and indeed have done immeasurable harm at Glasgow docks already. So at present I am staying here to be employed on the Master's party. He is organising the willing parties of the college into an executive to manage a national petition arising out of the Archbishop's appeal for renewal of negotiations. I'm expecting to go to Didcot with the petition this afternoon. I'm inclined to think this impartial push for peace for its own sake is the best thing to be at. If there is danger of starvation it will be time to begin strike-breaking, which at present can only be provokative [sic!]. [14]

The philosophy teaching at Balliol in Austin's time was in the hands of the Master, A. D. Lindsay, Charles Morris (Lord Morris of Grasmere), Professor John Macmurray and Henry Brooke (Lord Brooke of Cumnor) who deputized for Morris during a sabbatical year, so that in his first year Austin was not taught by Morris. All had been brought up in the Kantian and Hegelian traditions as interpreted in the Oxford Idealism of the nineteenth century by such writers as F. H. Bradley and T. H. Green. Lindsay taught them not to see Kant as an obscure pedant but as a sensible man discussing sensible points, Morris to see Bradley as a partial throwback from Hegel to Kant. The latter had argued in his book *Idealistic Logic* that the logic of the Oxford idealists could be derived from Kant without passing through Hegel. Macmurray developed a synthesis of Kant, Fichte, Hegel and Marx and put it forward as Christian philosophy. Macmurray's most frequent remark to his pupils was 'I am here to teach you to think, not to get you Firsts in Greats'.

All Austin's tutors were agreed upon his reserve. Macmurray's comment is perhaps the most illuminating. 'Of all my able pupils he was the most aloof and most difficult to know. He did not give himself away either in his essays or his general conversation. I retain the impression that whatever he produced would be genuinely his own.'

In the twenties Kant became a major interest. Bradley, and possibly Cook-Wilson, were studied. But, according to Austin's friend Hodges,

> The younger dons were searching for something different. We did think the attitude of the older dons to science was ridiculous. It was certainly knowledge in itself in the full sense and not a Hegelian 'first approximation'. So if I were to guess about Farrer it would be that he, like others of us, felt that he must start afresh, take a critical attitude to the ruling philosophy and think for himself. At the time, Farrer was probably not definite himself and not prepared to share guesses, particularly with his tutor. [15]

By 1927 Austin's Anglicanism had become Catholic both in belief and practice: he had made his first confession, was in the habit of going to High Mass at St Barnabas and, after the Jenkyns examination, made a retreat at Cowley. He wrote to Hodges that he had been running away from the idea of the priesthood for three years, indicating that the reasons for his hesitation were partly intellectual.

In the two years while he was reading Greats his preoccupations were twofold: he was anxious to clarify his belief in God and to decide how best to speak of Christ; he wanted to see if his beliefs were compatible with ordination. For if, as he wrote to Hodges, he had been avoiding the idea of the priesthood for three years, he must have had it in mind shortly after his confirmation. Then there were the practical questions: should he be a lawyer, a classics tutor, a priest? And, if a priest, what kind of priest – academic or parochial?

The material for his religious and theological difficulties is furnished by two letters to his father, one dated 20 November

1926, the other undated but on internal evidence (the mention of the Jenkyns examination) likely to have been written in February 1926.

> I am trying to get through Alexander's *Space, Time and Deity*, in the hope of making out why men ever want to be realists and what precisely the doctrine means. It is the worst written volume I ever attacked: most of it is bad considered as system, though there are a good many sensible and acute passages in it. The conception of Space–Time looks like becoming the *pons asinorum* of the philosophy of the future. I'm not at all certain that I'm on the right side of it now. [16]

Austin continued to think seriously about scientific theories, publishing near the end of his life an acute book, *A Science of God?* As a schoolboy he had learned no science. Alexander's conception of God as a step in the evolutionary process would hardly appeal to him: no one throughout his life maintained the doctrine of divine transcendence more stoutly. The reference to 'realists' looks like a combination of Balliol and Bradley. He goes on to his central perplexity:

> The philosophical atmosphere has odd effects on people's personal religion and while I can't profess to perform the startling feat of John Findlay,[8] who has a practising religion without a personal God, still I find that the form of religious thinking is to a certain extent modified; particularly it is real hard work to keep Christ himself in view. The Communion is the only sure and unfailing hold. And all this not through a lack of intention or through any intellectual problem. It just seems to occur. Everything seems swallowed up with One who *is* the Unity and harmony into which we enter in prayer, *is* the focus of all ends in which we see the meaning of everything particular, *is* that will into which our will is merged insofar as it is good: and though the character or quality of this One as our ideal is drawn almost wholly from the manifestation of him in Christ, though Christ is really the norm by which we determine the good in ends and so find their unity in the One End, the revelation which gives meaning to the idea of the pure will, yet to worship God as Christ, seems strange and requires an effort, and in prayer I do not think of him, having put what knowledge of him I have into the God I worship. The personality of God is not as the personality of man; it seems to change its form as we look at it like

28

the Pleiades; when we think of him as our Ideal, he stands clear-figured before us, a Person built up of all good qualities. But when we see him as the whole in which we ought to and partly do find ourselves organic parts, it is as when we look at the constellation less particularly – we see something wider but less clearly defined – and we say he is a personality still but not in the same sense at all as we are persons – a person by analogy[9] merely. Again regarded as the end or as the whole, he shows as almost impersonal: we see not a constellation but a blur of light. Is he as much impersonal as personal? One thing is clear, in relation to us he is personal but as we externalise his sphere outwards from us he seems to lose something of that personality. If one says he is personal in relation to us, is that enough?

Such speculation does not seem valuable, but it appears necessary. A fresh point has occurred to me. Christ is held to be, if anything the power by which we are saved from ourselves and brought into communion with God. But whereas Christ is the assurance of the will and power of God to bring us back to such communion, and though for this assurance to be real the divinity of Christ is to be believed, though he made the assurance sure by his life and death; yet in communion with God such things are not consciously remembered – they appear rather as a propaedeutic. The union which is at once God and with God seems self-causing and it is not God under the aspect of the Incarnate Christ who will be naturally thought of at all, but God as the over-person, the second form of the Pleiades as I described it above. Does all this seem to you unnatural or strange? Because it looks to me as if St Paul wouldn't think such religion qualified as Christianity at all. And Protestant saints and preachers always talk about communion *with* Christ. St Bernard's love songs seem even further away still. All this you must understand is not meant as bright new theorizing, but rather a description of practice. To preach like St Bernard would be for me entirely disingenuous. [17]

We may find some illumination to the development of Austin's thinking at this time in his Bampton Lectures:

I had been reared in a personalism which might satisfy the most ardent of Dr Buber's disciples. I thought myself as set over against deity as one man faces another across a table; and I hoped he would signify his presence to me by way of colloquy, but neither out of the scripture I read nor in the prayers I tried to make did any mental voice address me; anything would have satisfied me, but nothing came. I owe my liberation from this impasse to reading Spinoza's *Ethics* as far as I remember. Those phrases which strike me now as so flat and sinister, so ultimately atheistic, *Deus sive Natura* [God, or call it Nature] – God insofar as he is regarded as being the substance of the human mind – these phrases were to me light and liberation. Undoubtedly I misunderstood Spinoza. Here anyhow is what I took from Spinozism; I would no longer attempt with the psalmist to 'set God before my face'. I would see him as the underlying cause of my thinking, especially those thoughts in which I tried to think of him. I would dare to hope that sometimes my thoughts would become diaphanous, so that there should be some perception of the divine cause shining through the created effect, as a deep pool settling into a clear tranquillity permits us to see the spring from which the waters rise. By so viewing my attempted work of prayer I was rid of the frustration which had baffled me before. And this is why, when the Germans set their eyeballs and pronounce the terrific word, 'He speaks to thee', I am sure indeed that they are saying something, but I am still more sure that they are not speaking to my condition.[10]

The spell of Spinoza did not last. In the spring of 1927 Austin was to write at least a partial recantation, not only of Spinoza, but also of Immanuel Kant. Probably, the puzzlement about how to think of Christ remained the cause of his hesitation about taking orders.

He was by now emerging from the comparative isolation of the earlier years of his undergraduate life.

You may congratulate me on having come out of an enormous bout of philosophizing, which has had tiresome effects on my powers to sleep and do regular work, but admirable ones on my general state of mind, especially in establishing faith on its own foundations, where the ebb and flow of metaphysical speculations ought not to be able to touch it any more. This is a great gain since even when you are not sure it stands condemned, still you feel its position to be problematical and dependent on any turn your theories may take in the future, which is just as disastrous as belief and less progressive. So now I am going about saying that if only people would think their philosophy out they would discover the scope of its views and realize that it does not touch religion. This little victory pleases me a great deal, because the curse of this intellectualism is that it destroys desire by challenging the grounds of it before it has time to act and then leaving it hanging on an infinite regress of problems to be considered. All this, and how bad it is, I see more and more through the present example of the people I live with here whom I am constantly envying for their impulses without seeing a way to liberate my own.

For instance, a man ought to love God, not think it right to get into harmony with the universal values; he ought to be simply dependent on the affection of his friends, and at least be free from the miserable fear of being unfelt by, and unfeeling of, the world of his fellows, a sort of moral solipsism. Hodges encouraged me, who now finds himself coming out through the full thinking of his philosophy to the recovery of a religious sense which had run dry for years. With such an example before me, I hope to get back freedom inch by inch. *Inter alia* I am going to give myself bodily into the hands of the Cowley Community to do with me what they can for three days after the Jenks[11] is over, to say the hours with the brethren there and to be put through a systematic course of meditation. You don't know how happy I am. I feel less the slave of Reason than I have any time these four years, I should think. I tried a great cul-de-sac in religion of the universal 'ought', saying to myself that faith was a divinely given thing and that all the recipient could do was to practise those things which on full reflection he believed right in religion as much as in other things, since nothing is in our power but our moral wills. Which was no doubt St Paul's view before he was converted. But full consideration yields no positive results such as to be a ground for action, still less the power to perform them. Whence this palinode at last. But don't suspect me of plunging into irrationalism: philosophy is the deliverer and not the chain, and I more and more want to go through with it. It is absurd that no warnings are any use in these things; here have I been living on the simplest fallacies, with warning boards stuck all over the New Testament against the attempt to live by the good rational will. I used to be enormously baffled by our Lord's sayings to the effect that good deeds must proceed from the heart, from a love of them, and that this Pharisaic attempt just to do as an outward thing that which is according to your notion of right is a mere hypocrisy after all. So Aristotle is proved right againt Kant and all the moderns who uphold the latter against the former. But I used to ask, 'Though this is all very well, how does it help us to decide what we ought to *do*, and *that* is all that is in our power? I am grateful to Joyce for having once defined for me what sincerity is, and how it excludes the suspended judgement. [18]

He had made his recantation: and so vigorously comments on a sermon heard in Balliol chapel:

> He is able and interesting, but wholly bad. For in fact he holds to and preaches the merely natural with a pious mystical reservation to the effect that after all it perhaps carries with it something more. This naturally does not please my present frame of mind. For instance, he won't say that the soul either does or does not survive consciously to itself, but is sure that self-sacrifice is bound to survive as a living influence among men. Thus the crown of the Lord's life is not a (rather fishy) ascension, but Pentecost when he returned to live in his following, and this fuller 'immortality' is compared with the immortality which the poets and monarchs of the world try to attain by their works, not their spirit. Such was the ambiguity of his terms. Just what he meant I don't know, but he seemed to me (like other pious rationalists) to try to satisfy the conflicting demands of desire and reason by using words in a double sense, of all silly and childish proceedings the most extreme. This sort of thing will convince no one. We must (I'm a prophet already!) go through with reason and see what it does, and then just say of faith that it too does and says these other (not contradictory, but supplementary) things. [19]

In the middle of philosophizing so, Austin was faced more acutely with the question of whether his beliefs were compatible with ordination. In March 1927, Austin told Hodges of his resolve to seek orders. Hodges himself had become a Christian, in principle an Anglo-Catholic, though not yet received into the Church. Before the end of that Hilary term Austin learned of Hodges' difficulties and their discussion, recorded by Hodges, illuminates the difficulties of both men.

> What was directly on my mind was this [Hodges writes]. God is inaccessible by any kind of human effort, whether science, philosophy, morality or art; but God has made himself accessible in the incarnation and the sacraments. From here we somehow got around to comparative mythology and here comes the bit which I remember clearly. I spoke of Christianity as the supreme instance of the world-wide fairytale of a god coming among men. Austin said,

'Oh then, you're a Loisy[12] modernist and it's all right.' I replied that
that was not at all what I meant. My point was that in this instance
and in no other the fairy tale had actually come true. What
everywhere else men have tried to imagine, God has actually done.
That and nothing less is what Christianity is about.'[13] About the
same time I urged Austin to join me in working out a Christian
philosophy for our time.

Austin had also told Hodges of a *furor divinus* which had fallen
on him towards the end of the term while he was trying to
concoct an essay, presumably the bout of philosophizing which
left him sleepless.

> He had scribbled and scribbled and lost several nights' sleep. All his
> objections had been brought down like a house of cards and he had
> gone reeling off after the end of term to be put through the exercises
> at Cowley. He was now ready to join me in acknowledging the
> insufficiency of human reason and accepting the light of faith. He
> thanked me for the timely encouragement I gave him when he
> came to see me. But he would have to hand me the baby of Christian
> philosophy to mind alone – that promise at least was not to be kept.
> [20]

The problems which he had dismissed with Hodges were to be
crucial in much of his future thought and writing. Austin said
he found it hard to worship God as Christ, while he found it easy
to see God as the harmony in which all good converges. In
August 1927 he wrote to Hodges expressing admiration for
Benedetto Croce. Croce was himself a non-religious humanist,
but the idealist tradition tended, while denying a 'personal'
God, to give the name of 'God' to the absolute reality, and he
reacted more or less religiously towards it. Hodges comments,

> This body of ideas remained alive in Austin's mind through his
> Cuddesdon and Dewsbury days, as a question he had to face. How
> does one justify the Christian teaching about God in view of this?
> The discovery I had recently made when Austin came to see me was
> about the incarnation. Now if Austin's difficulty was about the
> relation of God to Christ, his remark 'Oh then, you're a Loisy
> modernist and it's all right' shows that he had felt drawn towards
> an interpretation of the Christ story as a human way of imagining
> God. What I did was to persuade him that it wasn't a human
> imagining but a divine reality. I think that this solved for him the

deeper question which was in his mind, the question about the relation between God and the created world, especially mankind. This continued to be a leading theme in his exchanges with me for years afterwards.

For example, one day in 1930 he visited me in Sheffield and we went out to a place on the moors called Ringinglow. There he elaborated an argument which we agreed to christen 'the Ringinglow argument'. 'If', he said, 'God is to be more than just the power which energizes in his creatures, if he is to be so over-against them that he can have reciprocal dealings with them, there must be events in the world's history which stand out as being God's action towards us, i.e. not just his universal action in creating and sustaining, but his subsequent action in opening up contacts with us. But that can only mean something like an incarnation and a sacramental system. Thus the acknowledgement of Christ incarnate is the only way we can make sense of a God who is effectively personal in his relation to us.'

I remember too in other instances how anxious Austin always was to secure for the creature a relative independence, an ability to be something really distinct from God, with whom God can then enter into contact. In a word, forget the incarnation and you sink the creatures in God; make the creature really distinct from God and then God can reach out and touch him as he does in Christ. The over-againstness of God and the creature can only be secured by having a real action and interaction between them. Can we then conclude that Austin's problem was not merely about Christ, but about the meaning of God? [21]

We may conjecture that Austin was reacting against the tendency of idealism to see the creature as simply an appearance of the absolute. He was trying to see his way to believing in a real action of God in Christ and a real world for it to be exercised in, a world in which things go by their created energies as themselves – and this was indeed the theme of his last philosophical work, *Faith and Speculation*, as the true yet dependent existence of the self was one of the themes of *Finite and Infinite*. There is an interesting parallel in the introduction to William Temple's *Christus Veritas*, where Temple admits his difficulty in reconciling his philosophical idealism with his belief in the incarnation of the Word. In 1917, of course, Temple's idealism was more deeply rooted than Austin's ever was. An idealist philosophy always has problems in assigning unique significance to any particular event, since it sees the world of phenomena as appearances only of the absolute. Oddly enough Professor M. F. Wiles in his essay in *The Myth of God Incarnate* has difficulty in assigning any particular act to God (*plus ça change, plus c'est la même chose* applies to much of English theology).

During 1927–8 when Austin was reading theology he lived in Oxford in term time in Ship Street. He continued to go to St Barnabas with Hodges and to talk with him about Christian philosophy. It was plain that they were an ill-assorted pair of parents for that child, Hodges the less disciplined mind always chasing off after some hare or other, whereas Austin had chosen his own path, the reconstruction in modern terms of the ancient and medieval philosophy of being, which culminated in the publication of *Finite and Infinite*. Hodges remembered a walk by the Kennet later in the 1930s when Austin pressed on him the merits of Descartes' doctrine of the human soul as an approach to the true doctrine of finite substance, to which Hodges retaliated with a Kantian doctrine of the known self.

Austin did not abandon the orphan child of Christian philosophy. In the exhaustion of March 1927 and the experience of human insufficiency his course was settled: he would pursue both human reason and theology to their limits and this he would do for the rest of his life.

By March 1927 he had decided on the priesthood, but other ways of life had been considered. In 1924 his mother had suggested the law as a possible calling for him. She asked whether Anglicanism, which seemed so attractive at Oxford, would wear well in the strains of a wider life and a tougher environment. If he were to become a lawyer an obvious course would be to join his father's friends, the Marsdens in Blackburn. In 1924 it was not yet a pressing question with Greats still three years ahead, but by 1926 the question was more acute: he had considered the prospects of the priesthood, what he called 'donnery', and the law. Three important letters survive in which he modestly tried to assess his capabilities and his duty. In May 1926, with a year to go and the apparent possibility of teaching classics at New College, he writes,

Personally I'm inclined to think the priesthood might be a happier destination. But (Heaven!) the idea is *carni gravis* [burdensome to the flesh] and I don't know what I shall do about it. It hasn't got much relish in it, though no doubt a good deal of the relish of salvation. I confess it has an uncomfortable 'Where shall I go then from Thy Spirit' feeling about it. I turn and twist and convince myself of this and that, and still there it is, like a spot in the eyes that remains whichever way you look. In my devotions I find it hard to think anything but this my duty. A plague on these serious forcible men that will enslave you with a word, use their influence and give no reasons. For I put it down to Butler,[14] to whom I was talking early on last term about the merits of donnery, when he simply said, 'Of course you know what your duty is – to be a priest.' *Nec plura effatus* [He spoke no more].[15] Is this sort of thing fair? Meanwhile, however much I protest, *haeret lateri letalis harundo* [the fatal dart clove to my side][16] and won't be shaken out. Others alone can judge our capacity: there are twenty men who can teach New College classics, while the Church is in straits for priests. But the lust of the flesh and the lust of the eye and the pride of life are, put it how one will, rather nice. Three professions in about as many months is pretty good going, isn't it? [22]

To clear his mind he talked in November of 1926 to his father's old friend, Mr Marsden of Blackburn. He with great honesty pointed out to Austin how strange he would find office life; but Austin was more concerned to discover what his duty was and the kind of life for which his abilities fitted him. He compared himself to Proteus (the Greek mythological monster who could assume many shapes). He began to analyse his character: to consider in what direction his life had been tending. He was clear that he was not a practical man, the kind to make great decisions in the outside world. (In this he underestimated himself, as he showed when he became Warden of Keble.) What then of the priesthood? His influence on others, he thought, was small. His former tutor, Cyril Bailey, pointed out what indeed was patently obvious, that wits were needed to defend the faith and that he might become a college chaplain and literary divine. Here at least he might honestly fulfil his duty to the best of his power, and exercise his originality in speculation. At least, he reflected, he did not appear to be so personally unattractive as to be unfit for the position of a don, and he was as conscientious as most people. So he concludes

*Quaecum ita sint* [therefore], a *relegatio in insulam*[17] or banishment to the North would rest for justification not on capacity but an attempt to amend this defective being. On the other hand it is moral effort alone that can amend it, and that may be exercised anywhere. I ought perhaps to choose a profession on the basis of what I am, or likely with reasonable probability to become, and hope in such profession to acquire some moral energy by the time I come to die, and not take out a vessel (complete with passengers) because I know nothing of navigation and hope that a few storms will teach me the art. If then, as it rather seems, I am to be a don, I'll just put myself on the world and if the New College job doesn't come to anything I'm prepared to go to one of the newer universities if I'm wanted. If I seem to have been neglecting the moral issue my principles are simply these, that one should do what is most useful, best for himself, and at which he is best. I wonder why this kind of thinking makes me sleep. [23]

Blackburn and law were ruled out: in the event banishment would be to Yorkshire, not to Lancashire. Meanwhile ahead of him was the Trinity term and Greats. After the mental and spiritual conflicts of two years, he found it difficult to settle down to philosophy. He writes:

I am beginning to give up the pursuit of the truth for the pursuit of a good class in Greats, a more immediate object, and am revising books when I have time. I wonder if to all men and for ever philosophy is the formation of schemes which give momentary satisfaction and are immediately swallowed up in the slough of crude intractable material.

However, this fatigue did not prevent him from achieving a brilliant first in Greats. He wrote to his father from Cuddesdon on 9 August to 'ostentate' his Greats' marks, which had just arrived. After listing the details, which ranged from a pure alpha for Greek prose to beta double plus for logic, he remarks:

. . . the main thing in examinations is not to know too much. In my logic paper (and philosophy generally) I had got too much in my head and got down wretched fragments; in my history I just put down all I knew. My Greek history was by no means the overflowing of a full tank but the very violent and complete pumping out of a poor little pool. I just succeeded in covering the paper. I got minuses in my unseen [alpha minus] and translations [alpha minus] by doing them (for ostentation) in under half-time. But I am surprised they marked my history so high; my logic was a crasher. I am said to have given the best all-round performance, though it is doubtful what this means. It probably included the pure classics, which ought not to count. [24]

The Liddon award to graduates for the study of theology was given to him on the strength of these results.

CHAPTER 4

# Balliol and Cuddesdon 1927–8

*

Farrer spent the academic terms of 1927–8, Michaelmas, Hilary and Trinity, in Oxford, living in lodgings in Ship Street by himself. For his last year of Greats he had lodged in Holywell with a friend, Stephen Kirby, a fellow scholar of Balliol.[1] The Long Vacation terms of 1927 and 1928 and the Michaelmas term of 1928 he spent at the Anglican seminary at Cuddesdon before being ordained as a deacon by the new Bishop of Wakefield (J. B. Seaton), who had been his principal at Cuddesdon. Cuddesdon (now amalgamated with Ripon Hall) was a nursery of bishops and of the austere Tractarianism of the 1880s. It had none of the flamboyance of the triumphant Anglo-Catholicism of the years between 1920 and 1930. For Farrer Cuddesdon had the great virtue of being a place where after the strains of four years he could relax and pray within a framework of Catholic discipline.

The place itself, in a small village among gently rising hills, is delightful and refreshing. The pattern of life had changed little for forty years or more. From the recollections of Cuddesdon men we can build up a picture of the day: matins at 7.30 a.m. was followed by Mass, which was voluntary, at 8.00. After breakfast there was half an hour for meditation, with intercessions once a week. Two morning lectures were followed by Sext, which was also voluntary. Evensong for all was sung daily in the parish church. On Sunday the seminarists attended the 8.00 a.m Eucharist in the parish church (the Principal of Cuddesdon was also vicar of the parish), usually celebrated with great speed by the Bishop (T. B. Strong), who would end the service as the clock struck 8.30, having entered the church at 7.59. (The students went by rota to lunch or dinner with him – and found him an excellent and entertaining host.)

The principal, J. B. Seaton, was held in great affection. He had great pastoral gifts, and was thought to look like Tenniel's Duchess in *Alice*. When he became Bishop of Wakefield towards the end of 1928, the college students went in a bus to his consecration at York Minster at which Bishop Gore preached. The other members of staff included the chaplain, 'Toby' Manson, later to be a member of the Cowley Community, who was 'hearty' at breakfast, to the annoyance of those who preferred silence. The vice-principal in Austin's day was E. J. Bicknell, the authority on the Thirty-Nine Articles, a learned, large and eccentric man. He could be heard talking in his bath – 'Come here, sponge', 'Now the other leg'. Kenneth Kirk, then a Fellow of Trinity, later Bishop of Oxford, was Farrer's tutor. For many men the abiding factor for many years was David, the major domo (or butler), who with his wife maintained a close and affectionate relationship with the students. The college had a certain reputation for austerity. There was no alcohol except cider, and that perhaps only on Sundays.

The few 'Spikes' (as Anglo-Catholics were termed) at Cuddesdon had little encouragement. The students were in general of central churchmanship with a 'high' inclination; they tended to become more Catholic at Cuddesdon. It was a friendly and loyal community, with a great affection for the place itself. From the standpoint of today the students might seem immature. There were few older men, most having come straight from their universities, and they were less involved in the problems of society. The depression of the thirties was still in the future. The spiritual life was taken very seriously and there was a strong emphasis on meditation and regular prayer.

What did the young men, mostly destined to be parish priests, make of the appearance in their midst at the same time of the gentle, ingenuous Farrer from Oxford and the considerable intellect of Michael Ramsey, the future archbishop, from Cambridge?[2]

In residence at Cuddesdon, in a smaller community than Balliol, Farrer was able to move more easily among his contemporaries. They recognized his outstanding intellectual gifts combined with a transparent honesty and humility. They also observed his amiable eccentricities. On a continental tour organized by the principal, a friend was amazed to wake up and see him lying on his back and revolving his legs in the air as if riding a bicycle, an exercise by which, he explained, he hoped to develop his rather slight physique. He still had the appearance of transparency that he had had as a schoolboy, and one of his friends remembered him vividly at Cuddesdon 'if only because in those days he looked like a faun'. He had an impish humour, he excelled at table tennis, and, on a more intellectual level, would hold forth on the lawn, his eyebrows arched upwards as he propounded the most superb theories. He was at the time the only student to use the enormous leather-bound folios of the Fathers, stretched out on his stomach on the library floor.

Farrer enjoyed the congenial company. His social life blossomed. 'All taps' he wrote cheerfully 'is vanities and yet one may as well go in for a full fruity social vintage rather than a thin sharp solitary vinegar.' Describing his first impressions, he went on

> I get on very well here. Really the chaps are magnificent and I feel a worm before them and no man. I spend my time laughing, repenting, praying, reading Kirsopp Lake,[3] designing a far better church than ever before and a Crocean doctrine of the Trinity. The vice-principal is a very cautious and sound man (has he not written the standard work on the Articles?) and is careful lest I should be carried off by Dr K. Lake's errors. He primed me with Headlam before he allowed me to touch the dangerous matter and besought me not to take it too seriously. I don't. But am utterly unable to come down on either side of the fence yet. Ancient history was nothing to this. [1]

He continues in good health and spirit, enjoying the freedom to stretch his mind.

> Tell father from me that a youth here heard a preacher in Oxford (a don of sorts) produce the phrase 'from the beginning of Time to the end of Eternity'. O Kant, where is thy Critique? I have been laughing at this for nearly twelve hours. And the same man in the same sermon described how all the clocks in Jerusalem were striking twelve as our Lord led the Apostles across Cedron to Gethsemane. Oh dear! – I've got to lunch with the Bishop today and no one can tell me what is the proper time to leave. [2]

The life of a seminary, however, necessarily involved the strain of conflicting points of view, particularly in those days when there were three types of Anglican, each with their own divisions: Catholics (post-Tridentine and Tractarian); Modernists, anxious to rewrite the Christian religion without miracles and to reconcile science and religion; and the Conservative

Evangelicals. At Cuddesdon the varieties of Catholic predominated.

> I find them [Farrer writes] interesting and intelligent like the rest of mankind, but they tend to be interested in the wrong things, points of ritual, whether we ought to believe in the Immaculate Conception or the Scout movement. I don't see how anyone is ever going to have a properly balanced view of things who has never felt the pains of real scepticism. What is the reason for not worrying about the papacy and the use of incense except the necessity for holding on to the existence and character of God? [3]

He makes his feelings even more explicit in a letter written to his father from Oxford in November 1927 after his first term at Cuddesdon:

> I should always rather be with intelligent (and moderately good) men than with good (and moderately intelligent) men, when in any case one isn't dealing with real life but either academic or theological hothousing. I find the academic hothouse much more breezy. Goodness without interest is intolerable. It isn't an interest in itself but a quality to be found or made in interests which are material to it. Heaven preserve me from ever teaching in one of these closed seminaries. To be in a university would of course, be another matter. But the seminaries aren't awake. To come back to Oxford is to walk into fresh air. I have no doubt Cuddesdon is necessary discipline for the rest of life, but as life I had rather die than prefer it. But you mustn't think that one makes no conversation in Oxford but epigrams. At the moment I feel entirely antipathetic to monasticism and all its works. [4]

He did not always feel so impatient. In the two terms after taking the Theology Schools – in which he achieved his third First Class and came near to ruining his eyesight – he was more relaxed. He was excused from taking the General Ordination Examination on condition of writing a thesis on ecclesiastical authority (a subject for which he did not greatly care) and apart from this he had two terms in which to read, pray, expand his wings and answer the questions his Cuddesdon friends kept bringing him. There were, however, necessary hurdles to be surmounted on the way to the clerical life.

> You will be happy to hear [he writes in August 1928] that I am being taught to sing (or more particularly to chant) by a member of

the Oxford Cathedral choir. He commends my voice and the accuracy of my pitch and gives me sensible advice about voice production. I find it easy to make only too much noise, so that I shall have no difficulty about being heard. We have, too, an old actor to give us elocution. He represents a tradition long dead even on the stage and has the most grotesque ideas about emphasis, climax, etc. He is preposterously theatrical and makes our stomachs ache with suppressed laughter. Yet he is useful for giving us an idea of the range of devices at the speaker's service. [5]

A further hurdle was the composition of his first sermon, to be preached to the staff and his fellow students, whose comments would follow. He had a distinguished predecessor: 'Yesterday Michael Ramsey preached to the brethren and gave me great delight to think that there will be at least one major prophet in our time.' Of his own performance –

Oh, that sermon! It was too compressed and contained matter for three; sprang far too many notions on an innocent audience; was made to flow too smoothly and would have gone through the heads of an audience like water through a pipe; ought to have been gathered into several climaxes driven home instead of being a simple rise and fall; was in fact too literary, not in the sense of being academic or obscure but in the way it was handled; a moral essay and not a sermon. All these things I saw myself when I came to deliver it, and heard them again from my hearers. I've since tried a reworking of the first third as a single sermon and I think I see now how it ought to go. If every sermon one thinks of has matter for six, that is a reflection of some comfort. My delivery was approved! [6]

Farrer, in fact, already had the gift of saying much in few words. He seems to have been treated as a fount of wisdom by his contemporaries. 'What am I doing?' he writes,

Never, I think, have I been so didactic to the world in general. I was engaged on a thesis on Immortality for Kirk,[4] but couldn't get on and had to leave the main argument for experimental treatises on my own. I was just beginning to see some light here when an intelligent lad came to me in a muddle about the doctrine of the Trinity. Now as this doctrine is my own chief practical belief, it grieves me to find other people treating it as a weird intellectual muddle somehow forced on us by the Incarnation but of no direct bearing on life. Well, I left Kirk to write this boy a fifteen-page effort on the matter. This began to be handed about the day after it was written and Lister[5] came down on me for enlightenment on what is religious truth and its relation to scientific. This has run me into twenty-three long, close pages, and it's just done. Besides all this I am in the middle of a section of Thomas Aquinas and have a treatise of my own on his theory of knowledge broken off in the middle. And I am supposed to be writing a short thesis for the Principal in lieu of the deacon's examination. Do not however imagine that I'm working hard, for one can be very occupied and quite lazy. [7]

The syllabus of the Oxford School of Theology included seven compulsory papers on the Old and New Testament and two on the early history of Christian doctrine. Candidates for first and second class honours were required to do two additional papers on such subjects as the philosophy of religion and church history. New Testament Greek was compulsory, though Hebrew was voluntary. Such a course was for Farrer almost perfectly designed to meet his needs. His perplexities had been about the relation between the being of God and the particularity of the incarnation of Christ. For a year he would be plunged in the study of what claims to be the revelation of the Divine Being in the particularity of the acts of Christ, and some of his developing thought he communicated to his parents. It was for him a time of intellectual adventure, not simply working through a syllabus.

In the sphere of theology, the mystery religions of the Near East and the Gnostic systems were being much discussed, and it was not unfashionable to suppose that St Paul turned Christianity into a mystery religion. Farrer was impressed by St Paul and quite unconvinced by the mystery religion hypothesis.

> The source of the terms he uses seems a purely antiquarian matter. But isn't he amazing? It would not be difficult to show that his foolishness and readiness to fly in the face of contemporary wisdom was really the most inspired philosophy: certainly one could trace back the modern philosophy of will and personality to no other source. Paul was an excellent Crocean. I think the Corinthian epistles are the best. The greatest crime of the Corinthians was that they could hear the first epistle and not repent. [8]

He moved on to the study of Gnosticism, convinced that the atmosphere in which the early Church grew up was indeed one of mystery, that St Paul was not a rationalist, and that the original meaning of the sacraments and the incarnation should be considered in the light of Gnostic logic.

What [he writes to his father] is more probable than a hearty sacramentalism, grace running through a succession of inspired men, what less probable than a quiet and sensible religious individualism cemented by natural deputed authority? And it looks as if the Christian religion, lifted out of this mental atmosphere, becomes a fish out of water and the rationalistic arguments used against the sacraments and ministry just as destructive of the incarnation, if one is to be consistent. Does not this happen in 'enlightened' Protestantism? We allow that the content we give to the idea of God is simply not philosophy and cannot be; it is not exact information, or even vague information, but just the best myth. Christ is the poem that was history. His Eucharist the myth become bread. The sacramental ministry is on the one side human, on the other part of the divine mythus which is Christ's living body, the Church on earth expressed in living institutions. All the scandal to the Protestant and the blasphemy to the papist arise from the cause of all heresies, confounding the two natures. Catholicism adds to the myth that was history things that simply can't be history. But Protestantism has still something to stand on while there is still any one single rational element in the Faith from which it can start. But philosophy will no longer support so much as the existence of our God nor science the continuance of our consciousness. No logic can forbid us to establish the antithesis God – creatures because God is so far perfectly empty of content, but when you go on to say 'God is' you must realize that this is poetry, that, considering the other attributes you are bound to give him, his 'being' cannot be predicated in any category known to us nor have we any means of determining it. So that it is as true to deny that he is (in any sense of the word we possess) as to assert that he is in he only knows what sense; and the part of wisdom is to do neither, but to accept this as an element of the revealed poem of divine truth. There is no way in which we can conjecture the manner of the resurrection (let us not say immortality – a pseudo-philosophical term) which is not either unthinkable as philosophy or improbable as science; so that we shall refer enquirers not to Streeter's treatise, in which – poor devil – he sets forth the psychological, biological, and philosophical evidence, but rather to the rhyme of Bernard de Morley, assuring them that the resurrection life is not *nothing;* that it rests in God, and that we have divine poetry to give us a vague foretaste of what it will feel like, so far as we are capable of realizing it, but for the rest whether it can be called consciousness, individuality, or even existence, we do not know: but it is something, it is good and it is for us. Let us not tire ourselves in vain by beating in the void the wings of the mind, but turn back into the circle of the myth, being assured that this is something which reason can never take from us, because she gave it us not; and that it carried its own truth immanently within itself. Apply this doctrine – and you must – to the Holy Eucharist, and I shall take you to High Mass, confident that you will not be offended.

He signs himself 'Mythically and historically, Your loving son, Austin'. [9]

Farrer had, in short, come across a way of thinking that upset the established dogmas of the academic and ecclesiastical world and was enjoying himself in exploiting it. What Austin had in view was the old kind of Liberal Protestantism which proclaimed the fatherhood of God and the brotherhood of man and marked St Paul as the villain of the piece, the man who Hellenized Christianity with sacramental dogmas. So when he talks of rationalists he does not mean those who pursue theology rationally but those who dogmatically exclude the miraculous and the sacramental, and he is delighted to find that the New Testament does not belong to the mental world of the rationalist. Much of this letter of course one could tear to bits easily. The talk of God cannot be mere poetry if Christ is the poetry made history. And if we can make the antithesis God–creatures we are not saying nothing about God, and the mental atmosphere of the New Testament is not Gnostic – the Word made flesh is abhorrent to Gnosticism; and we do know enough about God to say that he so cares for us that he will raise us up.

This youthful letter, too clever by half, as Farrer himself was to admit a week later, shows how he was already moving towards the problems of theological language dealt with later on in his *Finite and Infinite*. It also shows how, even in 1927, his belief in the resurrection life was as marked as it was in his later sermons: 'It is God who raises the dead' – was his touchstone; traces of Oxford idealism linger, but by September 1928 he had begun to read Aquinas.

Another letter produces some resemblance to C. S. Lewis on 'Spirituality' in *The Screwtape Letters*:

I failed to say what I intended to say. When I protest against the 'rationalism' of all the 'Protestantism' I can understand [he means liberal Protestantism, not the classic Protestantism of Calvin or Barth], I mean that it applies an arbitrary rule or standard to dogma and practice, it judges by an external criterion. For instance, what on earth is spirituality? The Protestant seems to have behind him a critique of the religious understanding which supplies him with an *a priori* concept of what will do and what won't. If spirituality means (as I think it ought to mean) the good in religion, then everything must be considered on its merits; there is no abstract principle which will automatically rule out this and that. I find people who think they are being spiritual when they are employing thin and airy images in their thought. They have no objection to saying that God is the Ground of all being, but are terribly upset by the idea that he could be this consecrated bread. There is no reason in this. No one suggested ever that he could be the bread except 'in a certain sense and context', but then neither is he the Ground except in 'a certain sense'. It should be an axiom that we know nothing about him *absolutely* at all. Everything about him is poetry, metaphor without a key – even the statement that he was incarnate in Jesus. The justification for so astonishing a belief is that the religious conscience recognizes it as the sort of truth it requires and that it is no more poetry and paradox than the other things that we say. As for the statement that 'He is Love', it seems to me so dangerous that one can hardly trust it with people who do not understand that in a thousand senses he is not. Unspirituality consists in making capital out of those points in the given metaphor which are not relevant, as for instance when from the statement God is love the ignorant go on to think of him as suffering the pangs of love or as an individual to whom a sentimental or erotic attitude is appropriate. What safeguard is there but a well-worked-out system of mythology (as in the full Orthodox faith) in which each fragment of metaphor is connected up with a whole body thought out by the mind of ages on the basis of the original revelation? Then the wrong applications of the single metaphor are corrected by the rest of the doctrine as the statement about God's being Love is corrected by a knowledge, say, of the Athanasian Creed. That symbol is most spiritual in which the wholeness of the Faith is most fully focused. That is why the myth of the Eucharist seems to me the most spiritual of all the mythology at our command. Here, of course, I am applying 'spirituality' to the terms in which we express our faith, to 'objective' spirituality. 'Subjective' spirituality or fervour may be present or absent in any religious exercise. Now as to 'Is religion poetry?' Certainly not. But God being in his ultimate reality unknowable, our experience of him *clothes itself with* creature-elements. Religion is an independent value and activity, as God is a reality *sui generis*, but it expresses itself entirely in the other values and activities – in morality, thought, poetry, the good, the true, the beautiful, but none of these is religion and none of these is God. I like to use the word 'myth' as a special term for elements of our life or our knowledge which are used to express what is religious. Does not morality become to the devout an enacted myth in which he has experience of God or union with God (which is the same thing)? And yet morality as such is not religion. Is it not the same with philosophy and art, yes and history too, when they become the utterance of the Logos?

But to return to the specific Christian revelation, which was the myth made history. We cannot say that Jesus was divine merely because he was so good or so wise – our data are quite insufficient: his transcendent goodness and wisdom are dependent on the transcendent part he had to play. He was not even a very great man unless he was a man playing the part of being Christ and God, that is to say *being* a myth, which is beyond all reason. The multiple sense of scripture (according to the ancient commentators) was in his life.

I'm afraid I used Gnosticism wrongly for sacramentalism, for a tendency which in Gnosticism reaches a caricature of itself: but if there was not something akin to Philonism in the way of thinking in which Jesus grew up, he is impossible! Was there not Philonism in the Son of Man Christology? Or even more in the idea that one could be an ordinary man and at the same time (in a second sense, as it were) that Heavenly Being? Did not degenerate Platonism in ceasing to be philosophy become the true 'logic' of religion, and are we not right in viewing our faith through the eyes of the early gentile Church? The question of origins, where Rabbinism came from and when, is surely a secondary matter. One does not need to establish that Jesus had read the pre-Philonians (if there were any) if he embodies Philonic principles. As for the symbolical acts of the ancient prophets and the ancient Jewish ritual, they seem to me to be just very imperfect sacramentalism; I don't suppose they had made up their minds what they meant. For instance, could Isaiah have decided for you whether the coal of his vision cleansed him *realiter?* I really didn't mean to tie revelation down to discreditable religious developments, but only to suggest that the same religious logic was to be found in the degenerate Platonism and in Christianity. I think that will do for today. [10]

This outpouring may be taken with a letter to his mother of the same date.

I hope father is not annoyed with my controversiality. I am only disputing with everybody possible in the hope of making up my own mind. He need not be afraid that I shall say any of the things I now say in a year's time. But I will have a connected and rational theology or perish in the attempt. [11]

Here is the seed almost visible which would germinate into *Finite and Infinite.* When he says we know nothing about God absolutely, we are to take it that our knowledge is never expressible in completely straightforward terms and that one metaphor on its own can and does mislead: analogy is to be corrected and supplemented by analogy and we are the best clue to the nature of God since our experience of God clothes itself in creaturely elements and we have the best knowledge of creaturely existence in ourselves. With these thoughts seething in his mind, Farrer's tutorials must have been exciting. Unfortunately no comments from his tutor have survived.

Meanwhile his friend B. C. Butler[6] had joined the Roman Communion. To assuage his father's fears that Austin might follow him, he wrote in the long vacation of 1928:

[Butler] was never one of those who are half-Romanists in the English Church: he was always moderate and sensible, and it was because of this clarity that he rejected any impossible compromises when he saw that he could not stay as he was. I think you must allow young men under 27 to be intellectual chameleons. He took a year's lay work in which to make up his mind and there he is. And now he makes no attempt at proselytism, but is more gentle than before. In fact he apologized to me and hoped that he mightn't have used undue influence in our talk. His simplemindedness is, I admit, excessive. He is really living in a Holy Roman Church of his own mind which his lips confess to be almost non-existent outside it: and

49

yet he has gone over to find the Church as the visibly embodied idea. This is Realism – to believe that the Church is something prior, self-existent, and not the form in which the spiritual life of its members attains active expression and only exists as such. I can't make this intelligible because I can't understand realism anywhere. I think you are a realist about Faith and that's where we differ. Thus you say: all those who pin their faith to Jesus should recognize one another whatever their beliefs – apparently supposing a self-existent object of faith identical for them all, although their faiths differ enormously. This I can't understand. There is only one thing in which we all share – the belief in God as a bare notion. This belief is mediated through christological doctrine and so receives its positive expression and value for life. But the mere occurrence of the term 'Jesus', in whatever context, really cannot be said to make people co-religionists. They all share faith – undoubtedly, and this if you like is the main thing – but what makes religion to be a particular and definite religion is not its faith but the beliefs in which that faith expresses itself and through which it impinges on conduct. And the fact that one's belief makes some use of the idea of Jesus does not carry one far – he may be preaching another Jesus entirely. If you say – well, at least the history is clear – yet people differ entirely in the interpretation of it, unless of course you are going to reduce religion to ethics and then there will be some real identity. So that to your statement that creeds merely divide, I should reply that nothing else can conceivably unite. My creed is really the only precious thing I possess and certainly the only thing it is worth anyone's while to borrow from me. There is no doubt that we fight about a word, and that by 'creed' we mean different things. The spoken creed is the grand link in which many men realize that their creed is one, as in the Sacrament that their life is one. And how can they join in the second if they don't in the first?

I'm glad you rubbed into me my own remark on the exhausting nature of religious exercises, for it confirms me in my opinion that one has to balance different sorts of activities one against the other, and that too much 'Religion' may mean sterilization. I am feeling very strongly now what a farthing taper this life is, to be burnt carefully by inches – and if you burn it at one end, you must burn it so much less at the other. I dare say it would be better for Butler if he prayed less and philosophized more. I read four and a half hours of Plotinus yesterday and I've got a headache today. You see you have come too late to warn me off Plotinus. He is fascinating. [12]

A week later, and still from Cuddesdon, Farrer reopened the correspondence about Butler, and revealed much of what he felt about current theology in 1928:

> Butler did not introduce the subject [his conversion] himself, and when I asked him for the main considerations that had sent him over, he answered quietly and with perfect candour. It had been, as usual, Realism concerning the doctrine of the Church, together with the conviction that only Rome at present could be relied upon to keep a firm hold on historical reality and full Christology together, even though she has not yet arrived at a proper synthesis. He suspects the tendency of Anglican theology: and, of course, if Anglicanism gives up metaphysics with the pre-existence and incarnation, we shall all have to go to Rome together, since I'm convinced there's no *via media* for the honest thinker between these things and the liberal synagogue. Not of course that this is anything against the prospects of liberal Protestantism in this world, since the world prefers compromise to thought. (I must point out that you and Wheeler [Robinson] are not liberal Protestants in this sense). However, we're inclined to believe that the English Church will hold up. If only these miserable Anglos could get down to a little thinking instead of studying the Sarum Use and mumbling unintelligible formulae. As it is, the Modernists with a contemptible philosophical position have it all their own way. *Magna est veritas: num praevalebit?* These immoral pragmatistical Spikes will produce a very awkward reaction soon, in which of course the baby will go with the bath-water. [13]

He gives an indication of what repelled him by writing to his mother a list of phrases that should be anathematized:

> I long to see an anathema book of the liberalist cliches, posted up on the college chapel door so that neither the Master nor Barry[7] nor anyone else could ever use them again. 'Whosoever saith ... "We feel that in Jesus we have got something so big that ... " "We cannot help feeling that somehow the cross is at the core of the Universe." "Let us avoid antiquated phrases and say that the man Jesus has the value of God." Whosoever saith these things, let him be anathema.' But what stuff is this to pour over one's mother's ears on a fine May morning! [14]

Gone were the days when the unsophisticated first-year scholar could say, 'The chapel is well ordered and everything decently done.'

As the time of his diaconate drew near, Farrer's enquiring theological mind considered how he might make contact with his future parishioners, no doubt stimulated by lectures on the Sunday School given at Cuddesdon by Phyllis Dent and Father Langford James. He also visited Dewsbury – the parish where he finally decided to serve his title – where he saw the Sunday School in action. For him every issue seemed to become a theological question. His regard for his mother's understanding of such matters is shown in the following:

> We have had lectures for three days continuously on modern Sunday School methods. They give the impression that the laity doesn't know anything and isn't likely to for a generation. It must be lovely for the liberal Free Churchmen who don't feel it the least important that they should. Do you teach your mothers the first thing about the Christian faith or do you just edify them? And what way of teaching do you find of avail? Are they fed with the letter of the New Testament? Or with tasty bits only? Does one teach them to pray sensibly? I want to know about these things for myself. I'm just trying to understand how on earth ever to get anything across to anyone and especially trying to find out what the Divine Friendship religion and the worship of the historical person of Jesus as a spiritual companion means, because apparently this is the only thing the simple people understand and I can't understand it at all. I'm sure it must be the same thing as my religion in the long run, only I can't get the bridge and can't translate. I remember people trying to put religion to me under this form when I was small, but I think it was always strange to me and I couldn't get on at all till I understood the Mystical Body through the Communion, but that seems entirely different: you enter into and submit to the operation of Christ, but these people who talk about the Friendship seem to be outside him, to have him over there, so that they can shake hands as it were and talk. And they experience an external 'presence' that would certainly put my hair on end and wouldn't appear to me to have anything to do with religion, because we don't worship something that may turn up here and there, but the one God in whom and from whom all things are. If you can give me any enlightenment on this topic, I wish you would, since there will be no harm in my understanding my parishioners. I haven't written

52

this as a polemic against this form of worship, but so that you may see my difficulty. Of course (let me add) I understand what is meant by Christ's having performed the act of redemption, and being our example and giving himself in the renewing of our mind by the infusion of his: these things are not meaningless to me. But the word 'friendship' amazes me – can you explain? [15]

Farrer was in fact, and always had been, theocentric. He started from God and even when he saw God as the Absolute, his problem was the relation between God and Christ. Most people when they are Christians are Christocentric and begin with Christ, and then their problem is how in this particular man God is revealed.

Almost up to his last day at Cuddesdon, theology and philosophy stream from Farrer's pen. In the last letter to his father before he left for his ordination at Wakefield he writes:

If I philosophize, let me remind you that this is for a very simple and evolutionary reason – that the Devil has kept me running for life 'on the philosophical side' for some time, and I've developed this sort of behaviour for the very same simple reason that the flying-fish took to the air – to keep out of the way of the shark. So you may see that 'sanity', if I possess it, is not a virtue but a necessity due to a lack of virtue. I only wish I may now be of any practical use: which is a very different matter.

I've delivered up my thesis on 'Authority in the Church', in which I came to the most lamentable conclusions more or less involuntarily. For instance, that episcopal divine right is an idea expressed in a visible order; the business of the hierarchy being to keep such a check on 'life' as to keep it within the limits of a possible viable church so as not to remove the possibility of the sacramental objective presentation of her doctrine and sacraments; and on the other hand by redefinition, which does not affect the essence, to modify the sacramental truth with great caution and conservatism, yet enough to enable it to be the doctrine and form of a living and developing church.

If you see what I mean you will understand that it is a rank piece of idealism about the sacraments and the faith, and reduces the 'inviolability' of the creeds to their capacity for being regarded as fixed and objective, that grace may be mediated thereby in a special mode: and I submit that every religious body has a truth which it puts to this use and that there's nothing like being clear and definite about it. Anyhow, no *Quod semper, quod ubique* on any liberal understanding of those words: though the sacred body of truth must have a wide basis both in time and space.

I know you'll pray for me all that you can about this time without my asking for it. As I am still running a race with the Devil on the philosophical side and shall be ordained with a quite large question unsettled and no hope of settling for months, you may be sure that I am proceeding with a due sense of human fragility and as prepared as I can make myself for almost anything; but I'm not worried just at present. [16]

Farrer was not to remain at Oxford but to go north, for reasons which he describes with great clarity. After his decision to take orders in March 1927 there was no further talk of his teaching classics at New College. But some time in 1928 he was offered and declined the chaplaincy of Corpus Christi College.

I have refused the Corpus job [he writes to his father], on my own decision, and with the Master's[8] strong support. The real objection to it is that it is not a whole-time priest's work. The college has about sixty members and it is always a small percentage to whom a chaplain can be of any serious use. If I took it, I could only do so with the intention of doing theological research and so becoming a theological tutor at last, and I don't think this is decent or right to start with. You cannot research profitably into the philosophy of religion – the only conceivable branch of study for me – until you know what you are talking about and the sphere to reveal that to you is the practical life. Or at least it is so for me. Some people no doubt can be mystics quietly by themselves in corners, but I'm not endowed that way: at least I feel so and can't give reasons. And besides this I don't know whether you have seen, but I suppose you have, the profundity of my scepticism. My faith is a very small and tender plant in a very vast expanse of unsheltered desert: religion is a wild and almost preposterous experiment to me, which I must try out on the most stringent testing ground I can find before I shall have any peace. A bad reason, you may think, for taking Holy Orders: I don't know, but I am convinced that in any other line of life my faith would never assert itself against sceptical indifference. I must give it the most bracing air or it won't grow at all. If I don't live for religion, I shan't live by religion. If you ask me whether I'm such an utter empiricist as this: whether I am prepared to say 'experience will decide', perhaps I shall say 'no'. The test is not pragmatical:

only it is by experience alone that the 'innate ideas' imprinted on the mind can be drawn out into the light of day and recognized for the eternal truths that they are. Of course I know that one can live for religion without becoming a priest: but I haven't written this as abstract doctrine, but as what I feel for myself, which is the immediate point. [17]

He concludes by likening himself to Proteus, giving an entirely different set of reasons whenever questioned, 'which must be a little confusing for my friends'.

In the same vein he writes later to his mother, reaffirming his decision to go into parochial life.

I do hate making up my mind. I had decided once and for ever that real work in a parish was the proper thing to start on: and now that I have to refuse a chaplaincy up here, I cannot remember why I decided to do so, except that I was sure I was right when I did. Someone has to be up here, and think things out for the other chaps: and if I have any brains – but then have I? One doesn't know. And then it seems indecent to swell the ranks of the Oxford Three Hundred[9] after having railed at the scandal so long. I am most inclined to stand by the notion that real work is a better school of virtue and piety. If I stay here I shall be as indolent in my religion as I am now: but in a parish there would be no reason for my existence apart from my religion. But then, if one is going to arrange life with the idea of stopping all loopholes for the Devil to get through, where is one going to stop? It seems a hopeless principle. I give it up. But meanwhile I seem to be refusing. To think of being ordained next Christmas! It is quite preposterous.

No doubt the ideal position is to be in a poor parish and to steal a few hours for study. Then you can think the real truth to yourself, and as for talking to others, you can give them the good old doctrine which you can interpret to yourself by your own philosophy. What must be impossible is an enlightened congregation to whom you have to deal out diluted liberal wash, an awful compromise which is neither honest clear thinking that will stand on its own legs nor the good old liturgical poetry. I suppose that is really why I like the Spikes: they deal out the raw material good and strong, and leave you to make the intellectual adjustment for yourself, while your Modernists insist on putting it in for you, and then they do it so vilely. [18]

This condescending view of one's congregation betrays some diaconal arrogance. Thirty years later Farrer's sermons were to show that he could state Christian truth on various levels without intellectual compromise and without sacrificing liturgical poetry.

The question remained – which parish? The first suggestion was a parish in Reading which Austin disliked, as did his father, to whom he wrote:

> Thank you for your commonitorium on Reading. I believe as a matter of fact that they want to give me an easy parish, because I gather that the Reading man is a bit odd, liable to blunder and make things difficult for an inexperienced youth. They want to set me to learn in a parish that is going well, with a man who can teach the art. I'm to go and look at Dewsbury, Yorks, this weekend. [19]

On 2 September he reported to his mother:

> I have settled with the man at Dewsbury.[10] I like him very much. He's a sensible man and not at all one to offend his congregation about trifles: is respected in his town; can preach a decent sermon, and takes the trouble to do so. He seemed to me very kind and considerate – and I am sure I shall get on with him – and I thought he was a really spiritual man. But how can one tell? Anyhow I felt some enthusiasm for him, which certainly I never did for the Reading man. His other curate speaks well of him. He must be rather more than fifty years old, and is married to a sensible Yorkshire lady who is duly submissive and won't, I think, interfere with the management. They live in a vicarage some way from the church. The other curate and I are to live in the church house, which is next door to it. The woman who looks after us is well spoken of. I am to get £190 and my rooms free, and to contract with the woman for what I eat, etc.
>
> They entertained me very kindly at the vicarage and the vicar took me a complete round of the duties on Sunday, and I read some lessons for him and heard him preach. I saw the Sunday School, which I think Ellie[11] would have approved of. There was the maximum of walking about, birthday celebrating, penny-dropping,[12] drawing, etc, but little rational instruction. They'd got a day-school teacher in charge of the youngest lot. I'm to specialize on the young and get some Scouts started (!). I am to do intensive visiting, but my mornings at least are guaranteed me for study. I'm

not to preach at present more than once a month. As for the other curate, he is in charge of the mission church! [20]

J. B. Seaton, shortly to be bishop of the diocese in which Dewsbury is situated, may have suggested some parish of this kind. On 23 December Austin was ordained deacon in the Cathedral Church of Wakefield to serve in the parish of All Saints, Dewsbury. It was a happy diocese with a Tractarian tradition in both the cathedral and the parishes, but a tradition that concentrated on the essentials rather than the externals. It lies in the south of the West Riding of Yorkshire, a region as rugged as its inhabitants, where anything worth building must be founded on the rock, and at this moment in its history it was a region of great poverty and distress. Here indeed he could try the experiment of religion on what he had explicitly desired, a stringent testing ground.

# CHAPTER 5

# Borealia Regna: Dewsbury 1928–31

*

It was appropriate that Austin Farrer should begin his ministry in Dewsbury, north of the Trent. His father had held his first pastorate in Blackburn, beyond the Pennines. There seems to have been a tradition that Cuddesdon men should begin their clerical life in the challenging surroundings of the black northern towns. Michael Ramsey went to Liverpool parish church; others went to the great Tractarian parishes of the north, such as All Saints, Wigan, or St Elphin's, Warrington.

The years between 1920 and 1930 marked the high peak of the Anglo-Catholic movement in its more flamboyant aspect. In later life Farrer was to celebrate at St Mary Magdalene's in Oxford, meekly following the directions of the Master of Ceremonies; he was at home wherever spiritual goodness poured out. Yet he was at heart a Tractarian; for him the things that mattered were communion, prayer, confession – the hard disciplined backbone of the Catholic life. The North had parishes of this kind. Both Wigan and Warrington parish churches, for example, had had their daily Mass and regular penitents for twenty years or more before they used eucharistic vestments. It was a very different world from that of London and the south of England.

Nine miles south-west of Leeds is Dewsbury on the River Calder, huddled near the other woollen towns of the West Riding. Its population in 1962 was 52,963. It is mentioned in Domesday Book and had a woollen industry in the thirteenth century, but its great expansion came in the Industrial Revolution. There is a tradition that Paulinus, the first Archbishop of York, preached at the parish church of All Saints in AD 627, and though it was largely restored in the eighteenth century, the church still has Anglo-Saxon carvings. The Calder where Paulinus baptized was, in 1928, a black stream with visible fumes rising from the surface. There is also a tradition that Robin Hood died in Dewsbury and was buried in Kirklees

Park, where there are the remains of a Cistercian foundation. The parish consisted mainly of the back-to-back houses of workers in the staple shoddy industry. There was a great auction for rag-selling, and the town reeked of the hydrochloric acid used to destroy the cotton in woollen rags. There were miners from the nearby Thornhill pit (where one of the worst mining disasters of the century took place) and also workers from the large blanket mill of Wormald and Walker. When Farrer went there the Great Depression was well on the way. There was already a soup kitchen in the church day school. The slump had spread from the mines to the woollen mills, and many people were trying to live on the equivalent of fifteen shillings a week.

The parish of All Saints contained the parish church and the mission church of St James. St James, in the Flatts area of the town, served a district made up entirely of rows of small houses, pubs, corner off-licences and fish-and-chip shops. It was common in Victorian days to build a mission church for those who, it was felt, would not be at home in the parish church.

A description of the parishioners of the mission church made by a contemporary resident of Dewsbury gives a vivid picture of local conditions.

The parishioners of the mission church were artisans working at the local boiler foundry or in the textile mills. Conversation would be of weaving, 'donnin' and 'doffin' mules,[1] cloth at so many picks to the inch,[2] dyeing and colouring. But the drab terraced houses were kept spick and span by the occupants. Everybody knew everybody else's business and very frequently added to the truth. Tragedy was shared by all. The houses were composed of one room downstairs and one bedroom in which all the family slept: screens were erected, often no more than a clothes-horse, to separate the sexes.

One short row near the mission was of 'better class', as it had two rooms downstairs, the living room and the scullery. There were no bathrooms or indoor toilets; each house had to share one of these with at least one other family, more often several families used the same one. There were no gardens, and the washing had to be stretched across the street to dry. Pulleys were fitted on to the walls at bedroom level and the clothes-line threaded through the pulleys, one at each side of the street. When the line was filled with washing it was hauled aloft to dry. The streets were paved with either granite or Yorkshire stone setts. There were in the town some 110 factory chimneys. Each chimney belched forth thick black smoke, so that a dark grey haze hung over the town. The pavements were black with the deposited soot, either eddying in little whirlpools in the summer or forming disgusting oily slime in winter.

Farrer's time in Dewsbury covered the slump of the late twenties, when married men were earning 37 shillings per week weaving and glad to get that. Many mills were working three days a week so that the workers were able to earn money three days at work and draw three days unemployment pay. Frequently four days were worked and so no unemployment pay could be drawn. Children with patched trousers' seats were a common sight, as were bowed legs due to rickets. Tuberculosis was rampant; most people knew the dreaded cough. Life began and ended in these back-to-back houses: there were no maternity hospitals and no funeral parlours. Everything happened in the downstairs room. Life had to go on in these tragic times and meals were eaten with the dead either on the bed which had been brought downstairs or covered with a sheet on trestles loaned by the undertaker. The doctor was fetched only as a last resort. Most doctors employed an ex-policeman as a debt collector. The doctor was paid for his services at so much a week for many a week after.

Although there were public houses in the area, drunkenness was not rife for the obvious reason that money was scarce. There was the occasional inebriate, a source of fun to the neighbours, a source of pity for his wife. The thrifty and the slatternly lived side by side.

There was a church house where the assistant curates lived, a gaunt building, now demolished, next to the church and a noisy tramway junction, It had perhaps once been a hotel: there were still numbers over all the many doors, a stone staircase, and green-painted walls sweating with condensation. My vision still persists of Dr Farrer in those days rushing out of the church house with his cassock, surplice and hood over his arm, his scarf rolled up in his hand, dashing across Church Street to cut up South Street and so on to Vulcan Road and St James! [1]

For most of his time in Dewsbury Austin shared this accommodation with the Reverend J. E. Farmiloe, who became his lifelong friend. He appears to have begun his ministry at the parish church and later often to have worked at St James' as well. At All Saints there was a very respectable Matins congregation. St James' had a sung Eucharist rather like the modern parish communion, with the English Hymnal and vestments. The building itself was on two levels: on the street level was the church and in the basement the Sunday School and a hall for social functions. (It would have been here that Austin as a deacon heard the poignant words from a Sunday school teacher, 'The next boy to throw a Bible at me goes out'.)

Although the Community of the Resurrection was near, it had made little impact on the churchmanship in Dewsbury, which was a Nonconformist stronghold. There had been considerable concern when the vicar, Canon Wolde, had allowed the Mirfield Fathers to celebrate High Mass with incense at the time of the Anglo-Catholic Congress. The local newspaper was up in arms against such practices. Canon Wolde, a fair-haired man in his forties, was of German descent and had had a hard time when he was appointed in 1916 in the middle of the First World War. By the time Farrer came he was well respected. The church was in good heart. The previous year it had celebrated its thirteenth centenary. The Canon had started a mid-week communion at 6.30 a.m. so that mill workers could make their communion on the way to work. The mills started work at 7 o'clock.

The great event in the year was the Sunday school anniversary procession on Whit Tuesday. The Sunday school scholars, teachers, choir (robed) and the clergy (also robed) would assemble in the Sunday school, which was also the day school. The procession would wind its way through the streets to the church for a special festival Evensong, then back to the day school for a tea of specially baked currant buns with gallons of tea. The band then led the children to a field in Savile Town near the cricket ground, where games were organized until 8.00 p.m or so when the whole proceedings would end with a dance for the more energetic.

If it were ever true that Farrer needed bringing down to earth, he had come to the right place. North-east Lancashire and west Yorkshire, the Pennine community, is a unique enclave. The people are strong-willed, cheerful and full of humour, sometimes rather grim. To survive in the Depression and the environment they had need of these qualities. They came to love Farrer and he to love them. Years later he would speak with affection of the black-leaded fireplaces and the smell of home-baked bread. His letters to Farmiloe over the years were full of queries about the friends he had known.

Next in importance to the people in a deacon's life is the incumbent who gives him his title. Again Farrer was fortunate. Frank Wolde was warm-hearted, learned, able, conscientious and business-like. The Wakefield diocesan registry records that he was an MA of Oxford, ordained priest in 1898. He was instituted to the benefice of All Saints, Dewsbury, on 28 November 1916, appointed Rural Dean of Dewsbury on 1 January 1917, and became an Honorary Canon of Wakefield in 1921. He was appointed to the Rectory of Barton-le-Clay in the Diocese of St Albans in 1932.

On Monday mornings there was a staff meeting. Canon Wolde and his two curates ploughed through *Essays Catholic and Critical*.[3] Wolde and Farmiloe listened with delight while Farrer sharpened his critical teeth on the contributors. Wolde used also to insist that his curates took a complete day off every week to get right out of the parish. Farrer often stayed in the parish to read and was duly rebuked for this. For exercise he ran daily in vest and shorts round Savile Town and Thornhill Lees. (In later years he would be seen sprinting across both quads in Keble College on the way to the chapel, and indeed to most of his engagements.)

The life of a parish, and even more of a mission church in a poor district, depends on assiduous visiting. Farrer (considered in Oxford to be shy and nervous) visited assiduously in the Flatts, and enjoyed his friendships. He also visited the general hospital, the fever hospital, and the TB sanatorium (needed all too often in those days of depression and malnutrition). When visiting invalids at home he was sometimes found reading on the stairs because his patient was asleep. The parishioners had many occasions to remark his absent-mindedness. In his early days at Dewsbury the envelopes containing his Christmas cards and, indeed, other letters rarely bore a house number; one was once addressed 'Halfway up George Street on the left-hand side', and another 'Opposite corner-shop, top of Springfield Street'. Later on he used to cycle round the parish, collect the house numbers he required and post his mail in a more normal style. The bicycle indeed was a problem; he would make visits on it and then walk home to the church house quite forgetting where he had left it. It stayed at one home for two weeks because no one knew whose it was.

In his sermons Farrer was already searching for illustrations to clarify his meaning, the art he exercised so brilliantly in his later sermons. One of his servers remembers him using the difference in the scale of maps: on one scale England might be a mere dot, but on a really large-scale map you might even mark the cat sitting on the top of Tommy Jones' fish shop.

He was at his best with young people and left his successor a lively group. With them he produced a Yorkshire dialect play, 'Our Bessie', which was a great success, toured the district and even went as far as Huddersfield. He was known to take part himself, appearing once as the Angel Gabriel in the Bethlehem tableaux of the King's Messengers (the junior branch of the Society for the Propagation of the Gospel (SPG)). During one of his talks to the King's Messengers – on Spiritualism – there was much hilarity when the lights failed. He was also an enthusiastic leader of the Dewsbury parish scout troup. Every Saturday afternoon he used to visit Staincliffe County Hospital (for geriatric cases) to give the chairbound old ladies an outing in the hospital grounds. At first he wore his Scout uniform for this duty, but when he found that the sight of his bare knees upset one old lady he took to wearing his cassock. With his usual thoroughness he visited the Scout camps and on one stormy night almost lost the Dewsbury troop.

I peered [he writes] from tent to tent. Nobody. Thinking they must be gathered around a neighbouring camp fire I went to the next troop. There I learned the truth – they had been washed out by the rain, soaking up through the spongy ground, and were with another troop camped in Cawthorpe village school. There I found them strewn about the school furniture in sleeping bags and blankets. This disarray of bodies we resurrected for prayers; and then soon had a very sound sleep, for which I for one was doubly thankful. Yesterday was gloriously fine, and the scene was beautiful. We lazed and played in the sun and had it warm on the back of our necks. I am sunburnt. We slept in tents and had a very warm march back as we had come, though with four miles' aid from a bus, else we would have been late for the Sunday school procession. It was as before, except that I walked as the idol of St James instead as the parish satellite; the weather was splendid.

Then tea unclouded by any feud on the butter on the buns question. Unbelievable tales were told about certain boys' bun consumption. Then very ragged S S sports on a field, done (glory be) by 7.45 p.m. [2]

The butter on the buns feud roused from Austin a ciceronian piece of rhetoric:

> I have had a let off this afternon. There was a meeting at St James' to make arrangements for the Whitsuntide Feast. Now, I had been warned that a well-rubbed sore was going to be chafed again. It was this. The snaky and calamitous Aunt Eva protests that since the children are supplied with unbuttered buns, it is invidious for the teachers to subintroduce private stores of the lubricant for their own consumption. To this it has now been replied that the church merely supplies mankind with buns: but that it is open to the whole ktisis [creation], whether teachers or children, to bring not only butter but pepper, salt, mustard, marmalade or German sausage, if it pleases them, as an opson [delicacy]. Moreover (these say) there are some to whom the butterless consumption of buns is physically impossible. As a point of right (it may be retorted) this may pass; but we are not under law, but grace, and the weaker brother must be consulted for. For the Apostle himself says that all things are sanctified by thanksgiving: but the luxury of the butterful is likely, nay certain, to kill the spirit of gratitude in the butterless. But that a Whitsuntide bun should not be sanctified is absurd. And therefore, etc. . . . But this is not allowed conclusive force; since the section, greasing and reglutination of buns can be so accomplished that the butterfulness of the few is invisible to the butterlessness of the many. Nay, say the first, the principle of deceit is not to be admitted in any case. This topic, I am told, nearly rent St James' last year. It did not appear this year. Can it indeed be that I have made Aunt E. fear my mockery? That would be an achievement indeed. I still keep up the plan of conducting St James' business meetings in a spirit of farce, and find that it works fairly well; but what would the Vicar say? [3]

One hurdle for the new deacon was swiftly surmounted – his first sermon. He wrote to his mother on 7 January 1929 – by then a deacon of fifteen days' standing:

> Well, no: you certainly can't have my last sermon because I destroyed the MS immediately after preaching it. The text was St

Mark 1.9, our Lord's baptism; but it was all about his faith in responding to the Messianic call, and about the purpose of God as something experienced and pushing one on from behind to do things otherwise absurd. This was in the parish church last night: it was approved, though the Vicar is reserving various criticisms of a practical sort which I've not heard yet. [4]

A week later he wrote to his father of the impression he had formed of the vigorous Yorkshire character, 'the perpetual wonder of Yorkshire self-conceit':

They think that Yorkshiremen go to Heaven *ex officio*, I think. Even my DT penitent[4] recovering vigour and appetite begins to strike a balance between his sins and his good deeds, and finds a decided preponderance for the latter. I'm quite perplexed and don't know how to get at them. How can one preach salvation to people who think they are saved? They think that religion is meant to be a kind of spiritual cup of tea, and if you can get on without it, that's rather creditable: and if you can be moderately kind and moral, you are fulfilling the Law of God. The DT man 'would rather do a good turn than a bad one any day'. There's evidently nothing to be done along the line of telling people that they can't do without religion, since they take the liberty of setting up their own standard, and how can one get into their heads the idea of regeneration and new life or religion as an end in itself? They would only think you meant enjoyable emotions, and if you talked about the whole of life as the sphere of religion, they would either think that this is just one of the things that the clergy say but obviously aren't true or they would interpret it as moralism – that serving God doesn't mean saying prayers but living a decent life. I don't see how anything but crude spikery is ever going to do any good with such people – man's first duty is to hear Mass and communicate; and in order to enjoy the mystery you must submit to confession and absolution and believe what you're told. That might be better than believing nothing. They don't disbelieve, either. I wish they did. But I'm beginning to talk nonsense. Obviously one must be content simply to study people at first; there must be some way of getting hold of them. [5]

Insights, surprises and new experiences were gained during hospital visits:

My first case was a miner probably dying of DT, who had been picking up snakes off his ceiling and rats off the floor the day before

65

but was rational when I saw him. He showed signs of contrition, was trying to pray, and was firmly convinced of one theological truth, that we don't know what's good for us. It was only as I left that I learned from the male nurse that this man's mistake on the question of what was good for him had been concerned with floods of beer. This man was in a separate cell, which made spiritual conversation more easy. The next man I had to bawl at in an open ward. He was old and deaf, and it took five minutes to get him to understand anything; and when he did he merely remarked that all parsons go to hell, which is, I dare say, a probable opinion. He was slightly dotty and obsessed with two ideas – that he was destitute, and that the nurses wouldn't sew a button on his night-shirt. Conversation was made more difficult by his tiresome habit of ranging the ward, they said. My third man was an old saintly creature slowly dying in agonies, and a marvel of pious patience. [6]

Yorkshire funeral customs, too, could be surprising and indeed grim to the unprepared. Farrer described to his mother what he called 'an orgy of pathos':

The little girl in the Bethlehem tableaux died shortly after. She was a thoughtful little girl and threw herself very much into the part. Well, they had a lovely funeral, with plenty of children there: music, candles, flowers, a plain-song chant. Everyone behaved very nicely: there seemed to be a general disposition to pray. But now what has changed my mind about the affair? Something I heard this afternoon. The mother had said to one of our teachers, 'Well, I never knew that we were so respected. We have had children coming in all day to see Phyllis [the dead child]. And her little brother [aged four] seemed to understand about it, too. He was even taking off the handkerchief for them [from Phyllis's face]'. From another source I heard that a little wretch . . . the most charming, irresponsible, ill-brought-up little rogue in our school, had been acting as guide and scouring the Flatts for small children who had not had anything to do with Phyllis and taking them along. This is not all. For it now comes out that there was diphtheria in the house at the time, although then unknown. Phyllis's sister was taken to fever hospital on the night of the funeral. There is nothing to be done now except say as little as possible. Of course I was taken to see Phyllis's little corpse, which was a very serene and decorous one: and I so loathe highbrowism that I was not in the least disposed to protest. After all, it is purely a matter of taste and custom. The little brother was running in and out, and I thought, 'It doesn't matter, he is too small to understand anything.' But it never occurred to me to warn her against promiscuous infant visitation. She seemed and is indeed a religious woman, although not a strong one. The Vicar has not yet heard this tale: he will be furious. [7]

House visiting was equally testing:

I've come across more queer birds in Central Street Yards. What of a Spiritualist, a Welshman by birth and a speaker with tongues? As a Primitive Methodist he acquired the gift of so talking that he did not know what he was saying. The Holy Spirit was speaking with his tongue: the brethren were edified. Then his wife became too much for him and he left her and began to live in adultery. The Prims did not like this, so he became a Spiritualist and exchanged the Holy Ghost for the Spirits of the departed, who cause in him the same phenomenon, called 'going under power'. It is produced by gazing for half an hour at a glass of water, but is sometimes spontaneous. He said that nine mediums out of ten were impostors and the Dewsbury Spiritualists were a bad lot: he would rather be with the Prims, who have got the Alleluia in them. In the next sentence he defended the Spiritualist position from a pantheist argument, saying God is everything. He did not pretend to know what spirit speaks through him, though others, he says, have that gift. I saw his mistress and deplored his taste. He had the usual arguments about the impossibility of living with his wife and that it could not be the will of God, but I insinuated that it is just possible to leave a wife without taking a mistress. This possibility he did not seem to have considered. I told him he was certainly excommunicated from Christianity; though I wasn't quite clear whether, seeing he had children by his mistress, it would do much good for him to leave her now. We parted on the best of terms; he lending me a Spiritual manual for training the young – horrible nonsense, sentimental angelolatry. I'd like your opinion on this *casus conscientiae*. Not that it matters practically, since he is taking his own advice – but to be separated from two women can hardly be much improvement on being separated from one, can it? The woman was a dull, passive creature, made to admire rather than to be admired. They were near the starvation line, as he had his other wife to support. Their two neighbours were below it. There are a great many people in

Dewsbury living on tea and bread with a certain amount of margarine. [8]

Not all visits were so harrowing; and Farrer's descriptive talents reappear in yet another record of his adventures in the parish:

My new area of poor houses I find very entertaining, though sometimes tragic. It was a great joy and surprise to find one young woman who railed, with a very primitive idea of wit certainly, but quite like a cockney. Her husband (to whom she was evidently very much attached) was shaving at the time and she spared no opportunity that the conversation offered for hinting obliquely that she wished he'd cut his throat. She also wished passionately that she'd never married him. I asked him if she was always like this, and he said, 'Nobbut before strangers'. He was a big good-tempered youth, had been brought up a Romanist, been in the navy, and escaped both Church and Service to marry this Protestant wench at a registrar's office. He got out of the navy by the simple device of borrowing his neighbour's sputum-pan in hospital; so he got himself discharged for consumption. He claimed that he was not irreligious (his wife certainly hadn't a grain of religion in her composition), and his quarrel with the Church was on the ground of liberty and authority. He knew a great deal about the Holy Scriptures, but his wife wouldn't let him get away with that. 'Ay, and d'ye know why?' she said, ''E were given twenty days when 'e were in t'navy and there was nowt else in t'place to read.' 'Well, lass,' he replied, 'I didn't have to read it, I'd not ha read it if I hadn't found it interesting. Folks don't know', he proceeded naively, 'but it's a queer book is t'Bible, and there's a lot of right interesting reading in it and all.' I was glad to find that he regarded the early part of the sacred volume as fabulous, and he told his wife off when she raised the chestnut about Cain's wife. [9]

The secret trial of Farrer's life in Dewsbury and his chief perplexity was the Sunday school. His great aim was its improvement. The half-trained teachers, the well-meaning volunteers and the toughness of the children all combined to depress the new curate, who wanted to effect a revolution and to produce shining well-instructed pupils. He wrote to his parents to share his perplexity, dismay and occasional triumphs:

I find myself suddenly becoming superintendent of the boys'

Sunday school. I can't teach boys (that's agreed) but I have some hope of improving the methods (e.g. I've already introduced 'expression work' by writing after the lessons), and at least I mean to make an effort to substitute worship for 'opening' and 'closing' the school. I made up a short litany with a response, and they really prayed with that, I think because it was they who prayed as much as I. I joined the hymn by some phrases to the Litany and they sang it decently for once without ragging. I'm surprised at the lack of common sense and powers of simple generalization in teachers who know the boys well and, inside their own notions, can teach them quite decently, indeed, to my envy and admiration. But laity will be laity, I suppose. [10]

Depression was tempered by the recollection of his own attitude to religious instruction as a child:

I'm getting very fed-up with my weekly lantern-services for children, in fact they're no good. The slides are idiotically chosen (e.g. pictures illustrating the parables as incidents in Christ's life). The pictures distract from the words, the words from the pictures, and hang me if I can get morals out of the narrative. Our Lord's life doesn't mean anything to children, and doesn't mean anything to anyone in small bits. All I can do is to have back four or five pictures when the story is finished, and say prayers appropriate for each. The slides are modern and realistic but put together in the most idiotic way, and the supplied lecture shows that these people learn nothing: it's just a confused 'harmony' tricked out with modern cliches and purple phrases, talks about 'personality' and produces a confused mythic rigmarole. So there's your S S Union. Meanwhile the weekly fixture must continue and the children come, because it costs threepence to go to the cinema, and the lantern's free. But what can you do with children after all? If they pick up a few chance impressions that's all you can expect. I sometimes try to recall my own childish religion, but I find that it had only two parts: a bad conscience, and a sense of bewilderment at something they were trying to teach me but I couldn't grasp. As for the child's alleged natural and joyous sense of a present deity, it wasn't there! [11]

In dismal mood again he describes another parish's Sunday school anniversary, which he calls 'the anniversary of *nothing*'. He is perplexed by the problem of how to approach the children.

You can make them think and answer questions and draw childish conclusions, but there never seems to be any real point that it is possible to bring home to the infant mind. The Vicar says 'Don't worry. If you have made children feel at home in church and provided them with an entertainment which they vaguely suppose to be intended for their good, that's all you can expect to do.' It is certainly all that as a child I ever experienced, and perhaps after all childish religion involves a considerable amount of make-believe or unreality as certainly most adolescent religion does, if indeed it is true that one has to feed them with a vague idealism about renewing the face of the earth, at an age when they have no power to do anything. How curious that people's desires and ideals contract to the reasonable just in proportion as their faculties expand to the adequate. I was reading one of these booklets about how to inspire the young with piety written by one of your youth-movement liberals – a great deal of invective against those who would make church life an end in itself, with a lot of talk about vision and world renovation and idealism . . . And practically, what did it come to? That if your young men should come into contact with foreigners, they should fraternize and not condemn. But Dewsbury lads do *not* come into contact with foreigners. Also, thank goodness, they break all the psychologists' canons by being quite untouched with idealism, else I should not get on with them so well even as I do. Do you not think that there is something to be said for truth and fact: something to be said for the old plan of keeping the young in their place and pointing out to them that the important part in the world is not to be played by persons under thirty? Why all this unreality? And is there nothing to be said for the ancient virtue of humility and to go back to where we began? 'We are but little children weak' is a pure if strong and unpalatable dose of 'know thyself' after all, is it not? Is it possible that education according to the findings of psychologists sometimes means education through playing on vanity? [12]

Still in 'reactionary mood', he criticizes

people who talk about education, assuming that the end or ideal of education is given, so that it is possible to have a pure science of method concerning the means. There is no doubt that one way of making railway lines can be proved more efficient than another: and one might say that the antiquated methods were wasteful, stupid and not adapted to the material they work upon. That is because there is no doubt about the end. But is it so in education?

People talk about the sheer inefficiency of older methods – that they were not adapted to the nature of man. But it is not possible to consider method and material *in vacuo*, and the truth seems to be that we have just decided to create a different sort of product, and this we assume and forget that we've assumed it. Of course the old cast-iron methods were inefficient for creating young Greek gods: but so are ours for creating an absolute sense of duty and humble submission to authority for the good of all, and the rooted belief in the objectivity of a law divine. Success and failure attend all endeavours: and you soon discover by questioning a few people that the old methods did not bore, antagonize or drive into revolt a much greater proportion than the new. The children who spent the whole Sunday in religious exercises did not consider whether it was amusing or not, because it was suggested to them that that was not the point: and so they imbibed the idea of absolute law, which was just what people wanted to teach them. Every age decides to create something quite new and individual, and the method follows with it. The ideal of 'efficiency' and 'scientific method' in education is, as an ideal, as absurd as the political idea of efficiency. Efficiency must be to an end. One can't get out of the responsibility of fixing the end by devoting oneself to the method. [13]

These are prophetic words and would apply to much that is said about education today. Yet with experience Farrer's expectation of instant success lessened. He became almost pleased with his Sunday school once he realized that they were children and not undergraduates. After some months he could write:

Sunday school is rapidly returning to holy obedience and would be better still if it weren't for pestilential special services – Dedication Festival, SPG, Armistice Day, and I don't know what, so that one can't enforce a continuous policy. Still today was almost a model performance and they loved St Telemachus in the arena. Their lust for blood is insatiable, and we have a martyr weekly butchered to make a Christian holiday. But on Advent, the Sunday after next, there will be a general move up of classes and all will return to primal chaos again. [14]

A greater anxiety was preparation for confirmation. Austin took the boys' classes and no doubt the vicar took the girls. From this experience he learned much about human nature.

My confirmation people will keep dribbling in. I have now fifteen of

71

them and have closed the list. The (apparently) worst boys always seem to have the most personal religion: the dull, working Sunday school prize-winners the least of all. The boys of 14 are the most flippant; those of 12–13 drink in with open eyes. Those of 16–21 are all serious and with a sense of sin; but they have all run so long in the groove of childish devotion (with one exception) that one has to dread an atrophy which it is too late to overcome. Several are from Nonconformist families: these all have a better idea of private prayer than the others, but a meaner idea of God. But taking them as a whole, I am surprised at the degree of natural piety, and a bit ashamed too. My own religion at their age was nothing but a sense of guilt. [15]

This was stringent testing ground, and at times he was distressed by those who lapsed.

Wretched man that I am! The exclamation is due to a visit to one or two lads, one of whom I prepared for confirmation a year ago and I have seen scarcely at all. O that I had my time over again to give much more of it just to getting to know these people, instead of writing lectures for students, and fighting the Devil, the most foolish and selfish of all preoccupations. And then one discovers that the Devil just doesn't matter, but like all quite simple discoveries it takes so long to make. And that anyone's mind should be so absurdly built that he should make it through the roundabout of German theology instead of believing St Paul quite simply when he says that Christ nailed the powers of evil to the cross. O perversity! I have used two and a half years learning about these simple truths, instead of being any use. But these complaints are vain. This lad I saw in the street the other day and invited to come and see me with his former pal. He explained with some confusion that he had changed pals since then. So I told him to bring the new one (a person totally unknown) and he took it as the naturallest thing in the world. Both are shop-boys who spend their spare time teaching each other music or walking in the countryside. [16]

As he reflected on the perversity of the human heart, so he was brought face to face with the perversity of human life, with festivity in the midst of poverty.

. . . Some weeks ago I went with the Scouts to parade about at a function called 't' Gawthorpe Maypole', and was surprised to notice that the chief enlivening element – that is the clowns who hopped about at the sides of the usual weary procession of chariots carrying infant prigs dressed in white with 'Love', 'Peace', 'Joy' written across their hearts – that these clowns nearly all bore the parts of beggars, draggle-tailed girls, ragged children, all the forms of poverty: you'd think this rather a bitter jest in a region where twenty per cent draw some form of relief, but I suppose *inveterata hominum consuetudo sibi inferius aliquid semper conculcare* [it is an inescapable human habit always to trample on something lower than oneself]. [17]

It was not all work. He had one day off a week to go right away from the parish, which, typically, he felt he did not deserve.

But it's certainly a relief. There's decent country to the south and I got a good walk over frozen snow-covered fields on Wednesday. Farmiloe goes miles away by train, but I don't like that, and I'm going to stick to the neighbourhood until I'm sick of it. It's ordinary hilly country of about the same scale as Rickmansworth, but of course wholly different. [18]

There were visits outside the parish, including those to nearby religious houses, one of which produced an explosion of wrath against the 'sugar' and 'mythicity' of some nativity tableaux presented by the nuns at Horbury:

O Lord! Is this Christianity or Hinduism, or is it that I am a miserable rationalist and Christianity is this? So I reflected, turning my face to the wall and inly groaning. St Anna sitting on a stool, in a scene of melting distances, roseate clouds, cypress trees and purple pampas-grasses: pink and golden lights predominating. To her enters the Blessed Virgin, aged six in white and a gauze halo. St Anna registers prophetically: dim blue lights: enter vision of very Murillo angels with golden heart, cross, spear, thorns, nails. From windows opening into the back of the hall, the sisters chant about the Rose of Sharon: tapers and incense, cherubs and gilded wings, culminating in the adoration of the shepherds and magi (conflated) . . . One could have a perfectly unreal and Christmassy presentation of the Nativity which would yet tell the truth essentially, and I've no desire to throw rotten eggs at the Blessed Virgin, and legend has its place – but this wasn't a piece of meaningful drama about an event but a mannequin parade of mythological characters, and one can only assume that those who got it up worship the characters and not God in the event. I don't care very much whether it's the Virgin

73

Mary or our Lord – but I don't worship a dear-man-god whom I can take from the pages of a gospel and breathe into the figure on my crucifix, who has got loose and floated to one somehow down the ages, who stretches human and caressing hands to me from the wall, but I worship God the Son seen in his *life* as man, and *work* of salvation, and I can't see that this has anything to do with the nuns' Jesus worship, nor can I see why, if one admits Jesus worship, one should rule out Mariolatry: if the divine is not centred in the *work* but in the perishable accidents of amiable individuality, that very life that one has to lose in order to gain Life – then there is no principle to exclude the adoration of Mary, Joseph, Anna, Joachim, or Jesse himself.

Drama is an ideal form for the presentation of the Gospel mystery, but worship should be directed to the soul of the drama, which is the Son of God, but not to the characters who play it. We should worship the soul of the drama – but that soul is all focused upon one of the characters and not diffused through the satellites. For all my protesting, I felt a strong temptation to surrender to the Nunnery, but I think that's the Devil. [19]

Popular devotion was always a problem to Farrer, whose theology was Trinitarian and theocentric. He included Glover's[5] liberalism in his condemnation because he excluded Mary from our Lord's legend on the ground that the latter was historical, Mary's was not. We find the same perplexity in almost his last letter to his father from Dewsbury, 'I am trying to get hold of the idea of the Saviour–Friend because I can't find any way of expressing to people the idea of God as *here* as an available power and apprehensible reality, but I haven't got there yet. If you've experimented with it to your people you might tell me how it goes down'.

More to his taste than Horbury was Mirfield, the mother house of the Community of the Resurrection, which owed its origin to another scholar of Balliol who became chaplain of Trinity, Charles Gore. It was therefore appropriate that Farrer should be invited there to lecture to the ordinands on the New Testament and to introduce them to the developments of Form Criticism, His first impression of Mirfield during a visit in March 1929 was favourable:

The fathers are men who do a lot of work outside and have lively minds: there are scholars and even a philosopher among them

(Father Thornton), and their religion seems to have a monastic severity: no trendy saint-worship. It doesn't seem as if women can be trusted with the monastic life – they always run to piety. Or are there exceptions? [20]

Of his lectures he wrote:

I perform on Tuesdays, Thursdays and Fridays from 11.50 to 12.50, attend the office, lunch with the college and return by the two o'clock bus . . . Now I have got going nicely, except that I can't get the stuff in in the time. My class is almost twenty, but I am to have forty for the next lot, beginning Tuesday week. I find that it is not impossible to interest them. In my reading I have finished Bultmann, and potted him with my annotated NT. [21]

Later – perhaps in 1930 – he was to have doubts about the combination of lecturing and parochial work:

The Mirfield course drags on. I do not bore the young men, but I have yet to find whether I really convey to them what I want to say. I prefaced the second course (on the history of Jesus in the synoptic gospels) with a discussion about the Person of Christ. What do we expect *a priori* to find if this is indeed the history of the Incarnate Word? They thought me heretical for insisting on the two *phuseis* [natures], or rather the two wills, and distinguishing St John from the synoptics as the story of God when he was man confronted with the story of the man in whom was God. I should like to have a debate with some of them about it, but I can't decently, since it isn't my subject, spend time on it. [22]

Meanwhile in 1929 he had written an essay for the priest's examination and was ordained priest by the Bishop of Wakefield in his cathedral on 22 December. The essay was on what he termed the 'supercilious' question 'For what truths did substitutionary theories of atonement stand?' 'I would have liked', he said, 'to defend the scholastic position, but courage failed me and I tried to expound the truth instead, a very dangerous course. May all be for the best. I put my trust in princes, that is, in the Bishop.' That trust was not misplaced.

Farrer was also improving his knowledge of German. Twice he went to Germany, once on a light-hearted visit to his Balliol friend James Woolcock, who in 1930 was ICI representative there. Woolcock took him (by tram) to the Palatinate Wine

Festival, the *Durkheimer Wurstmarkt* (sausage market). Farrer professed to see nothing unusual in the sight of a woman in a strait-jacket hanging head down from a scaffold amid lots of *Pfalzer* (people of the Palatinate) swilling beer at long wooden tables, and the Ghost Railway with its entwined couples or the other side-shows.

> Eventually [Woolcock reports] I took him into a trellised-off small area where they sold cheap German champagne, *Sekt Buide*, where we were the only guests. Having filled our glasses the two girls in peasant dress joined us, while a third insisted we buy woolly dolls for the girl friends we had apparently mislaid. While I had to do most of the chat, Austin did quite well. When I took him away, having refused a refill, he admitted for the first time that this was something he had not experienced in Dewsbury. I did once visit Austin when he was a curate in Dewsbury (between Wake and Huddersfield, as he used to say) . . . Austin walked me around. He also emphasized what a rough town Dewsbury was. It was nothing . . . if a wife, being beaten up by her husband, was ejected from the front door of a terraced house with such force as to end up crashing in the front door of the terraced house opposite. Coming as I did from the very tough Stockton-Middlesbrough area, I could not admit to being unduly impressed. [23]

A second visit to Germany was a more solemn occasion. He went with the Bishop and several other pilgrims to the passion play at Oberammergau and was deeply moved.

> In the morning we went to the English church (in a club-room or something) at a quarter to six. We presented a most edifying spectacle to strangers for many of our number (not I, I'm glad to say) knelt in the street outside. They could not hear anything, for the priest, who was a furious spike, never raised his voice.
>
> The play began at eight and continued till 11.30: then again from two to half-past five. I had the German of the play in a book, and being used to reading German, but not to hearing it, could only follow by means of the book. Anyhow, I shed pints of tears in spite of it – I was resigned to that, for I'm an awful fool at that sort of thing. As a spectacle it is glorious. I always wanted to hold the scene up in order to admire the colours and groupings. The tableaux are ravishing. As for the playing, the best actor was the crowd. It produced the most marvellous effects and seemed to be alive. The

characters are not really characters in a psychological sense, except perhaps Judas who is half comic and (but hardly) Pilate. The part of Christ makes no attempt to act out the motives or inner feelings. I felt that no one but a peasant could act a part of such simplicity – expressing throughout simply the ideas of love, dignity, and unity with the will of God, as expressed in the various situations. It is above all the Christ of St John's Last Supper, but with a dash of St Luke. It was beautifully done: the Last Supper scene was the most expressive. The crucifixion was as good as it could be: but the taking down from the cross and the lament of the faithful the best part of it. It is this extreme simplicity in the characters which gives the play its effectiveness – Mary simply *the* Mother, Christ *the* Man, and so on. I could not conceive of any professional actors being able to acquire this. [24]

During his time at Dewsbury Farrer had learned German, read the German Form Critics, seen the strains and tragedies of daily life, and worked on his lectures. Of his personal thoughts on theological topics one or two are preserved in letters to his parents. On the subject of 'evening communion' he writes to his mother:

> I've no comment to make on your defence of evening communion, since if what you say is true you've proved your case. But I shall find out what the Roman clergy here do, for they are always a good test on practical matters; it's certain they won't have banished young mothers from the communion of the Church and equally certain that they don't celebrate the Eucharist in the evening. I don't feel strongly about fasting myself, but I feel strongly about law as such. What one wants is evening communion for those who need it under special dispensations, but of course it's nonsense to talk about that with us, for we haven't the authority sufficient. But do you think one ought to worry about whether things are helpful or not? Unless the gift of God in communion is limited to what we feel, and the physical accident of remembering breakfast is going to frustrate omnipotence. Isn't it terribly irreligious to begin experimenting and trying to make the divine self-giving taste better? Isn't the duty of man to accept the divine ordinance in the Church and to make such personal preparation as he can, and for the rest to trust the Gift and the Giver? Once begin asking whether it's helpful or not, or whether something else would be more helpful, and where are you? That sort of thing destroys the nature of a sacrament,

degrading it to an edifying stunt. I go to the communion trusting in the promise of Christ, but not expecting to feel something. That defeats its own object. But you can see now why we wish to have a Church that will speak with authority and will fix these details for us: not because we expect more uplift but in order that we may not blaspheme by thinking about uplift. This was the good element in Jewish legislation: do the law because it is the law, not because it'll do you good, but because it's the appointed means of salvation. It is noticeable how the Romanists, who are taught on this plan, are free from self-regarding ideas, and have their thoughts concentrated on God and on the Church: and the chapel people who've grown up on the opposite tradition will always be telling you of their own piety and spiritual comforts as a sort of merit. This is their great defect, as wakefulness and vigour are their great virtues. I notice this in visiting. [25]

On his return from Oberammergau he presented his mother with a statue of the Blessed Virgin. Her pleasure in the gift reveals a broadmindedness in a Baptist lady of that time. It evoked some of Farrer's own thoughts on the use of images:

I am glad that you like the image which I bought for the same reason that makes you like it, that is, because it is beautiful and not as an object of veneration. As for the meaning of it, she is there represented in the moment of the Annunciation, making the act of faith and submission that enabled her to become the mother of Christ, and whether one regards that as history or not, it is a symbol of grace which will not be forgotten; and I don't see why anyone should feel any antipathy to it. I often wonder, by the way, whether anybody ever does, even symbolically, pray to images. A crucifix does not so much represent to me the object of prayer as the perfect intercessor into whose mouth, so to speak, we try to put our prayers by conforming to his attitude of spirit. Hodges said the same, and could not believe that anyone could pray to a crucifix, but only with it. It is different with the presence of Christ on the altar, which, being wholly mysterious and inexpressed, can symbolize the Divine, But I suppose a Romanist might use your image as we do the crucifix, or as we say the Magnificat, as an expression of the attitude of Mary when she accepted the calling of God. Excuse these irrelevances – unless they serve to show what the thing meant to the man who carved it. [26]

Of greater theological interest are his reactions to reading Emil Brunner's book *The Mediator*:

> This man [Brunner] is the Truth. He is Barth with the rhetoric pulled out and thought inserted in its place. He just restates the good old faith, but in such a way as to leave one saying, 'Well, and why not?' What are these cobwebs that the modern mind has got into it? Understand that there is nothing historically or philosophically reactionary in him. He has of course his EITHER – OR, but it is a real one. Did a divine and unique event happen in Christ or not? If it did, it is no use or sense trying to reduce this to common categories of the spiritual. If it did not, we shall not be believing in Christianity but in a 'general religion' or a family of it with certain historical roots. Then he has another EITHER – OR. Is the human and natural *continuous* with the divine, so that to get back to the roots of one's own spirituality is to meet God as far as it is possible for man? Or is there a *breach*, so that it requires a genuine coming of God, a definite setting up of a new relation by a new act to bridge it: the first says Brunner is (pious) paganism, the second Christianity. The first says that man is all right at bottom, the second says that he is a miserable sinner and there is no health in him. He has a most masterly display of the real uniqueness of our Faith, without denying any of what the History of Religion people can genuinely allege. Of course if Christianity really is unique then the real thing in it must be the unique thing; not therefore mysticism, spirituality etc, but faith determined by a definite view of the relation of God to man. I cannot get round his arguments. [27]

This is by far his most explicit rejection of idealism and he reinforced it by recounting to his father a conversation he had had with Hodges:

> I found him fairly patient of Brunner's doctrine: but he disconcerted me by asking what, after all this decrying of mysticism, we were to declare the End of man to be. Is it not a plain fact that religion (a) adds the activity of prayer and contemplation to the others, interpreting them by it, (b) promises it as the staple of the final bliss of man hereafter? We then settled down to try for a distinction between the gentile breed of mysticism and Christianity and said, 'Mere mysticism is, like solipsism, a short cut, I, as I am, and by myself can enjoy God. Christian mysticism says that only the whole

79

creation redeemed into a real union, and myself as a part of it, can fully do so. Therefore:

1. We need a revealed (apocalyptic) plan, showing us how the world is coming to such a consummation.

2. Because we cannot see God *through our own essence* (mysticism in general really asserts this) we need one in whom God is made visible and vocal.

3. Because we do not (this from our ground-proposition) stand on our own feet, we need a Body.

4. Because we are on the Way and not at the End, because travelling is our chief business at present and the end is only reached through its attainment by all the destined travellers, there arises the social, moral, active element stressed by Calvinism (to do the will of God is better than to 'see' him).

On this view then, the Christian faith can be seen to arise (logically) from a sort of dislocation of simple mysticism. Would this satisfy Brunner? Perhaps it excludes his principle of Radical Evil . . . no, I think not, for it is just because man is not, as such, continuous with God that sin can mean real alienation, so that the need for atonement runs parallel with that for revelation. All this is really very obvious but it cleared my mind . . . [28]

He had, in fact, acceped Brunner's position about the breach between God and man, the radical discontinuity between divine and human existence, and this set the stage for asking how God is to be known – by revelation only or by revelation and by man's apprehension in his limited nature as rational theology discusses it. There could at any rate no longer be any question of the world simply being an appearance of the Absolute and so the relation between the transcendent God and his creatures must be restated. This set the stage for the problems to be dealt with in *Finite and Infinite*.

There is one further small and tantalizing fragment, bearing no date, simply the word 'Dewsbury' to place it between 1929 and 1931:

I gravely disapprove of the bad optimism that denies that evils come in any way from God, from whom all things come in so far as they are real, and there is a reality in all things – all things *can* be seen in God. If one says that sickness comes not from God but from bad drains, one will have to say equally that health comes from good ones. It is certainly the Will of God that we shall struggle to overcome all evil, but it's no good pretending he doesn't put the bunkers on the course . . . One must remember too that fatalism diluted with a vague idea of special providence is the fundamental religious conviction of the poor, at least so one is told, and to touch this is to touch the ark, and the superstition of the poor is more true than liberal enlightenment.[6]

It must always have been plain to his friends that Farrer would eventually return to the full-time study of theology and philosophy. In August 1930 the opportunity came.

Kenneth Kirk wrote me a mysterious note, saying that if I received in a few days an Oxford offer he hoped I'd accept it because, though not perhaps tempting at first sight, he thought it was the very thing. He couldn't say more as he was not supposed to know about it yet. In three days it came. St Edmund Hall wants a chaplain and tutor with an option of teaching philosophy or theology (!!!) to start in October 1931. The vice-principal is a Cuddesdonian whom I know slightly . . . St Ed. H. is an ancient foundation (there used to be many Halls). It is not a college, because it has not a body of Fellows to suffice to teach the students. It has a principal, vice-principal and chaplain. There are 130 undergraduates, about thirty theologicals, the rest all sorts. They are not necessarily stupid, though frequently needy. The dons teach what they can and send the students out to other tutors for the rest. In other respects it is like a college. It is an advantage, I think, to have no SCR [Senior Common Room] and to be in a sympathetic atmosphere and yet to be honourably placed in the university: above all to be *both* chaplain *and* to be allowed to teach philosophy. I expect to land this fish, (a) because Kirk suggested it, (b) because I haven't heard of a rival, (c) because it is about 'my weight' and (d) because I shall not have to fear rejection for suspected over-clericalism. It has a daily Eucharist and other (to me) spiritual amenities. As for temporalities, it pays £350 and rooms, and this is apart from lecturing fees, etc. So if mother is hoping to see me married she had better produce a few candidates – oh, but celibacy may be a condition, I haven't found that out yet. In any case it wouldn't stop my accepting it. Still, there's many a slip.

So the offer of appointment to St Edmund Hall was confirmed and duly accepted.

# CHAPTER 6

# St Edmund Hall 1931–5

*

Dewsbury had shown Farrer a new and fascinating world, but few men have been so obviously destined for an academic life. He was now back where he belonged, to spend the next thirty-seven years of his life in Oxford. When Austin joined St Edmund Hall as chaplain and tutor in the Michaelmas Term of 1931, it was a charming and remarkable place, an ancient academic society without the full status of a college, the oldest surviving hall in Oxford, which was beginning to surprise its collegiate contemporaries by taking on a new lease of life in numbers, academic results, and sport. The principal, Dr A. B. Emden, who might be described as High Church and High Tory, had only been there a year and was the youngest head of a house in Oxford. The government of the hall was entirely in his hands. As the first lay principal it was his decision to have two tutors in Holy Orders resident in the hall. His friend, Kenneth Kirk, had recommended Farrer.

In 1931 the tutors at St Edmund Hall were John Brewis, a historian who was vice-principal (later Principal of St Chad's College, Durham, and Vicar of St James, Piccadilly) and Ronald Fletcher who was tutor in English literature and had been chaplain. But in 1930 Fletcher married and moved out of hall so Farrer took his place, and was also to be tutor in theology and philosophy. Farrer's other colleagues were the senior tutor, George Brewis (father of John) and Dr Herbert Hunt, tutor in French. In 1931 the undergraduate members of the Hall numbered 115, together with five graduates. In 1935, when Farrer moved to Trinity, the undergraduate numbers had grown to 150, with nine graduates.

While Emden remained Principal the college was virtually under his benevolent despotism. He loved and served it. Farrer described with amusement the dressing down he received when he accepted his fellowship at Trinity because he needed the money to get married. Emden found it hard to see how anyone could leave St Edmund Hall. It was a small closely-knit society, quite different from the gigantic post-war corporations. Indeed, so easily did the Principal administer the college on a paternal basis that there were no formal meetings of the tutorial staff. Any business matters that needed to be discussed were dealt with over coffee in the Principal's dining room after dinner in hall. On one of these evenings Emden suggested that Farrer might write for use on St Edmund's Day and other hall occasions a *Hymnus de Sancto Edmundo*. Within a few days he had produced the finished article 'in seven impeccable verses' composed during a session in his bath.[1]

The services in chapel on weekdays were Holy Communion followed by a very much curtailed Matins, Evensong (said); on Sundays Holy Communion with hymns at 8.30 a.m. and sung Evensong. Vestments were not used but for Holy Communion there was always a server wearing a gown. Brewis and Farrer shared the pastoral work, with Brewis reaching out to a much wider range of undergraduates and Farrer dealing with a smaller and perhaps more intellectual circle. Out of nine ordinands in the Hall, seven were members of the Rugby team.

Farrer is remembered as a frail bird-like figure, moving with the agility he retained all his life. As at Dewsbury he still went running by himself. An ex-pupil recalls that 'in moving over short distances from his rooms to the chapel or the porter's lodge, he rarely walked but trotted with curious short paces, eyes ahead, a shy smile lighting up his face'. In the afternoons he would frequently invite undergraduates, usually singly, to walk with him for an hour in the Parks, Christchurch Meadow or beside the Cherwell. His shy attempts at getting to know everyone produced some amusing episodes, as when he invited some freshmen to tea and was observed blowing up the gas fire with a pair of bellows.

Those who went to him for tutorials, however, found him very different. On his home ground he was clear, incisive, and understanding. He stimulated his pupils, plunging them in at the deep end and insisting on their reading the most radical authors, though with brief and telling hints about the bias of particular writers. He was always ready with sympathetic help for those in difficulty. Essays were read right through without interruption, though every now and then there was a furious scratching on a note pad with a quill pen, which could be unnerving, a warning that some astringent comment would follow. Sometimes he would sit on a chair beside his desk and play with the cable of a desk lamp, twisting and turning it to a perilous degree, his face a study in expression as the essay was read to him: pursed lips as he mentally debated a passage, eyebrows shooting up almost out of sight with a look of feigned amazement as some dubious argument attended his ears.

Two of his earlier pupils give a vivid picture of Austin settling in at St Edmund Hall:

I began to read theology at St Edmund Hall in the summer of 1931 and was sent for a term to William Wand, then Dean of Oriel. Already it was known that a brilliant young scholar, Austin Farrer, curate of Dewsbury, was coming to the Hall as chaplain and theological tutor next term. I was to be one of his first pupils. He was slim and fair and, except for traces of age in his face in later years, changed remarkably little in appearance over the time that I knew him.

He quickly invited me to breakfast, and the ice was broken by the discovery that we both came from Baptist families. I had an elder sister who had gone as medical missionary to India with the Baptist Missionary Society. She was working at the Farrer Hospital in Bhiwani in the Punjab. To my surprise and delight Austin remarked that the hospital had been founded by his aunt, Ellen Farrer, who was the Dr Farrer of whom I had so often heard my sister speak with deep respect and affection.

I owed more than I can say to his keen and penetrating mind in tutorials to which I instinctively responded, though I doubt if I fully appreciated what was being gained at the time. His reading of the Scripture lections in chapel was a delight. I can still hear the intonation of his voice bringing me an understanding for the first time of the epistle for Sexagesima as he gave expression to St Paul's words of protesting sarcasm, 'Ye suffer fools gladly, seeing ye yourselves are wise.'

Conversation [on walks with him] flowed easily about everything under the sun, but rarely, if ever, did one finish the walk without receiving from him some illuminating yet seemingly casual comment, beginning a train of thought which in retrospect led to a growth in the understanding of life. I never knew him pious in the pejorative sense; but his whole attitude to men and events was informed by holy wisdom. He could, nevertheless, be sharply caustic if nonsense was spoken by one who, in his judgement, should have known better. Sometimes the walk would end with tea in his rooms if there was more to be said than the walk had given time for, or if books had to be consulted and a reference pointed out. I still treasure a plan of daily meditation for a week which he drew up for me as a result of one such walk. [1]

We have also a vivid picture of him from the memory of Gordon Phillips, later Rector of Northolt, incumbent of the chaplaincy to London University and finally Dean of Llandaff. He came to Austin in 1933, a scholar of Brasenose, having taken a first in Greats.

I had never heard of Austin in my Greats year (1933) . . . . but when F. W. Green of Merton could not take me I was sent to Austin. So I went, as a superior person from Brasenose.

My tutorials with him were, alas, only too exciting. He treated me, absurdly, as an intellectual equal. We both found little to satisfy us in the prevailing Oxford tradition in philosophy and theology and both of us felt a little in the 'Collingwood'[2] position – a detached and rather irritating arrogance. In philosophical theology we combined a sort of detached neo-Thomism – or rather anti-Platonism – with a sort of Barthian and biblical passion. I suspect at *that* time (he had only recently returned to Oxford) he found in me almost the only like-minded person he had yet met (*longo, longo intervallo*) and tutorials were like a wild movement *Allegro vivace* from an eighteenth-century sonata for two violins. He used to be rather apologetic at setting me essays on the usual hackneyed topics, such as 'Discuss the authorship of the Pastoral Epistles', and as a trained logician I had much fun turning received solutions, of e.g. the Synoptic Problem, inside out. I used to emerge from tutorials in a state of intellectual exaltation – a mood which carried me into my theology finals and gained me a third. The papers seemed to me, at the end of five years study, trivial and easy. I cannot think I ingratiated myself with the examiners by asking in the purest Farrer/Barth manner whether the questions were capable of being asked at all. He was heartbroken at my failure and never wearied at attempting to win me back into the academic life he thought he had been responsible for taking from me. I think he tried to get me to half a dozen vice-principal jobs in the years just before the war and after. We remained great friends all his life. [2]

One memorable dictum is preserved by his pupils. He remarked with great seriousness on the difference between the orthodox and the heretical mind: the orthodox tried to understand revealed truth so far as possible, and then beyond that point just adored God, while the heretical mind was determined to accept only what it could master.

When Farrer lectured on eschatology, his main theme was that 'there is an anticipatory experience of the age to come' and that Jesus was prepared to be crucified on an eschatological issue (Mark 14.62). The whole subject suddenly became clear, important and authoritative. His hearers began to appreciate him.

His letters home at this time describe the pastoral duties of the chaplain of St Edmund Hall – what Farrer referred to as 'chappery'. 'Yesterday I preached my sermon for this term, not at all to my satisfaction. I did not and could not know what to say. It's odd, also, preaching from one's place, so that the young man on either side could read one's manuscript if he would: and in a chapel so small that to raise the voice at all is at once to become ridiculous.' [3] As for getting to know the young men, he admitted ruefully, 'I can face northerners and cockneys and aesthetes, but running blues are not really possible.' He went to the Sunday evening service at the University Church of St Mary the Virgin and commented:

> There was a good number of young people there and I believe that Barry[3] was giving them the right stuff, though I myself have ceased to understand the terms such as 'Life' and 'the Heart of the Reality within Experience'. 'Oh dear,' I thought, 'I shall never recover touch with youth.' I have thoughts of trying to write down my intellectual history when young as an undergraduate, so as to remember what it was like being young: but I shall not find the time. [4]

Still, he persisted:

> I am trying to entertain the freshers to tea by batches, three sets of these a week. I say 'trying' because sometimes they neither answer nor appear, while on one occasion I thought I had invited a freshman but caught one of the fourth year. I successfully pretended to expect him.
>
> I find that some freshmen will talk fairly honestly about spiritual matters, which is a load off my mind. I have passed the

feed-them-all-with-buns stage and gone on to selected individuals. I think they really expect it of the chaplain to do his job, although, of course, they are shy about how he'll do it. I am less in despair of getting there with the help of God than I was a month or two ago. [5]

As his experience widened, his audience grew and his humility deepened.

A great deal has happened this week, but I can't see the wood for the trees. I used to think it was a great matter if someone was ready to come and discuss truth with the chaplain: but now it appears that everybody is ready to do so and the only question is how to select because one can't have an hour's (or two hours') discussion on Life with everyone every week. I must be more conscientious about dividing my time. Equally of course one discovers that such discussions may not lead to anything: but at least it is something that the chaps should consider that Christianity is a thing to be considered. Today one of my best pupils who has been all over the place appeared at the altar, but that I need hardly say was the Vice-Principal's triumph if anyone's, for I made a complete mess of trying to get hold of the man months ago and John beautifully cleared it up. I still make muddles and frighten chaps off. It is an odd life and time passes at such a fearful rate: chaps develop so quickly and a term is so short a time to do anything in. [6]

Farrer developed an interesting method of preparation for confirmation, of which he wrote:

The boy considering confirmation has decided to be prepared. Another I told you about, who was mucked up by the [Oxford] Groups,[4] has, under the influence of an ordinary decent Christian undergraduate, made some repentance and come to see me of himself to be put in the way of studying what is this Christianity which he has rejected. I have set him on reading St Paul, and then we are to discuss what he finds there. I am coming to the conclusion that all books except Scripture are bad: Scripture answers most purposes as long as one retains the right to talk it over with the boy afterwards, but this latter is very important, and apart from this it would be better to refer people to modern books than to the New Testament. The Hall has been showing great piety this term, so far as frequenting the chapel goes. [7]

## A Hawk Among Sparrows

It was not always simple:

I have to kill the freshers in four weeks. This week I have entertained 16, lunched twice and picked up by roundabout recommendation an Indian student; a Christian of the second generation – nationalistic, not at all over-zealous, inclined to a vague scepticism. Must I become proficient in Bergson (a philosopher I contemn) to answer the fellow? [8]

There were also times of despair or near despair:

Some of my children appear to be walking according to the truth, as St John says: others not so. The wretched boy who was a groupist and then confirmed seems to drift further and further into reaction. But it is awful if to convert anyone you have to convert their family and their best friends at the same time. That's about what it is. Another boy, an aesthetic Spike, spent the summer in Germany with an atheist tutor who spent the whole time preaching to him that there is no God and that Goethe is his prophet, and he has come home full of aesthetic pantheist bosh, as silly as anything can be: so silly and yet a young man cannot see it, so what's the use of reason? And when he does see it, it will be five years hence, when he is out of reach of the influence that might steer him in the right direction. There is a natural trend in men towards badness and lies. I'm very pleased with a Communist–Atheist pupil who got into prison during the vacation (for a week and only for creating an uproar in a cinema against a war film). It is not *that* I'm pleased with, but with his getting thrilled with philosophy and with an obvious religious type of interest, I've got him going with Spinoza, who gives him God in peptonized form. I am being a Spinozist for the present and trying to make him one. We will not smash the idol for a while yet. The freshmen continue in numerical godliness. We must proceed to the bun stage immediately. [9]

There were also occasional visits to the local hospitals and the workhouse, in which John Brewis was the leading spirit, Farrer in faithful attendance and the young men of the Student Christian Movement as helpers. It was not really Farrer's *métier*.

Yesterday John took me down to the workhouse to see some zealous youths giving a service in the casual ward. It was a curiously patchy performance – a mixture of sporadic, violent efforts to get on

88

to the plane of the hearers and of bits of stuff far above their head. The casuals were tolerant and some of them seemed to like singing, especially the Welshmen among them, of whom there were several. We sat about talking after. The old men were quite friendly. After that the Vice-Principal (bless him) made off to a tramp's mission at the other end of Oxford, but I departed to be in time for Evensong. [10]

He describes confirmations by T. B. Strong, the Bishop of Oxford:

Yesterday I went to Cuddesdon where [two men were to be confirmed]. The Bishop took these two out in his car and gave them lunch before the ceremony. He was his usual self, fervour smothered under the coolest commonsense, and preached to them the extreme improbability of their perseverance except for their especial zeal and the peculiar grace of God . . .

And again:

The confirmation came off yesterday. The Bishop, as is his wont, poured pints of cold water on any indiscreet enthusiasm. He began by saying, 'It is in any case surpassing all that in the controversial atmosphere of a university three men should be found to come forward and profess adherence to certain principles and for life,' and, having laboured the point, went on to say that after all there was perhaps something to be said for it. He added that most persons confirmed probably lapsed within a couple of years, and having casually mentioned the Holy Ghost in parenthesis, concluded. I thought it was quite perfect. He will see them now privately, as his manner is, to warm their hearts a little more with direct kindness and a fervent benediction. [11]

The Bishop's combination of frankness and kindness was clearly contrary to the erratic inspirations of the Oxford Groups, of which Farrer was becoming increasingly critical:

The Vice-Principal is trying to steer the Hall SCM through a crisis caused by the Buchmanites having captured the machinery of government and using it against the will of the majority of members. They have behaved with surprising dishonesty – or rather not surprising, since they act from inspiration. The V-P keeps the confidence of all parties with an excellent tact. [12]

In lighter vein, he was 'miserably disappointed' in a Groupist cleric he entertained to lunch, hoping to hear all about the Groups from him.

> Instead he jumped up and said he must go, as he had promised to escort a young lady to see the boats . . . Here was a Buchmanite with an obvious duty to convert me: and there was I plainly (if hypocritically) nibbling at the bait. To leave such a chance for such a cause! Fortune paid him out. I do not think he made a good job of it. For having some time later taken myself to the towing path and found a place where the boats could be seen, and there were no men with death-dealing weapons to shoot into the air and shatter my ear drums; I looked up and there was this youth with a young lady and an older one. He was unnecessarily pink, he was talking fast in a forced tone and grinning foolishly, and though I was perfectly visible to the naked eye at ten yards, he was not seeing me or anything else. [13]

Further disapproval of the Groups is in a letter to his mother:

> At a meeting of theirs that I attended, by grace I was enabled to say nothing. The more I admire their zeal and their success, the more I am convinced that the end aimed at is not good, when one has got it. I can't approve 'enthusiasm'. When people think that the primary seat of revelation is in their own affections and wills, it causes them to be portentous and immodest about their experiences and their projects. They cease to live in this world that the rest of us inhabit. They become a conspiracy to swear reality away. I do not feel happy in their gatherings, and I cannot persuade myself that is only because I am a sinner, but also because when I walk out I seem to walk back into a different and better world. [14]

Life, however, was not all undergraduates, Buchmanites and conscientious struggle. Although he leaned at first heavily on John Brewis, there was the constant flow of Oxford personalities, the dons and friends, the grave, the eccentric and the entertaining. It was refreshing to meet Hugh Lister again, a great friend at Cuddesdon who had done work as a priest in Hackney[5] and as a Christian Socialist and Trade Union organizer. He had been ill with tuberculosis. 'Hugh Lister came over quite suddenly to see me yesterday, having finished his tuberculosis period in Switzerland and now resolving on what to do next. He wants in fact to spend some time completing his

theological education and, he says, learning to say his prayers.'
[15] In June of the same year Lister returned, 'turning up
suddenly in a car with his mother, and motored me gently
round Otmoor and up to Brill, more light, more leaves, more
buttercups than you would believe. He has got the roughness
out of his throat. I began to believe in his tuberculosis cure.'
[16]

It was a duty to call on Dr Wheeler Robinson, Austin's
father's principal at Regent's Park College, and it was the first
call he made on coming into residence.

What [he wrote to his mother] should I be doing on a Sunday?
Writing to you for a start. Besides that I have paid Dr and Mrs
Wheeler Robinson a call. I found the salon in a fairly prosperous
state, several young men – his own students, I think – as well as
many more young women being present. There was no other
senior except myself. Both Dr and Mrs Wheeler Robinson did me the
extreme honour of talking to me during tea; with Wheeler I did a
stroke of business by betraying to him the name of a Baptist
freshman here. With Mrs Wheeler I discussed Oxford and Regent's
Park. She complained of friendlesness in Oxford . . . When all had
been eaten and drunk we made a circle and indulged in the tasteless
amusement of telling anecdotes. Perhaps I should not complain had
my own fallen less flat. [17]

On a later visit he was amused at 'Wheeler on his own hearth,
giving heavily sound opinions to his young men on sundry
questions, and attended to with awe'. Wheeler had sent him a
pupil to tutor in the philosophy of religion. 'He is really quite
promising but too deferential. Who teaches Wheeler's young
men to regard their instructors with a look of dumb awe?'

However, Farrer's most pungent observations were reserved
for Anglicans. Of Brewis he wrote, 'A remark of John's after the
Principal's garden party in the quad last Thursday. "It is
encouraging to find some easy ones among the divine com-
mandments. I am continually surprised how little I feel tempted
to covet my neighbour's wife." The don's wives are an odd lot
indeed when you put them together.' The Warden of Keble was
dealt with more remorselessly:

Dr Kidd did very amusingly in the pulpit of St Barnabas this
morning. On getting into position he found a stole hung over the

pulpit rail for his use. He glared at it in a shortsighted way, rolled it up deliberately and put it in one corner of the pulpit, glared at it again and put it in the other. Then he got out his manuscript, set it on the rail and glared at that, decided it was too low down to read, so climbed down the stairs and made prey of a couple of hassocks; climbed in again and put them on the rail, and his notes on them. Another glare did not satisfy him, but when he had added an open Bible to his pile he seemed at ease. Meanwhile the Vicar of St Barnabas was reading the notices but commanding very little attention. Dr Kidd then began his oration. Having remarked that confirmation seemed a theme not inappropriate to the day, he went on to ask what on earth the rite meant, assuring us that though we thought we knew, we were wrong. He then examined all the views that had been held, and having, by a careful historical argument, proved that the word 'confirmation' means not confirmation of baptismal vows by the candidate, nor confirmation of the candidate's faith by the bishop, but confirmation by the bishop of the candidate's baptism, he threw in a pinch of exhortation to the effect that the gift of the Spirit bears no shadow of excuse for the futility of the human will – and left the pulpit. This, mind you, to a mixed parochial congregation. I had once heard him do this before, in my undergraduate days: but had begun to suspect my memory of dressing the tale. [18]

Nor did his own tutor, Kenneth Kirk, soon to be translated to a professorial chair and a canonry of Christ Church, escape Farrer's acute observation:

Kirk to lunch on Tuesday. He and I got excited like children, discussing a point of his, and walked up and down the room; and parted in the best of spirits. In some respects he is the most shameless man I know: as in openly smiting his opponents with ridicule in public debate; and in producing a point at lunch that he has come intending to discuss almost before we have had time to sit down at the table, which he did on Tuesday. He is a very odd mixture of the speculative and the practical. None of his friends can say whether he is more satisfied to have thought out one of the sublimer points of theology or to have confounded the politics of some persons who oppose his measure about the regulating of lodging houses of which he is the director. But which row he likes best, he certainly likes strongly, and has a refreshing zest for life. [19]

And again,

> On Saturday I lunched for the first time with a weekly lunch club that has elected me, to which Kenneth Kirk and N. P. Williams[6] and other lights belong, to the number of about ten. I have never seen Kenneth Kirk in such a humour; he was simply naughty like a perverse but very clever child, turning unanswerable ridicule on everything sacred or profane. He was obviously so much cleverer than anyone else there; no one could say anything to him. Then he suddenly rose from table, and said he must go straight home to bed since he was suffering from a bad attack of 'flu. This appeared to be true. [20]

Later on he wrote:

> Yesterday at the Lunch Club Williams held the floor. It seems Williams and Kirk cannot appear together. Williams was raising support to stop some old wretch crawling into a DD through a hole in the statute: someone must oppose it in Congregation. 'I wish Kirk had been here', he said, 'for I believe that is the sort of thing he rather likes doing'. This seemed to me a bit much (though it is quite true Kirk enjoys a little mischief-making). So I said I thought Dr Kirk would very likely return the compliment, and was immediately overcome with my own impertinence and the burst of laughter from the rest of the table. Williams was unruffled; and replied in his coolest and most precise tone, 'Very likely he would: but that would not be true.' It is awkward, I think, having a professor who takes himself a little seriously in a completely informal club such as ours. [21]

When Canon Ottley retired it seemed likely that Kirk would be offered the vacant chair of Moral and Pastoral Theology attached to a canonry of Christ Church.

> Kirk is bound to be a little anxious waiting for the Crown appointment to the chair of Moral Theology. It will be a crime if he is not offered it: but if he is, he has a £1000 to find from somewhere to recondition the canon's house where Ottley (if his colleagues are to be believed) kept too many daughters, hens and rats. There is a regular Pied Piper saga about the last, as well as a tale about his asking in a cathedral sermon 'What do we hear?' and being answered by his cock from outside: also of an unsuccessful attempt to hide Ottley's fowls when the King was in Christ Church gardens. [22]

A high spot for excitement would be the occasional irruption of Bamforth down from Ampleforth, fresh with the convert's enthusiasm. Of an early visit to St Edmund Hall we hear:

> Bammy is off again. He fell upon the Principal and devoured him: he attacked the Vice-Principal and cornered him. I blushed and trembled but they liked him: the Vice says he is a nice fellow and that his manner would never deceive or distress a person of sense. I had my friend the Dominican (Father Gervase Mathew) to lunch with him. Bammy was soon testifying to his papal and Italianizing principles. Imagine my amusement, then, when the friar very gently and gradually came out on the other side and deplored medievalism. I skirmished in to back him up, having put on the tone of an enlightened Romanist, and was exploiting the situation to my own satisfaction when Bammy suddenly leaped from his chair, smote his knee and swore, having realized that he would be six minutes late for an engagement with a Jesuit. This man was to show him the new convent of Capuchins, then Bammy was to take tea with the Benedictine prior – so you see he has not been wasting his time. He did four religious orders in one day as well as visiting Ronnie Knox in the morning. So the friar and I went for a walk and came to a most edifying agreement on a number of topics. [23]

Another old friend was Hodges, referred to as Bert. They met in Oxford when Hodges presented his doctoral thesis – 'They gave him a gruelling hour, but sufficient indication that they would pass him.' Later Farrer and Hodges spent a holiday together at Lyme Regis in Dorset, walking with enthusiasm and talking with equal zest. 'Bert walks in a coat, waistcoat and necktie and will not be persuaded out of them. I tell him he does not deserve to be well. I raised my complaint to Bert that he always walks me out of breath, and he returned the accusation, so we've made a compact not to raise the speed on one another.' And after a day or two:

> Bert is behaving very nicely, not philosophizing beyond measure and becoming quite human from time to time in anecdotes about Reading students or his Sheffield relations. On Thursday we had a visit from Bert's professor, De Burgh, who spends his summers at Toller Porcorum, which is by interpretation 'Pigs' Toller', a village up beyond Bridport way. A sort of sudden man he is, full of experimental notions like Lewis Carroll's White Knight. Friendly

withall. I was glad to see him as being the hero of a saga I have heard at some length. Bert is not an uninterested spectator of his acquaintances. His way is to work them up into phantasies of interesting types, not without satire. [24]

In 1934 came the news that Hodges was to have De Burgh's vacant chair at Reading. Austin was very happy about it.

Other visitors to St Edmund Hall included Ivor Thomas, who came and talked of the power of the superior press. *The Times* he considered worked the last election (1931). 'If so it is an odd fact and food for reflection.' Cousin Hebe 'who brought to tea as chaperon Cousin Florence who kept lodgings in Southfield Road'; Cousin Cecily, 'a fresh jolly little person of nineteen'; Colin Hardie, with whom he walked the Oxford countryside and admired the trees in Wychwood Forest and watched the trout. He made the journey to Barton-le-Clay for the induction of Canon Wolde to his new living, and to meet the Bishop of St Albans, 'a giant seven feet high to whom I had to apologize for my cycling costume'. And we hear of a remarkable preacher without an 'R' in his mouth. 'He was very eloquent. It had not occurred to me that there were so many 'R's in the English language. He took as his text "The stweet and the wall shall be built, even in twoublous times" and repeated it frequently, especially "twoublous times".'

On his way north to Scarborough for a short holiday in 1934 Farrer called at Lincoln and saw Michael Ramsey. 'Michael was most kind to me. He talked about everything. I adored the Cathedral. I found one of my former pupils walking according to the truth. Michael is a great man in the College and holds his audience spellbound and I think he is less mad.' [25] Later he records reading the typescript of Ramsey's book *The Gospel and the Catholic Church*. 'I am very pleased with it: he says what I should like to be able to say.'

Now that his Balliol friend and contemporary Gervase Mathew was at Blackfriars, Farrer became a welcome visitor at the Dominican House. It is possible that, just as Brunner turned him from Platonist tendencies (for which we have Farrer's own word), so Blackfriars may have helped to turn him to Aristotle and Aquinas. His first visit there was at the invitation of a young American friar from California:

When previously he lunched with me, he had been a fish out of water. When I went to them yesterday, I was like a cat in a pond, and he in his house and habit like a king. Monks 'come it' over you with a courteous humility, and you do not know the game so you can't do it back. I was used to prayers, the continual lections in Latin and English. My host apologized after for certain anti-Anglican passages in the lection: and discussed topics of controversy with perfect freedom and sweetness. For Vespers he put me in the chapel gallery, ran around two corridors and a flight of stairs and back again to fetch me a breviary, found me places and ran the same journey back again to be in his stall for the office. They sing beautifully. There will be forty in the house, mostly quite young; the place is built for seventy: everywhere spaciousness and decency but with severity. [26]

There were also the inevitable examinations and interviews for the award of exhibitions at the Hall.

We viva'd the select list this morning: all horribly dull except one gentleman whose essay I had had the pleasure of reading. It was a *cri du coeur*: it demanded a soul-mate, salvation by psychology and 'Life with a big L'. 'Oh, let the red corpuscles speed and bump!' he exclaimed in his first paragraph. But in the flesh he turned out to be a bright, sensible fellow and so charmingly admitted his penchant for talking nonsense that I believe we shall elect him! [27]

The two main influences on Austin in the four years at St Edmund Hall were the stimulus of his visits to Germany and his meeting and growing acquaintance with Katharine Newton, who was to be his wife. The one by reaction stimulated his philosophical thought and the other gave him the home background with which he was to live when, on his move to Trinity, he was able to consider marriage. In 1931 he was awarded the Senior Denyer and Johnson Scholarship, an award made to graduates to enable them to pursue the study of theology. Kirk advised him first to visit France to study developments among the French Catholic scholars, but Farrer preferred Germany and Switzerland, and in 1931 went to Bonn (Barth) and in July and August 1932 to Zurich (Brunner). He was impressed neither with Bonn, nor, more strangely with Barth.

There are so many things one cannot do in Bonn: as, for example, obtain access to the library catalogue; get a book you order today sooner than twelve o'clock tomorrow; get hold of a library order form without paying for it; enter the reading room in your greatcoat; buy a copy of Calvin's *Institutes*, though it is a set book in the University; find a laundry that will take in collars except on Mondays; buy a clerical collar anywhere – or at least they said I couldn't, but I found a shop where I bought one by the square foot – folded celluloid about 25 inches long and four inches deep, without stud holes. This with the aid of a pen knife and a pair of scissors I made into the collar I at present wear, and shall continue to wear until my laundry returns, and (though I shall certainly never wear it again) shall keep for ever as the sign of the only personal triumph I have scored in Bonn: the rest of my existence being a continuous series of failures to master Bonn's intractabilities.

Anyhow I have seen the great Barth in his house and twice heard him speak: nothing of any particular interest. I am inclined so far to write him down as a false prophet: not so much because he is a wolf in sheep's clothing as for the opposite reason – he is a lamb masquerading as a lion, a don tricked out as an Elijah. His thoroughgoing theology seems, when you hear him, less like the passionate conviction of a Reformer than the passion for notions of a don. Otherwise I walk, I sleep, I read (heaven help me!) Cambridge logic. I arrive home Christmas Eve morning by train. [28]

It must be remembered that Farrer had not yet read the *Church Dogmatics* and that in 1931 the struggle of the German Church against Hitler was still in the future.

He enjoyed Zurich more than Bonn. He allowed himself a day off.

I have recovered [he wrote to his mother] my appetite for food and print. At a quarter past one I put on the shirt I bought in Brittany and a pair of flannel trousers, cut through the confounded forest which the municipality has planted behind us, and ranged the divine country. It was very quiet: villagers in groups strolling about or drinking in inns. I touched the next lake to us, skirted it and struck back over the hills home again: saw various things growing wild, as purple columbines, the big spiraea (as in our garden), purple orchids, canterbury bells and a young red-hind: also Swiss bodies in a semi-natural state littering the shores of the Greiffen Sea. [29]

The visit was not without incident:

> Next, I have just answered an urgent summons to the police station, where they kept me standing on one leg for half an hour, asked me your maiden name and my religious opinions, made me cover much paper with execrable pens (I tried them all) and in the end robbed me of my passport and fined me nine shillings, because, apparently, I had not thought of paying them a call on my own volition. I had filled forms in the house and thought that would do. They promise me my passport back by post. I signed among other things a declaration undertaking that I would not earn a penny in Switzerland by any means, nor do an unpaid job. [30]

He mentions too, as he rarely did, the politics of the world outside in a letter to his father:

> I feel reasonably acquainted now with the affairs of the world. I am a partisan of Hindenburg and Von Papen, and I hope they defy democracy and keep Hitler in his place. Other things reach me through the post – as for example this morning a forecast of my income tax assessment, on which I must pay extra postage because the Manciple supposed His Majesty's crest would take a letter free all over the world, thereby putting himself in the succession of the lady who in mid-Paris protested, 'But I'm not a foreigner, I'm English'. I have just been rung up on the telephone by a professor's wife: German on the telephone is awful. But the worst of it is that I have, I believe, declined the invitation, because 'thank you very much' means in German 'No, thank you,' as I realized as soon as I had put the telephone down. I shall go anyhow, and try to appear innocent on this point. [31]

He had meanwhile been attending Emil Brunner's seminar, which began at 7 a.m.

> To end the session Brunner invited us all to coffee in a restaurant. I wondered what would be done, but ought to have had the sense to know that it was bound to be a discussion of some kind: that is how the Teutons are. So we were hardly sat down when Brunner got up, and after a very short speech called for criticisms from the Germans (who composed most part of the gathering) against the city and University of Zurich.
>
> They were soon ready, and spoke in order as Brunner named them: they would lift up their hands to draw his attention, exactly

as though they were in class. Many frivolous criticisms were made, as that Brunner should lecture at a more merciful hour than seven o'clock. This was received with applause: but when he called for a vote upon it, the early risers had the field. Then the critics turned against the Swiss character and manners. They complained that the Swiss were unsociable: that in discussion they sit back and let the Germans talk; that they are incurably bourgeois and settled in their ideas and do not even try to understand the extremes of German political idealism. Brunner (who kept standing, as in class, while the others sat) replied to these accusations himself: admitted some of the charges, but thought there was something to be said for common sense and balance, and compared the Swiss with the English in this: and reminded the Germans that they are half-way to Russia, where people take politics seriously indeed and discuss the last riddles of the universe with strangers in the train. [32]

Brunner's seminar, like his work *The Mediator*, impressed Farrer, though it did not convert him.

Brunner [he writes to his father] is dealing exhaustively with the status of the Gentiles . . . He seems to think that Luther wrote the New Testament: he says 'Luther had a masterly conception of this' and proceeds to quote St Paul. Calvin and Zwingli have not come on the stage. Meanwhile I do begin to see a little more what Protestantism means in the strict sense of the word, even if I am not convinced, and to respect it. He is an excellent lecturer and I follow him as easily as I could his printed text. I have heard him, too, in his seminar, which gave me new ideas about teaching and about the value for class purpose of the sharp antithetical theology which the 'Dialectical School' produces, although antithetical thinking is hateful to me. Brunner shows great anxiety to distinguish himself from irrationalists and Catholics: the former include Karl Barth. I should like to try to prove to him that the latter might, in principle, include himself. I went with David [Cairns] to his consulting-hour (no doubt the auctioneers and piano-tuners have consulting hours here). I made questions to him which he answered with a monolithic block of doctrine, designed not so much to answer them as to annihilate their basis. I just devoted myself to drawing him out on his own line. I have since written it all down and my stuff with it and hope to put the question next time in a form he will grasp. He is a very lively, eager thinker and honestly systematic, and in the main right, except for the antitheses.

Farrer's mind was also on the following term and on his own future path:

> I am now [he writes] on Bousset's *Religion des Judentums*. I shall also read *Haupt Problem der Gnostikismus*. After that Loofs in preparation for next term, and in consequence a flood of Patres. Then I ought to read Ritter or someone on Plato. Then I may feel free to touch the philosophers. You see I have fallen victim to a touch of conscience about my pupils. How I wish I knew what I really want to do! Kenneth Kirk would make me a Pauline Theology/Dogmatic History man, John Brewis, though more gently, a good practical chaplain, and I have no one but myself to make me a religious philosopher. I can never pursue anything to an end – though that is partly my idleness. I am much embarrassed to explain myself to the native scholars here. [33]

Although he had heard Barth and Brunner, it was Bultmann, whether heard or read, whose thinking challenged Farrer in 1932 to charting the road which was to lead him by 1940 to the completed manuscript of *Finite and Infinite*. His final letter from Germany also contains hints of his later Bampton Lectures. It sketches his future philosophical tasks if, indeed, those lectures and *Faith and Speculation* support the central section of *Finite and Infinite*.

> Let us discuss Bultmann. Is it as good as it sounds? His main point appears to be: revelation is not information, divine science, but an act. As when one's aunt dies and one knows no more than before about the specific nature of death, yet one says, 'Now I see what death is' – or she doesn't die but she rallies round and supplies £1000 in the hour of need, and one says 'Now I know what Aunt is' – although one knows no more than before about her humanity, femininity, or about the list of her characteristic attributes or the ramifications of her complexes. Now I suggest that a little philosophy makes the applicability of this analogy very doubtful. On what is the analogy based? It is based on a distinction between the intelligible natures of things and their significance as individual factors in our spiritual world. Very well: the distinction can be made. But it is none the less surely evident that I should not know the significance revealed by the particular act unless I already knew the intelligible nature of the agent, and what is more, the general type of act of which this is an example. As thus: if my aunt's death is

to enable me to say, 'Now I see what death is,' I must know quite evidently, first, that dead people don't revive, that death is the general lot of all, etc. So that the knowledge of significance is not without the general knowledge of intelligible natures. Or in the other case, I must know what is the significance of a gift of £1000, what is my aunt's income, whether she is sane, etc., or I shall not understand the significance of the act. And I must have a general understanding of the nature of persons and their interrelations. Well, in these cases, all that can be taken for granted, and doesn't seem worth mentioning. But the case of revelation is entirely different. Here we have got, not a striking example of a perfectly well-known type of act by a perfectly well-known type of agent but on the contrary an unique act and an unique agent. Therefore it seems to me to be no use saying, against the catholic verity, that in this act individual significance is all and the apprehension of intelligible natures unimportant.

For certainly if we can apprehend no intelligible characters in the act, it can have no significance: for this must be consequent upon those. And if you say, 'Oh, but as a this-worldly event the act of revelation has familiar intelligible characters, falls within known categories' – then how can we ever come to apprehend it as revelation, except on the Liberal assumption (which Bultmann would repudiate) that what is good and beautiful is in so far divine and the act of God? Now I propose to turn Bultmann round. First I admit that for the Apostles the saving facts were, very largely, what Bultmann says. 'Has He done this for us? Then . . .' But I say that they could apprehend this significance, precisely because their dogma of a historical–eschatological God was already there, supplying them with the intelligible characters and categories for seeing the act at all, and the agent behind it. This is, I think, historically speaking evidently true. Because Paul is familiar with the God who gave 'dispensations' in the past: because the eschatological scheme is firmly in his head: therefore he needs no scientific or rather philosophical ratiocinations about the intelligible characters of this act.

But as soon as the Church shifted on to other ground, as soon as the uniqueness of this act came to be emphasized and the alteration of balance that it had made in the historical–eschatological scheme to be perceived: then its intelligible characters had to be groped for, and it was seen that in and with the significant individuality of the act, its intelligible characters also, and those of the Agent and his relation to us, were given, but like all intelligibles needed thinking out. And so it is most evidently with the modern man. It is no [more] use trying to come over him with your 'significance' until you have enabled him to see the idea of such a God and such action on his part any more than it was for St Paul to try to get across to the Athenians an eschatological gospel in Pantheist categories. How lamely it comes in, that bit about the judgement and the resurrection.[7] How it seems to beat its wings in empty air!

We say then that the knowledge of general intelligible doctrinal notions logically precedes, and actually must at the latest be given with, the knowledge of the individual significance in the revealing act. And we say that the incarnation changed the apostles' intellected doctrine, and creates ours. But we say with Bultmann that the distinction between the individual significance of the saving facts and their general intelligible characters is a most important one. Theologico-philosophical speculation or doctrinal formulation can only concern itself with the latter, and ought to be purely formal; a mere exposition of the ways of thought necessary for thinking the significant facts and of their philosophical justification. But we cannot speculate upon nor construct the significance itself: that is perceived in mere contemplation at the best, and is declared to be mystery. The great fault of speculative theologians is pretending to establish the categories and proclaim the gospel itself in one intelligible act: to turn the gospel into theoretic truth. Then comes the reduction and the intellectual work is denied all validity even in its own sphere, and we are left with the dilemma of pantheistic liberalism or *Schwärmerei*.

So the business of theology appears to me to be with these questions. 1. What categories of thought did the apostles use? 2. Which are essential to the apprehension of the saving fact? 3. How can they be cleared up, modernized? 4. What is their general philosophical type and what is its justification? [34]

A formidable programme indeed. The first question is one for a New Testament scholar. The third and fourth become the question how men could talk about God – how, without knowing man and God in the cosmological relation (if we may anticipate), they could recognize the saving acts as saving acts and how in the pattern of human created life the refracted image of the divine life may lead to the apprehension of his act. The language is not the language of 1940: it still owes much to

Aristotle, Descartes and Thomas Aquinas, but it is the fore-shadowing of the great work which was to occupy his first years at Trinity.

Brunner had cured Farrer of his idealist attachments, so that as early as 1932 he saw salvation in the particularity of the saving act. He now found this at work in the growth of his religious strength. An undated letter, which appears to belong to this time, illustrates the attitude into which he had grown.

I find that what I really want is to believe, and to be rid of this misery of attempted self-salvation, which the mild sort of Catholic mysticism–pietism I was given as my working religion really after all is. Mysticism is all right – if it works. But it is very awkward when it doesn't, because one is up against a dead end. One has put his faith in a method: and what happens if one either fails satisfactorily always to practise it or practises it unprofitably? This is perfectly fatal to that sort of liberalizing Catholicism which is for spoiling the Church of all her spiritual plums and leaving the dry crust of sheer dogma behind: but it is not fatal to good pragmatical Romanism, for that believes in the sheer fact of Church and Sacraments as an extension of the sheer fact of the Incarnation: and this I believe is better Christianity than the mystical *imperium in imperio* which all liberals like to think of as the salt of the Church. (I don't know what Dr Kirk would say to all this.) [35]

The most important event of Farrer's years at St Edmund Hall, however, was his growing friendship with Katharine Newton. Her father, the Reverend F. H. J. Newton, was Vicar of Rickmansworth, where Farrer's parents were now living, and Katharine was in residence at St Anne's (then the Society of Oxford Home Students) reading Classical Moderations and Greats. On her father's side she was related to Miss Buss, the formidable pioneer, with Miss Beale, of higher education for young ladies. On her mother's side she was connected with the Des Anges family, associated with the Port Royal movement in France in the reign of Louis XIV. She had been a day-girl at St Helen's, Northwood, Middlesex, and became, so her headmistress said, a tactful and firm prefect and an original and thorough worker. At Oxford she was placed in the third class both in Classical Moderations in 1931 and in Greats in 1933. She seems from her letters always to have been nervous under examination conditions, but her tutor comments on her industry and interest. She then taught classics and scripture, first at St John's, Bexhill, and then at Maltman's Green, Gerrards Cross, where she had the nickname 'Frailty'.

Katharine's father read mathematics at Emmanuel College, Cambridge, and went on to Wells Theological College. He became curate at Chipperfield, where Katharine was born, and then was chaplain first to Bishop Jacobs of St Albans and afterwards to Bishop Michael Furze (the 'seven foot giant', whom Austin encountered at Canon Wolde's institution) before becoming Vicar of Rickmansworth. In 1932 he moved to Ashwell, where Katharine and Austin were married, and later to Blackheath.

The courtship continued through 1932, but Farrer waited to propose until Katharine had taken her degree. In 1932 he wrote:

> Katharine has forgiven me or I suppose she would not have had me round this afternoon to take tea with the lady in whose house she lives. Katharine strikes me as immature for a third-year student; a taste for poetical rhetoric (not unpleasant in itself) and not at all a good grasp of the real world of people and things. Her piety is of a romantic order too. [36]

Soon after this she went to lunch with him, determined to make an impression.

> I have never told you how Katharine came to lunch. She came in full force, eyebrows shaved, face à la mode, cleverly dressed. I was glad I had put on my better suit. She knows her business in life. She developed rapidly a high power of bright conversation: apart from one resolute blocking of a High Church opening, I let her rip. My pupil, Stephen Guest, said the responses and Amens with a deal of grace, and Ralph [Marsden] occasionally intervened. At a quarter past three she rose and broke the party up. Is she not a hard-hearted young woman and more like her father than her mother? Or is this only a social game? I lay awake all night thinking of it. [37]

However, during Greats in 1933 he saw a very different kind of Katharine.

> My children are still in the examination school dying of heat but keeping cheerful countenances; not so poor Katharine, whom I found outside the schools the very picture of woe and quite like a

child on the point of beginning to cry. You could not think of anything less like her in her splendour and pride eating ices with the young gentlemen on the Barges during Eights. She reported that she couldn't concentrate and was writing pure nonsense. I hope she is not in real danger of losing her third class. [38]

Farrer felt able to tell his mother all about Katharine, but at first he was anxious about the impression she might make on his sister Eleanor (Joyce had left home by now) and on his father and his donnish friends such as Kenneth Kirk. He was shy about being seen with her at Rickmansworth or Oxford, resorting to remarkable subterfuges.

We behaved [he says about a Saturday trip] with a great deal of unnecessary caution. It was particularly absurd how we got on to the same bus in seeming independence and travelled separately as far as Littlemore, where we both got out and joined forces to walk to Dorchester. She came here too on Sunday and there was a conspiracy by which I left the back door open and she walked in exactly at the same time when the young men had all gone away to lunch and we continued to sit in my dining room so that if anyone called on me during the afternoon I should appear to be out. We were rather, as Katharine observed, like children playing pirates. We had the most heavenly afternoon walking to Dorchester. I am very glad that Eleanor and she are being so nice to each other. Eleanor means to treat her as a sister: the rest will come. [39]

Meanwhile Katharine was settling into her life as a schoolmistress at Gerrard's Cross and waiting impatiently for the weekends when she could see Austin.

You ask how Katharine likes her school. I have heard that she finds she can interest her pupils, and as children she likes them: but I should gather that she finds it hard to settle into her place in the machine, having enjoyed so much liberty for so long. But that doesn't matter: it'll do her good. There is nothing more to be said about the woman. Complete calm prevails and may be expected to continue for an indefinite period. I am eating your apples at a terrific rate. [40]

In November 1934 Farrer writes about their future:

... about jobs, Katharine's and such like things, I have got the conviction that there is nothing to be *done*. We are all in the hands of God – I have got to do what I am called to do and I cannot play Providence to my own life. At present I am called to be where I am, keep my head and behave honourably. I gather she is to be two years paying off her debt. Anyhow, I am a priest and a scholar first: and I am not free to undertake to *do anything* in order to be in a position to marry, even if I were clear I wanted to – or even more that she is. I am certainly getting to see better what she is, and what she isn't. Meanwhile she in no way destroys my peace of mind, nor I hers, I imagine. She is getting on much better with her school, teaches with real satisfaction and tries to be good, the dear child. [41]

By the beginning of 1935 Farrer had assured his mother that he and Katharine would not correspond more than once a week. More importantly he had been interviewed by Dr Blakiston, the President of Trinity, who had selected him to succeed Kenneth Kirk when Kirk moved to Christ Church as canon and professor. The President of Trinity wanted Austin for the summer term of 1935, but Austin would not leave the Hall till October.

He [Blakiston] stood out stiffly about the Summer Term, but I got as far as plucking up courage to say I supposed I would have to stay in the Hall for it [John Brewis had been ailing for some time]. I began raising the banner of revolt against the rooms he wanted me to have – you see Kenneth Kirk did not live in them, he lived at home – and one of the present fellows had said to me, 'Don't let Blakiston put you into them on any account: it's just that he prefers a Fellow to be there because they look out on his garden.' Blakiston said about John [Brewis], 'He will no doubt be offered high preferment. Selborne (Anne's grandfather) is a very influential person'. Blakiston values himself on his knowledge of the English peerage. I nearly lost my temper and said, 'He may be offered it but he may not take it.' If I don't manage to behave better, Blakiston will begin to repent having me appointed. [42]

The appointment stood, however, and as Chaplain and Fellow of Trinity Austin would eventually be in a position to marry – though not for two more years.

Soon after this, Farrer took Katharine to Kew to visit one of his many aunts, recording it in verse,

*We took the train and went to Kew,*
*It seemed the only thing to do.*

## St Edmund Hall 1931–5

*Aunt suffered in her face to rise*
*Hardly a vestige of surprise*
*On seeing there before her door*
*The world's completest bachelor*
*So very well accompanied.*
*With scarce the flicker of a lid*
*She heard the name and welcomed us.*
*She was extremely courteous.* [43]

The engagement still had to be kept secret – it was presumably made after Katharine took Greats in 1933.

We did think of coming to Rickmansworth [he wrote to his mother] but we are both Public Characters there and it really wouldn't be safe. Except to Aunt you are to go on being as secret as a dumb oyster in a sealed tomb, as Katharine said, because it would be an awkward business with Trinity if the thing got round as yet. Katharine thanks you for your love and sends you hers.

During the Rector's absence [Katharine's father] on his summer holiday, the Ashwell pulpit will be occupied by the Chaplain-Elect of Trinity College. Mr Farrer insists that his motive is a desire for a quiet place to work in – but the Rector is equally insistent in attributing it to a generous wish to allow him a holiday. Miss Newton has a piece of literary work she wishes to do and has therefore declined a pressing invitation from a friend in Scotland. [44]

A little later he writes cheerfully:

I met John's Anne [Brewis's fiancée] on Sunday and remembered her perfectly from the party at which he had introduced her as having been about the only person comfortable and unbothering to talk to there. I am trying to find some fault in her so as to have some cards in my hand when John disapproves of Katharine (he always disapproves of other people's women) but I can't think of anything except that she has got an odd voice and is rather an outsize in women. Did you see that the President [of Trinity] has coughed up his information for *The Times* at last? [45]

He had not yet managed to tell Kenneth Kirk of his intentions, for he writes:

I can't go on holiday with Hodges this summer, much as I'd like [Mrs Hodges had complained that her son was overworking], what with the claims of Kenneth Kirk and Katharine on my time. I took tea with Kenneth last Tuesday. He was a bit pathetic and spoke of himself, particularly his lack of friends and suggested that we might walk again this summer. I felt less than ever like telling him of my secret and having his opinion (the sole one of value) on the best way of going about it: how long hence and so forth. Anyhow I shall no longer be afraid of inflicting myself on him in Oxford. [46]

Courtship was to bring more appalling dangers than that of revealing an engagement. Some days later we read, 'I see Katharine on Tuesday on her way through London and Hugh Lister after; and tomorrow I've my first dancing lesson. Oh dear!'

On 7 April he writes to his mother again:

On Tuesday I was in town, Katharine being on her way home, and after I had put her into the train at Kings Cross I went and dined at Sir William Lister's, for Hugh is staying there now. My heart dilated. Katharine was anxious to meet you as soon as possible and even thought of risking coming here next Wednesday had you been home. It occurred to me that you might meet her at Aunt Millie's some time, for example when she is on her way to Bexhill shortly after Easter. You might walk with her in the Gardens and call at Aunt's for tea. [47]

The meeting seems to have gone well, since we read on 12 May, in a letter to his mother on her birthday:

I am training Katharine up in the faith that you are always right (except sometimes on points of planting a garden border) and quite perfect (except about teaching your daughters to powder their noses), and she embraces the doctrine with fervour and forgets the excepting clauses, so that you see your Kingdom is on the increase. Not so absolute a Monarchy perhaps as in earlier days, but with more intelligent and spontaneous loyalty and a wider dominion. [48]

And in his last letter from St Edmund Hall:

I have had Gerald Hawker to stay. It is odd that he conducted a weekly instruction on prayer at Ashwell in Lent. Katharine, he said, on her return from Bexhill seemed to have sent up the family temperature whole degrees and they read poetry to one another. I had heard about it, of course, from Katharine. I have just heard from her that her programme this term is more pleasantly arranged, she has a fresh young colleague from Oxford, and she has an opportunity to meet me during the term. She very much enjoyed her lunch with Eleanor on Tuesday and coveted Eleanor's hat. [49]

So with tact and discretion Farrer had smoothed the path for his fiancée among his aunts, his sister, his family and his friends.

# CHAPTER 7

# Trinity College 1935–45

*

Only a narrow garden wall separates Trinity from Balliol, but the two colleges were worlds apart. Farrer has left his own account of his first encounter with a Trinity man. 'In my third year as a timid scholar of Balliol, I was walked round Trinity Garden, given a glass of wine, told what was what. My host I later discovered was a freshman.' But Balliol scholars transplanted into Trinity could flourish. Farrer followed Charles Gore and Ronald Knox in making this successful move.

In 1935 the undergraduates of Trinity were, so we are told, mostly perplexed by their new chaplain; some were fascinated as by some rare creature. They were earthy gentlemen with dogs at home and a common background of a very few public schools, which gave them the confidence of well-bred hunters. They must have been rather alarming after the undergraduates of St Edmund Hall.

The Trinity Senior Common Room, with twelve Fellows, was a closely knit and friendly community. Farrer's chief problem was the President, Blakiston, a magnificent, crusted old Tory with whom he never came to terms. The President had been offended when Austin refused to come into residence in the summer of 1935. There was a further disagreement about the room offered to the new chaplain.

> I offered to take the wretched room if he could find me another bedroom, the bedroom I had being almost windowless and quite insanitary. I objected on the grounds of health. Now it happens that two married Fellows who have no right to do so have retained bedrooms on the same stair. The President brought up the question; they failed to volunteer; results that the presidential wrath was diverted upon them and he gives me three rooms in the Garden Quad. The trick was all of Kenneth Kirk's contriving. [1]

Although he was not to come into residence at Trinity until October he preached his first sermon there on 2 June 1935.

John Brewis met me going out and gave me his best wishes for 'the first round of the Balliol *v.* Trinity Contest' and viewed as that the thing was a tolerable success as far as I can judge. How it scored in the more important match of Satan *v.* the Guardian Angels is of course a very different matter, though I think I tried to speak the truth. I stayed and dined after and talked to the President, who has to be conciliated, for according to Kenneth Kirk he was not best pleased by the ultimatum I lately sent him on my not coming into residence before October. I hope he will respect me in the long run for having an opinion of my own, as obstinate men generally do. He was quite gracious to me at table and shot out none of his withering epigrams. [2]

By 14 October he had settled in and wrote to his mother with great satisfaction about his rooms and their furnishings. The contrast between the aristocratic ease of Trinity and the sobriety of St Edmund Hall struck him when he went there on the eve of St Edmund and talked with the elder Brewis.

He made me a half serious defence of Etonians and the landed aristocracy in reply to some much less serious sighs I had uttered over the blue-bloodedness of Trinity. The Hall was just like itself, including a ten minutes' wait at one time between courses: this always used to happen and reminds one of shortage of staff. Trinity seems to crawl with unnecessary servants who are continually bringing round or fetching notes. I should like to see Emden or John put in to cleanse the place of superfluity. One could economize hundreds of pounds and no one know it. [3]

Farrer did not like Trinity Chapel as it then was. During Kenneth Kirk's chaplaincy, Blakiston had usually celebrated on Sunday mornings at the north end, with great dignity and devotion, with Kirk at the south end (the position known irreverently as the Lion and the Unicorn). Farrer also did this but, it was felt, with an ill grace. As long as Blakiston was there they had daily Matins in the college chapel and Farrer went on to Mass at St Mary Magdalene's afterwards.

I have [he says] with much misgiving dropped my present attempt to induce attendance at daily chapel because the chaps do quite sincerely find it farcical and irreligious as the President will have it done, and I'm afraid it would be just stirring up mud to press it until I am strong enough to present the President with the choice of

reform and a congregation: or no reform and no congregation.
Tonight I am starting a series of Sunday evening discussions – if
any one comes. Kenneth Kirk once made a success of these. I am
pinning nothing to this either. The wish to discuss topics of
theology is certainly not necessary for salvation. I wish though that
I were more group-minded. [4]

By 1936 he had, however, introduced a weekday celebration
on Wednesdays. He had a freer hand after Blakiston announced
his retirement at a college meeting in June 1938. He was
succeeded by the historian J. R. H. Weaver, a devout Anglican
with a Roman Catholic wife and a sister who was the Reverend
Mother of St Margaret's Community of East Grinstead. It was in
her presence that Farrer preached his famous sermon about the
Church of England being like a London Underground advertise-
ment for ladies' brassières – 'for uplift, for support, for ladies'.

At St Edmund Hall Farrer had lived under the guidance of a
vigorous principal whom he admired, and was able to fall back
on the help of John Brewis in any pastoral emergency. Now in
Trinity he was compelled to a new firmness and a new
maturity. In 1938 he was greatly encouraged by the arrival of
James Lambert to take Hinshelwood's[1] place at Trinity. 'I am', he
says, 'much comforted by Lambert's coming into residence: a
charming young man and an active and professing Christian'.
The same October he tried to breathe new life into Trinity
Chapel when fifty-seven freshmen came into residence.

I went straightaway and raised a platoon of loyal men to pack daily
chapel to prevent too hard a disillusionment of the freshmen and to
amaze the President. Then I got in on the tail of the Dean's *allocutio
de moribus* (address on our customs) to the freshmen assembled and
told them not to believe it, if people said 'no one comes to daily
chapel', while admitting I wished there were more. [5]

This had some effect for he can write a little later:

I have had the happiest and most encouraging beginning to the
term in being able to talk familiarly to my flock in chapel – and not
dully – in spite of my colleagues sitting by – and then I had a very
friendly party in my room, a score of young men full of goodwill,
eagerness, and ready to help. [6]

His attention was not confined to undergraduates. In his Balliol days there had been the Balliol Boys' Club, at Dewsbury the Scout Troop, and now there was the Trinity Mission. Like one or two other Oxford colleges, Trinity ran a mission in the East End of London at Stratford, E15. Farrer somehow did not take to it. Eric Knell (later Bishop of Reading), who took it over in 1936 until the premises were wiped out by bombing in 1941, says:

> Austin most nobly came to the summer camps which were part of my work there. I say most nobly, for he must have hated the whole thing, living in a tent, and trying to 'communicate' (as today's jargon goes) with a tough lot of East End boys for a fortnight under canvas. I always admired him for this, as James Lambert will confirm. [7]

Lambert himself adds:

> He took over from me with great reluctance (at the outbreak of war) the treasurership of the Trinity College Mission, and Eric Knell said they often had to wait for weeks to get their wage cheques from Trinity. Austin found this kind of administration just boring. After the war we ran a Trinity College mission in the Kent hopfields near the one Miles Sargent ran from Pusey House in the 1930s. Austin came for one weekend, so obviously loathed every minute of it, that we never asked him again., [8]

It is odd that he should have so disliked at Trinity what he had managed so effectively at Dewsbury. Perhaps he did not regard it as a duty he owed Trinity, whereas it was an unavoidable duty at Dewsbury. Also he was by then older and married; by the time of the hopfields mission he was 41.

At Trinity, Farrer began to move into the main stream of university life. He examined in the pass school in divinity in January 1936, failing ten candidates out of fourteen and coming across the remarkable assertion that 'Our Lord possessed a rather unusual degree of divine omniscience'. In the same term he preached his first university sermon – the Assize Sermon, at which he began by accidentally throwing over himself the glass full of water placed in the pulpit for the preacher. Apart from the official audience there were, he said, a few curious or idle people present – a great contrast to the crowds that flocked to hear his Bampton Lectures after the war.

He began to enjoy his new position. In later life he was considered austere in the Common Room. When seniority brought him to the vice-presidency he would sometimes gesture to the port and say, 'Oh, I suppose nobody wants any of this stuff'; but in his first year in Trinity he was pleased with his new wealth and surroundings. One Sunday he had his aunt and her friends to lunch.

> I polished the candlesticks and bought an azalea plant. I made Myles produce pheasants and ice-cream with hot chocolate sauce, and gave them Moselle to drink. We took a short walk through St John's Gardens and came back to drink tea. We lit the candles. The light was pretty on the shiny white walls, and they sat contentedly. [9]

He settled in to his work as chaplain, sending out invitations to the freshmen. There were almost fifty of them, all but ten from English public schools; of the remaining ten, half were Rhodes scholars and only five came from grammar schools. He had only nine pupils, which gave him more leisure than he had had at St Edmund Hall. He continued to run round the university parks instead of the meadows. He lunched and dined with the Fellows, beyond, he said, what his stomach could cope with. His servant was respectable and Jeeves-like, and his colleagues were friendly.

The Trinity Senior Common Room was engaging and entertaining, though the President was outwardly formidable; yet when bearded, said Austin, he was a very tame lion.

> Having spent last night feasting I have only scraps to make a letter. My colleague Syme[2] was being so very amusing we just sat around and listened. Among other things he had found in Alington's memoirs, now appearing in the *Sunday Times*, the most indiscreet statement that Blakiston had said of Gore, 'Oh, he is sure to get on, he is eloquent and well-connected,' and that Gore had called Alington a beast for repeating it to him. When Syme had talked continuously for three-quarters of an hour, Hinshelwood reminded him of his own conversation with the President when Syme had the influenza. 'Common Room is very quiet, President, with Syme away.' 'Oh it must be a very virulent germ that keeps Syme from talking.' [10]

Austin realized that there was no one in Trinity any stronger than he was – an odd sensation to a man who had till now been guided by Emden and the Brewises.

Meanwhile his discreet courtship of Katharine continued. In the summer of 1935 they were punting on the river near London away from undergraduate eyes, then back to London for supper 'in a little French place in Swallow Street . . . recommended for a decent half-crown dinner in reasonable seclusion'. That evening Katharine had told him that she would be able to leave Bexhill, which she had not enjoyed, for a better position at a school in Gerrard's Cross; this would also be nearer to Oxford. So he could now entertain her in Trinity.

> Katharine came here on Sunday. I think my reputation can stand it about once a term. We lunched in an old hotel up a yard where no one goes but parents and uncles staying up to see undergraduates, walked into college in the most unconcerned way possible, sat here a goodish while and made our own tea. We went out by the garden gate. None of my colleagues saw us. [11]

Fortunately, now that Katharine was at Gerrard's Cross, the bus timetable came to their aid, and (said Austin) . . . 'I have established the possibility of drinking tea with my aunt (in Burnham) and eating supper with my love the same night which is satisfactory so far.' He went on to give a dinner party in style to Katharine and her friends, the Yates, with whom she was staying in north Oxford.

> Mrs Newton, with sudden impulse hearing of this project, sent her branched, Sheffield-plate, old candlesticks in a biscuit tin and some silver sweet-dishes – unregistered. So we dined by the light of six candles; I don't know when or whether again I shall dine here with women in party dresses and give them fresh peaches, claret and Madeira. It was very pretty and pleasant, and everyone in good spirits and good temper. [12]

His mind was now made up and after this dinner he did not go to bed, but called upon his colleague Robert Hall, the only young married fellow, to ask his advice. Hall told him that the College suffered from a lack of married Fellows and advised him to announce his engagement about a month before his election to a statutory fellowship (when he had served his probationary year). Austin felt that he could count on Hall's support, and Hall was the strongest and most influential of the younger Fellows. So he would have good news for Katharine on their next meeting. With this settled he began to make financial plans with remarkable speed, aided by some luck in appointments. At the end of Hilary Term 1936 he went into retreat at Cowley before settling down to marking.

> I am going to make £100 with examining in the current year, for I have Lampeter (twice), GOE (thrice), Group D (twice), the Theology Diploma and the BD Qualifying Examination: and I suppose a Trinity Scholarship some time. I am going to be shamelessly chrematistic [money-loving] this one year, since I want not only to get and furnish a house but also, if possible, to extinguish Katharine's debt which her school lent her for her education at Oxford and with which she is meanwhile doing what she can. This is all very base, bourgeois and what not, but I think there is much to be said in favour of a clear start. It would be good, I think, to be married and at ease for a few years before the Socialists cause a financial collapse or the German army is ready to shake down the fabric of the world, or whatever else is the next chapter of our Apocalypse. It is no doubt very shocking how a Katharine to marry and provide for weights one's political interests on the side of the *possidentes* [the possessing class]. There seems reasonable hope of marrying in decency within 16 or 17 months, nor, so far as I can see, does my duty lie in any other direction. I should hate, I think, to be a married parish clergyman on the edge of want. [13]

He was not in fact as money-conscious as he sounded. In the same month as he wrote this letter Farrer was to show that his 'bourgeois' preoccupation with money was not to preclude care for others. His friend Bamforth had been invalided from Ampleforth and was for some time supported by the generosity of his friends, stirred into action by Farrer himself.

A last surviving letter before the wedding was a birthday message to his father:

> I have no longer any fears for my Katharine's fidelity, for if she will not marry me for myself she certainly will for my parents. I find she is resolved to have you at all costs. You do not need telling how much I wish to have you well and happy. I can't distinguish what I wish for you for your own sake from the happy debt I owe you for all I have and am. [14]

Farrer's fellowship was confirmed, his engagement announced, and the wedding took place at Ashwell Church on 15 April 1937. The service, taken by Kenneth Kirk, was followed by a nuptial mass, celebrated by Katharine's father. Her brother Arthur played the organ and John Brewis was the best man. Katharine had just recovered from pneumonia (she remained susceptible to chest infections all her life). For that reason they did not travel far but spent their honeymoon in Cornwall, a county for which they both retained a great affection. They moved into a flat at 72 High Street for their first home. What was most clearly remembered of their short stay there was the ingenious external cradle resembling a budgerigar's cage, which Farrer contrived for his daughter when she came – calmly, though seemingly perilously, poised three floors above the High Street traffic.

This promising future was cut short by the outbreak of the Second World War. For six years the university was not indeed empty – far from it – but most undergraduates were on short courses combined with military training and so the turnover was quicker. It was not uncommon, for example, for men reading Classics to do Classical Moderations (sometimes the full five terms – sometimes the shortened three-term course) and then return after the war to spend two years on Greats; and the call-up of the younger Fellows meant a greater work-load. So early in 1941 Farrer writes:

> Term has begun and our numbers have increased from last term and stand at seventy-seven . . . meanwhile the flight of Fellows continues. We have lost James Lambert, and Bruce Wernham is not likely to outstay the term. We shall be cut to the very bone. The College Mission at Stratford has been bombed, the church destroyed, everyone saved, including two hundred sheltering in the adjoining hall, the club rooms above it much shaken, probably condemned: a question to spend or not to spend several hundred pounds in fitting some of it for present use: very difficult, the work being more than ever needed: but what of the next bomb? [15]

During the war years the Socratic Club first began to meet under the leadership of C. S. Lewis. Farrer was often on hand to read philosophical papers or to answer philosophical questions (reported in the *Socratic Digest*). In fact this was almost the only philosophy he published at this time: *Finite and Infinite* had been finished in 1940. The meetings of the Socratic Club almost certainly helped in promoting the remarkable post-war efflorescence of Christianity in Oxford. Many of the men returning to

Oxford in 1945 must have heard Lewis and Farrer during their war-time short courses. And Lewis, of course, had a wider wartime audience through the BBC, his addresses to the troops and his books, *The Screwtape Letters* and *The Problem of Pain* in particular.

In February 1944 Farrer came into close contact with the war:

> I went into hall late and sat next to a man I did not know. 'Il y a trois mois,' he announced, 'que j'étais à Paris.' 'Then, sir, you came here by way of Spain.' 'That I cannot discuss.' He was an important member of the resistance movement. 'For the month of Singapore,' he said, 'we gave up for lost. Yet in that month I came into the movement. They were teaching my children lies about the history of France. It was with me not a question of feeling, it was a purely intellectual question.' He must have been running the most appalling risks, but he was perfectly composed: he might have been just returned from a long holiday. 'You cannot conceive how it feels,' he said, 'to be in a free country'. He was amused by our customs, withdrawing from the hall to common room for dessert and passing round snuff. 'That is what I admire in you,' he said, 'the instinct for tradition.' 'Ah,' said Hinshelwood, never at a loss, 'visit us in March and you will find the tradition without the dessert – our last apples are just running out.' Hinshelwood did best, sliding elegant French out of the corner of his mouth. Ewart, Professor of Romance Languages, was professionally competent. I was shy and premeditated, and the two medical professors did not risk a syllable. [16]

Like Christians all the world over, Farrer was shocked by the sudden death of William Temple in October 1944 after his short primacy.

> I do not meet anyone who is not grieved by the Archbishop's death. He was a great man and more than an ecclesiastic. He was able to convince the people that he cared for them, and no one doubted that his words and actions came from a candid heart: they were not Church politics. Where is there such another?

On the whole Farrer did not enjoy the war years in their public aspect. As Dean he had to sleep in college, which he hated. When his colleagues returned from the war, his first effort, almost, was to dispose of this dignity, together with a notice which said:

> The Junior Dean
> may best be seen
> from 10 a.m. to 10.15.

He used to go with other clergymen to help at a canteen for troops in transit at the railway station. What he did enjoy was working on an allotment near the house in 7 Manor Road to which he moved in 1939. He also composed a paraphrase of the psalm *Notus in Judaea*, as a more suitable victory hymn than the more flagrant patriotic effusions.

During the war years Oxford was something of a philosophic vacuum. The publication of the first edition of A. J. Ayer's *Language, Truth and Logic* in 1937, with its rejection of both metaphysics and theology, had provided added stimulus to philosophical debate, to which Farrer contributed the lectures which led to the publication of *Finite and Infinite* in 1943. But now most of the lively young minds were away and there were only rumours of the new Wittgenstein at Cambridge. So, apart from his teaching and lecturing and the occasional paper to the Socratic Club, it is not surprising that with the work for the Speaker's Lectureship, which he held from 1937 to 1942, he turned increasingly to the study of the scriptures. His speculations were at that time so unusual that they have put many off his philosophical books. It is astonishing that Anthony Flew, in his book about God,[3] demolishes whole hosts of lesser men and does not even mention Farrer in a footnote. In America his books are now required reading in many faculties, and have been since his friends from America introduced them. (Professor Hartt was using *Finite and Infinite* as early as 1945.)

R. H. Lightfoot had demonstrated that St Mark did not write his gospel as a handful of disconnected stories attached to a Passion narrative. Farrer went on to underline the seriousness of inspiration. The gospel writers used the history and legend of the Old Testament, usually as it came to them in the Septuagint, and they saw in Christ the promises of God fulfilled. How else, brought up as they were, could they think? Here was a new Moses, a new Elijah, a new Joshua; and so on. This is not to say that they invented: the events attracted the types, not the types

119

the events. St Mark was, Farrer thought, as good an historian as Livy, perhaps better.

The speculations of these years can be traced in letters to his father. They contain brilliant and stimulating speculations; when he thought he was wrong he was not ashamed to change his mind. He was breaking new ground in England: his Speaker's Lectures dealt with New Testament eschatology and the Johannine Apocalypse. They showed the consistency of his approach to the Apocalypse as a continuing and coherent drama rather than a random collection of visions. There is also a digression on the structure of St Mark showing that he was already thinking of Mark in this way over ten years before publishing a book on it.

In a letter to his father in 1940 he elaborates his 'provisional conclusions about John; the gospel is a paraphrase of St Mark, enriched from other sources, in just about the same sense that the Apocalypse is of Ezekiel. There are three Johns, the Zebedaid, Mark and the Prophet-and-presbyter . . . ' The letter is an excursion into the kind of literary speculation and analogy which Farrer himself did not see fit to publish at the time. But about six months later he completed an essay covering all four gospels. It contained five theses:

1.  The Apocalypse follows Ezekiel in order with excursuses into other prophecies.

2.  St Mark 1 to 12 follows the life of Moses, Exodus 1 to Numbers 27 similarly in order, supplying antitypes to usable incidents as well as the tradition he derived from St Peter allowed: but without serious distortion of the elements of the tradition thus symbolically arranged.

3.  St Matthew and St Luke, following St Mark, show some consciousness of the Pentateuchal type behind him (especially St Luke) and make their own typological addition (e.g. a law from the mountain).

4.  St Luke used St Matthew, and Q is a fiction of the critics, derived from the error of supposing the evangelists to be scissors-and-paste hacks like the Pentateuchal editors.

5.  St John followed St Mark but reshaping the material in the interests of a completely new and very rigid Exodus typology which can be proved to the hilt.

Michael Ramsey is reported to have approved thesis 2, but Lightfoot, who saw the same section, lamented that Farrer was lost to scholarship and reason.

These early efforts were to germinate in later years. (Indeed Farrer was to contribute an essay on 'Dispensing with Q' to the volume of essays in memory of Lightfoot.) By May 1941 he was 'almost as excited now with this literary criticism as at other times with philosophical problems'. He was applying his typological method to St Luke.

By Maundy Thursday 1942 he had got his gospel books straight, complete with an outline of the story:

1. St Peter used to give his scriptural instructions not by way of a systematic catechetical course on the Lord's Torah, but on occasion, recalling no doubt appropriate antitypes from the Lord's actions and Passion in commenting on the Old Testament lections.

2. St Mark put these instructions together into a continuous book by the natural method – arranging them as antitypes to a continuous Old Testament book, and so his gospel could be a substitute for the Apostolic voice, providing a new testament lesson to be read in order after the old. But by a *tour de force* of ingenuity he made it a double antitype to (a) a continuous text of Torah (b) a continuous text of prophets – the lives of Moses and of Elias – explaining clearly the meaning of this in the form he gave to the Transfiguration story.

3. St Matthew did what St Peter and St Mark had not done – he made a catechetical and systematic presentation of the Lord's Torah, by inserting it into the Marcan narrative in a number of great discourses.

4. St Luke did not approve of the procedure: he returned to St Mark, followed Mark's Mosaic typology through Exodus and Numbers and then in chapters 10–18 went on with Deuteronomy, arranging the Lord's Torah, as he had it in Matthew and other sources, as antitypes to themes from Deuteronomy taken in order. He telescoped the end of the Elianic typology so as to finish it off neatly before his Deuteronomy begins. So he weeded out the Matthaean insertions from Mark and put them together in his Deuteronomic appendix and then proceeded to the Passion.

5. St John, with all this material before him, struck out a new line

and took a new Old Testament type, *viz.* Genesis. He starts with the Creation of the World, goes on to the Lamb of God on Mount Moriah (Gen. 22) and then through the histories of Jacob and Joseph continuously. There is also a secondary typology of Moses' great signs in Egypt, culminating in the Paschal Redemption, which also runs throughout the gospel but in a mere outline.

This involves a pretty complete recasting of the gospel material to square it with the new typology. St John manages this principally by taking St Mark in parallel from chapter 1 to chapter 11, but with material from other New Testament books. To tell the truth, St John overcomplicates his typology.

I think this story can be proved to the satisfaction of any reasonable mind. The Elianic typology in St Mark is in many ways more interesting than the Mosaic, and the Deuteronomic arrangement of Luke 10–18 enables one for the first time to see what Luke was at (and of course to read the burial service over the Q hypothesis). [17]

Thus Farrer enjoyed 'being able to disprove hypotheses', but he can hardly have expected his treatment of Mark and the dispensing with Q to be immediately popular. He was convinced that the theories he put forward must commend themselves to reason. Here was the preliminary working out of the kind of ideas expounded later in his published biblical studies and of the presuppositions defended in the Bampton Lectures.

Most of Farrer's remaining wartime letters to his father deal with the Greek text of the Septuagint with great ingenuity in relation to St John. Another interesting piece of work came his way. Before his death in 1944, N. P. Williams had designated Farrer to publish his life-work on the Epistle to the Romans. It was practically ready for the press but there was much expert work required in checking the patristic citations, in which the elder Farrer helped the younger.

And what meanwhile of his wife and family? After his marriage Farrer wrote movingly to his father on his birthday in 1938:

I hope you enjoy your birthday as much as I do mine, now when everything smiles for me. I do not expect to be so fortunate always, but that thought does not take from my present pleasure. But I think too that nature is to be trusted and all things are good in their season, and that I shall be perhaps not less happy and on solider foundations if ever, like you, I can see a family brought up in mutual trust and kindness, all established where it is best for them to be and thankful to God for their parentage. I vividly remember from the time that we made and sailed boats to those later years when you have followed me and helped me in all my moods and interests as I think no father ever did. [18]

Hopes for a family were fulfilled in Holy Week 1939 when a daughter, Caroline, was born after a difficult delivery.

By September 1940, anxious that his parents and sister should be away from the neighbourhood of London for a rest from the sirens, he kept inviting them to Oxford.

You would not increase Katharine's burdens, for you will bring two competent females. It should be possible for everyone to have an easy time. We live very much enclosed in ourselves and I go on with my Johannine studies: a twenty minutes (daylight) warning has just ended. They bombed one of the aerodromes as usual, I should think by the noise, or perhaps the power station in the fields by Botley: they left two time-bombs there the other night which have gone off, not near enough to do damage. Katharine and I played chess, and have left the game unfinished till next time, and Caroline proceeded with her bath. She is splashing noisily. She has invented a new game today of roaring like a lion: I should think it would give her a sore throat. It appears to give her infinite pleasure. [19]

A week later he repeated the invitation.

I hope you have profited by the somewhat decreased battering of London, but still that you will all come here soon for a thorough rest. Blackheath has been smashed, including the Newton house. Our last news was a telegram saying that Mr Newton had removed to a house opposite, waiting for the front of the vicarage to fall down – or get shored up. There are many craters in a square of a hundred yards. Almost no one has been killed in the parish. Mrs Newton is away but on her way back unless we succeed in intercepting her. If you think of coming here there is no need to give notice: we are always ready for you. I know that you are pretty safe where you are, but I'm sure it would be useful for you to have a rest from the sirens and racket. We are feebly attempting to interest ourselves in emergency works. I have put myself down to do some all-night duty in a canteen at the station, where soldiers get marooned. Katharine has been giving away clothes and I have been discouraging her from trying to take anything on while she has Caroline to cope with. If you come here, we could set one another free for all sorts of virtuous activity. [20]

Letters in 1941 describe the Farrers succouring their friends and enjoying their daughter's beauty, playful mischief and singing games. It was an oddly enclosed world – the livelier philosophical minds away, a constant succession of young men coming and going – leaving Farrer with his mind free to meditate on his new scriptural interests. Yet he was still sometimes called upon.

Last night after playing chess with a sick pupil I was then carried off by a relentless young man who asked me at five-minute intervals:

'What is the Apostolic Succession?'

'What is the origin of the ceremonies of the Eucharist?'

'How do I answer Papists who deny the validity of Anglican orders?'

'What is the authority of scripture?' etc., etc.,

until half-past-eleven, was then rather indignant at my going away to bed and asked how soon he could come and start again. [21]

These were years of steady and unseen growth which led to his post-war blossoming as a pastor and preacher: scholar, of course, he had always been.

# CHAPTER 8

# *Trinity College 1945–60*

\*

In the years following the war, the practice of the Christian religion flourished in Oxford. College chapels – not only Trinity – were well filled. The philosophic world was busy bringing itself up to date with the latest news brought with evangelical fervour from Cambridge by the disciples of Wittgenstein and on the whole was not interested in Christian doctrine.[1] The revival was a revival of Christian practice, of prayer and communion, and not of Christian thinking. Prayer, worship and Bible study drew large audiences, but not so doctrine. It was as if the undergraduates could divide their minds into two parts, the one that listened to their tutors and the one that went to chapel. Many Trinity men remember the brief addresses Farrer gave at the Eucharist in Trinity Chapel (published as *The Crown of the Year*). Music and poetry supplanted politics in the undergraduate mind: and that remarkable constellation of Christians (C. S. Lewis, Charles Williams and J. R. R. Tolkien) were influential in the English faculty.

These were golden days. Farrer came to his full stature as chaplain, preacher and divine. In 1945 he took his degrees of Bachelor of Divinity and Doctor of Divinity on the same day. He and his family moved into the new house built over the gate between Trinity and St John's in St Giles, and the books began to flow. Much of the reading and writing were done in a room at the top of the house, to which he gave the Aristophanic title of Phrontisterion (thinking shop). The Bampton Lectures, published as *The Glass of Vision*, were delivered in 1948. They broke the tradition of the heavy academic approach and the tone of voice which threatened a half-page footnote in small print. Farrer preached to gratifyingly large numbers with a lightness of touch and a verbal felicity which never hereafter left him.

With an unusually large number of ordinands in the college because of the post-war bulge, there began the daily celebration of the Eucharist at 8 a.m. and Evensong at 6 p.m. which Farrer

maintained for the rest of his time at Trinity. The fundamentalists of the Christian Union did not altogether approve,
commenting sometimes in their characterisic mode that the
Chaplain was 'spiritually dead'; to which he replied, 'Of course
they grow up and they either become good Catholics or retired
Lieutenant-Colonels.' By 1950 he had won them over: they
attended chapel and he attended their Bible study groups. He
was also anxious to enrich the very plain tradition of worship in
the college chapel. During a university mission, when Father
Algy Robertson, ssf, was the college missioner, he decided to
take the opportunity to introduce Eucharistic vestments,
declaring with delight that Father Algy, who wore them for the
last Sunday of the mission, was 'not so much a stalking horse as
a clothes horse'.

The ordinary undergraduate was amused by Farrer's whim-
sicality: only the more perceptive were aware of his spiritual
depth and intellect. From his life of prayer there flowed the
teaching, the friendship and the priestly guidance which were
always available for his pupils. Those who shared his home life
were amazed by the depth of his intelligence and the quickness
of Katharine's wit. Their friendship was prized by this mature
post-war generation as they walked with Katharine round the
gardens discussing their problems or gave thanks in chapel for
the birth of a child. It was a friendship spliced with wit, as when
Farrer wrote to a future Bishop of St Andrews, then his pupil,

> I have had a communication from the Bishop of Oxford inquiring
> whether you are suitable to become a reader. Since you are
> accepted as a candidate for Holy Orders, *a fortiori*, one must
> conclude that you are suitable for the lesser office. So I took a
> post-card and on it I wrote:
>> 'It is not a fluke, that Mr Hare Duke
>> is a candidate standing for orders;
>> his manners and mind
>> are the joy of mankind
>> and his works of the angel recorders',
> and I sent it to the Bishop. [1]

The whole religious life of the College seemed to come alive.
Lecturers in the theological faculty might refer to the 'neo-
Thomist tradition at Trinity' or raise a laugh by referring to
Farrer as 'Jude the Obscure', but his delight in people, in life and

126

in thought was transparent. Its source was the daily discipline of his life of prayer. If one waited for him after the daily Eucharist, it became apparent that his meditation lasted half an hour. Accepting an invitation to dinner before a speaking engagement Farrer said, 'I will be a little late because I must take Evensong in chapel first.' When his host offered to have a taxi at the college gates to save time, then came the reply 'Oh no; I would feel sinful sitting in a taxi. I'll run.'

Some who attended the Bampton Lectures remember 'crowding into the gallery of St Mary's with lots of others'. The lectures inspired the same interest as Lightfoot's lectures on St Matthew and St Mark. In both cases they went to hear the message 'because of the outstanding divinity of the man who delivered it'.

Farrer's reputation grew outside the college as some of his books became known – biblical scholars might consider his work eccentric but no one could fail to be moved by the brilliant simplicity of the smaller books, such as *The Crown of the Year* and *Lord, I Believe.* The arrival of Hugh Maycock as Principal of Pusey House in 1953 opened the gates for Austin to preach to a wider congregation.

None of this fame detracted from his pastoral efforts in Trinity. By the Hilary Term 1955 there were usually about thirty at the Sunday Mass, the weekday congregation at Evensong was steady at sixteen to twenty, and the chapel was packed at Sunday Evensong. There were some Austinian touches. He had compiled a typological lectionary for each day, with the second lesson from the New Testament expounding the first lesson. Each day of the week also had a special prayer superbly composed by him. There were also seven or eight Bible study groups a week and two or three discussion groups.

To the average undergraduate at Trinity Farrer continued to be a remote and rather daunting figure, 'a brain on a stalk' as he once put it. He would pass them and even find it difficult to raise his eyebrows in greeting, and they would think – wrongly – that he knew and cared little about them. In fact his knowledge of them was detailed and careful. When he made Tuesday nights his open nights for undergraduates, many came. His advice was precise and to the point. An undergraduate who thought he might have a call to be a missionary, and therefore perhaps to celibacy, was told to go down for the vacation and (by arrangement) not write to his girlfriend for six weeks. When she was driven to tears by this procedure, he remonstrated, 'She really must have a little more fortitude.' An ordinand consulted him about the suitability of his girlfriend as a wife, and was told, 'Marriage is a matter of the inclination: but will she do the housework and cook?' He always married members of the college if they asked him to but was hesitant about it: 'You can do only good by baptizing and you can't do any harm by burying, but you never know what you may be starting when you marry people.' He insisted remorselessly on putting personal needs before any kind of show. Two of the Christians in college were sharing a room and did not get on well; the chapel-going undergraduates were anxious that they should make up their differences and present a united front, but Farrer would have none of it and wisely urged their separation, to their great relief. To complaints that a fellow Christian was so concerned with playing bridge that he failed to turn up to a weekly religious meeting, Farrer retorted that it was a good thing to be seen as a good bridge-player and a good Christian.

Farrer appears not to have been an outstanding tutor of undergraduates as far as ensuring that they mastered the necessary matter required for a good degree. Those who came to him as graduates found him stimulating and profound. He tended to ignore in biblical studies and philosophy what he thought merely trivial or fashionable and to ask his own questions in his own way. He was of course perfectly well aware of what was going on in the world of contemporary scholarship: it was simply that he did not care to write footnotes about it.[2] 'They will say,' said Katharine, 'that he spent his time writing books and never reading them.' His less talented pupils would emerge from a tutorial overwhelmed by the brilliance of his logic and the excellence of his English, but somehow forgetting how he had reached his conclusions. Those Americans who came to him with their doctoral theses found him a fountain of living inspiration.

Michael Goulder,[3] who was already ordained when he arrived at Trinity, provides a picture of Farrer from the point of view of a mature student:

He wouldn't stand for levity about Christianity – 'Our holy faith', as he called it – and would use strong language about clever philosophers who were causing his little ones to stumble. As a tutor he was brilliant, and one emerged from a tutorial laden with pearls of great price such as no amount of reading could have supplied. He knew how to extract the key sentence from a volume and to express the teaching of a school in a phrase. From Augustine (whom he always stressed on the first syllable, like his own name) he would cite *Ita suadet ut persuadeat* (God so influences that he persuades), the sentence which shows the great Latin father at the crunch between his doctrine of grace and his belief in freedom. He seemed to see to the heart of every thinker. 'Clement [of Alexandria] was too busy being a Greek gentleman to concern himself with such matters.' 'Bertrand Russell thinks he is a fly on the cornice watching Bertrand Russell behave.' 'The vital point is the resurrection [of the dead]: does Bishop Robinson believe in that?' 'X told me that God was the most powerful of our symbols. He has become a sentimental atheist'. He always listened with courtesy to one's essay however bad – unless there were jokes about scriptural authors in it. I once referred to St Luke as providing a chorus of Jews plotting Paul's murder (a remark which many modern critics would think mild), but not a second time. [2]

Several undergraduates lived with the Farrers very happily in the Gatehouse in these years. Farrer felt more relaxed in familiar company where there was no pressure. Certainly it was easier than at those sherry parties where he would entertain groups of ten freshmen at a time. He would sometimes drink pure water, having intended to flavour it with orange squash but having forgotten the orange, so giving the odd impression to some that he was drinking neat gin.

A most vivid picture of him is contained in a letter from Stephen Willink, who as college organist in the fifties came to know and appreciate him well.

His lectures rarely attracted queues. I treasure a letter from him which, after bemoaning 'a most terrible thing – I have a pupil in theology, beginning from the beginning', continues 'On the other hand NO-ONE came to my St Thomas lecture, so I have thirty-two free hours on a plate'.

Yet for us, a motley band of struggling Christians, the friendship which he and his greatly beloved wife, Kay, offered was incontestably Oxford's most precious gift. We laid at his feet our doubts and enthusiasms and never doubted that even the most intractable

129

personal problem, once submitted to his scrutiny, would be robbed of its terrors. 'Well, now,' he would begin, gazing fixedly at the carpet and knotting his eyebrows with a sort of benign ferocity: we were instantly comforted. The magic worked almost as effectively at a distance. Long after our departure from Oxford his pen would seek us out; here is a typical concluding paragraph: 'But I am shooting random shafts: and maybe this is just the advice that you least ought to hear. Which only shows how bad it is communicating by letter, and why you should come and see us: as for my going to Cambridge, I plead that I am busy, married and old'.

Above all, Willink remembers him at the altar:

> He himself used to say that nothing was more ridiculous than a priest celebrating Mass, nowhere so laughable a contrast between what a man is and what he presumes to do. Yet here this most self-forgetful of men seemed to clothe himself in a new authority as he entered and took us with him into the heart of the mystery. Obedient to the Prayer Book, he never failed to give us a two-minute homily after the Creed: these paragraphs might at first put a strain on our unbreakfasted intellects, but as our ears accustomaed themselves to that fastidious prose, we came to sense and eventually to share his love and understanding of the Eucharist. [3]

He continued to be at the service of his pupils with selfless patience when he could help them in any enterprise. One of his first pupils says:

> After coming down I kept in touch with Austin. During my first Anglican curacy in Gloucester I went to see him at Trinity to ask his advice because I felt inadequate in helping the sick and dying. Austin was just as patient as he had been with my intellectual problems. I remember him saying that he thought the important thing to aim at when ministering to the dying was to help them to live with God. When I was on the point of becoming a Roman Catholic I wrote to tell him and received a charming and affectionate letter. Subsequently when I did not know where to turn for help in the Roman Church he gave me an introductory letter to David Mathew, auxiliary Bishop of Westminster, who was a great help to me. [4]

His help, given at considerable cost, did not end when his friends had left Oxford. In 1966 he gave three lectures for

Michael Goulder on 'St Mark's Christ' at courses for the West Midlands clergy. As Katharine was by now dependent on his company[4] he drove the seventy miles there and back each day. He also accepted an invitation to open a series of four controversial lectures on 'Infallibility in the Church' – two by Anglicans, two by Romans.

> He was at his most brilliant ... Austin's remarks about fears of Rome becoming a 'fact-factory going full-blast' and about the infallibility doctrine being like 'King Ahab propped up in his chariot till the going down of the sun, least Israel be as sheep scattered upon the mountains' have a lasting pungency.[5] [5]

Not all undergraduates could warm to a man who would probably neither look at them nor give a response to their greeting as he hastened by. Many would have described him unkindly, but with some truth, as a remote and ineffectual don. On the other hand many recognized him as a scholar and a saint, and it was those qualities which saved him from being a failure as a college chaplain. The faithful gained from the chapel services, from the penetration and humour of his sermons, from the evenings in his rooms. But on the rowing man and the agnostic he made no impact.

Farrer's own version of what life was like in post-war Trinity is recorded in letters to his father up to the latter's death in 1954. In 1946 the college was becoming itself again: and what was called the post-war boom was on. In the Michaelmas Term he wrote of 'a general sense of happiness in the way things are going in the college'.

> I was beginning to feel that I was getting beyond pastoral usefulness, but now things proceed better and I conclude that it was only my own wickedness and the difficulty of the times. I find more sympathy in my colleagues and the most touching co-operation from some of the returned soldiers and others of the young men. They have formed a little society chiefly on the basis of prayer and friendship, intending to develop other activities of sacred study and good works as they may be moved. This is only in its infancy and it may prove a disappointment, but nothing could be more hopeful just now and I beg you sometimes to pray for us. It is the greatest blessing to have some sort of living nucleus through which to work instead of vainly and mechanically spreading the net over the

whole college. The most valuable person in this affair is a man who was slowly martyred in a Japanese labour camp ever since the fall of Singapore, and came out alive (which only half did) having sustained his own spirit and (though he does not say so) that of his soldiers through inexpressible privations: and he is as 'alive from the dead' in the New Testament sense. [6]

A small incident shows the increasing regard in which he was held.

Yesterday by a mere not hearing of bells I missed the evening chapel. A handful of people turned up and went sadly away again. I found out who they were and sent them apologies saying they must come again, to show there was no ill-will. Today I went into evening chapel to find all those who were there yesterday and what looked like a special muster of their friends. [7]

The immediate post-war years were a period of great activity – teaching, lecturing, gardening, serving the chapel and increasing pastoral work. He describes one crowded day:

Yesterday I taught all morning, did some lightning shopping at one o'clock, pulled all the nettles out of the fruit bushes after lunch, taught from five to seven, took chapel, came home to receive a message about imminent frost, went down after supper and covered all the strawberries with old black-out and earthed-up the potatoes, went back into college and taught until a quarter to ten, joined a Bible study group and afterwards said Compline with them in chapel. Wrote two documents to be read at college meeting this morning, ran home, and got straight into bed at 11.30. [8]

During the twenty-five years he was at Trinity, Farrer taught both philosophy and theology, and also political theory for historians. In the later years when theology teaching became more specialized and college tutors would send out pupils for some parts of the syllabus, Farrer continued to teach his pupils Old Testament, New Testament and Christian doctrine. His philosophy lectures included both classical and modern philosophers. He was at the heart of the discussion group which was concerned that philosophy and the Faith should meet,[6] and he ventured into the Greats school with lectures on Collingwood's *Metaphysics*, of which the first drew a surprising crowd. But as he tells us:

My 'rational theology lectures' in the theology school produced quite other results – five nervous looking men. As soon as I entered the room one of them shied and ran away, supposing that he had been about to hear Landon on *The Law of Torts*: a second held out until my first sentence, then fled after the other. The survivors and I had a good laugh. It was like the history of Gideon. I wondered if I should pour some ink into a pen-tray and see which of them would lap like dogs. [9]

At this time he began conscientiously to work to rule. 'There are', he said 'many things which I love to do when I have brought myself to begin, yet which I would not begin except for a rule. Setting myself to write is like forcing open a window which has jammed; but when it is open I enjoy the air and the prospect.'

This rule he perhaps needed as his influence and his activities widened. In September of 1947 he had been invited to talk to the seminarists at Ely Theological College. The Hilary and Trinity Terms of 1948 were the time when St Mary's was filled with an audience for Farrer's Bampton Lectures (published as *The Glass of Vision*). He had become famous; he was human enough to appreciate it.

I am tasting the sweets of glory, though I am able to tell myself that I know exactly the valuelessness of the ingredients that go into the charm and why they happen to work at this moment. But anyhow my three lectures have kept such an audience in St Mary's as has not been seen for I don't know how long, perhaps thirty years, at the official sermon. So much for glory. I only wish I had any reason to think I were doing any good with the audience I've got. A huge lot of people came to show me their good will: I could have wept to see so suddenly that I had so many friends. The oldest of the bedels told me he had not seen so many for a Bampton Lecture. They will not, many of them, stay the course, if only that they know they will be able to read it, should they wish. [10]

The same year he preached the Hulsean Sermon[7] in Great St Mary's at Cambridge, a most masterly exposition of his way of viewing the Gospels, to a congregation which no doubt regarded him as eccentric in opinion if not bizarre. He stayed as the guest of C. E. Raven, the Master of Christ's College and Vice-Chancellor. Of Raven he says:

He is a nice man, but has such an outsize actor's personality that (if you see what I mean) you can scarcely hear the words of the song because the band plays fortissimo all the time. I do not mean that his manners are bad: on the contrary they are perfect – as perfect as those of a Vice-Chancellor on the stage doing his very best. How ungrateful I am! No one could have been kinder or more attentive, he is genuinely amiable. [11]

In the long vacation of 1948 he again paid a visit to the hop-pickers in Kent, where he describes James Lambert and some of the young men from Trinity

heroically running a first-aid station and some other amenities for a camp of 1,600 hop-pickers: East Enders, gipsies, all sorts. James and his assistants are kept busy enough. I just stayed a night with them in their tent and said service for them and for a similar larger team in another camp. There were, I gathered, to be mission services in the evening, but with them I was not concerned. I was glad to have gone. I heard and saw such good of some young men who did not come out very strong in college. [12]

In his contribution to the *Apostolic Ministry*[8] Farrer had aligned himself with the leading Anglo-Catholics of his day. But his pastoral concern at Trinity began by 1948 to bring his heart and his head into conflict. He could not bring himself to refuse to communicate devout Scottish Presbyterians if they presented themselves at the altar. He was unwilling to behave in an apparently harsh manner on principles which he now felt were probable only. He did not feel himself to be an expert on the theology of the Church, and he was called to think about philosophy and to cultivate charity, to let controversial divinity alone and try to understand the Gospels. He had been on a committee of the Archbishop's which was negotiating with the representatives of the Free Churches, and his High Church friends depended on him for a 'no compromise' vote. But he had resigned. He could not be an unwavering party man like those whom he said were as cheerfully confident in their cause as if it were a cricket match. As a close personal friend of Gregory Dix and Kenneth Kirk, Austin felt deeply for the rites and ortho-doxies of an Anglo-Catholicism which was already beginning to look inadequate. As it came increasingly under attack he sometimes felt that something precious in his own spiritual life was being threatened, but he was clear-headed enough to know (in a favourite phrase of his) that much of it 'wouldn't do'.

In addition to the work and prayer which often filled his days, he began to take an interest in the church of St Nicholas, Abingdon. Built by the abbey to serve their lay servants, it had never had a proper parish attached nor been sufficiently endowed. Farrer was the first Fellow of Trinity for three-quarters of a century to take the duty in person. 'It is worth 10/- net. But I find I like doing it.'

Farrer was so content with life at Trinity that he did not feel at all attracted by two professorships shortly coming up for election – the Regius Professorship of Moral and Pastoral Theology (in 1949) and the Nolloth Professorship of the Philosophy of the Christian Religion (in 1950). The latter Farrer could have filled with distinction but did not want: it is attached to a Fellowship at Oriel; that college already had a Chaplain–Fellow, and he would have had to leave his new home in Trinity and live in North Oxford, abandoning his pastoral work. It would leave him 'without God, altar, or home in the world.' As for the former, moral theology was not his subject, although he did write the article on the 'Theology of Morals' published in *Theology*, May 1939, in the series of twelve which inaugurated Alec Vidler's editorship.

In a letter of 1 March 1949 he explains his views about the Moral Theology chair to his father:

It is a Regius Professorship: the King nominates, but the King in fact takes the advice of the Dean (of Christchurch) speaking for the College. The Dean asked me about it. I told him to try everything else first and that I would not think seriously about it unless the situation obliged him to press me. In that case, I said, I would take advice . . . But I am not at all clear that I would take it under *any* circumstances. I have only said that if the Dean is in despair, I will take advice. I could scarcely give him a more negative answer. In my opinion they have one unexceptionable candidate who would be likely to accept. I believe their real motive is nothing but friendship. They are familiar with me and see that I should have no adjustments to make to fit in with them, having been their neighbour so long. And Katharine they perceive is no dragoness. But I would rather stay here [at Trinity] for a bit, and so would Katharine. It is heavenly being here – I do not think I have ever been so solidly happy in all my life, what with Caroline doing so well, and my being able to do a bit more at the chaplaincy. I could not be happier than I am, except by being a better man entirely. So the last thing I am likely to do is to alter the conditions of my life in a hurry; you may be sure of that. [13]

Three weeks later he writes:

I think the business of the Moral Theology chair must have blown safely over. Then it seems there are no more rocks and shoals until some time in the middle of the next academic year, when Grensted's chair will be advertised (the Nolloth Chair of Christian Philosophy). Then I shall have to take advice whether I can let it go without condemning myself to teach pupils 15 hours a week for ever. [14]

In Hilary Term 1950 however, there was to be a mission to the university and Farrer did not like large-scale missions with episcopal oratory:

I find this sort of thing very strange and cannot co-operate without certain misgivings. By what warrant do I represent it as Christian duty, or indeed obviously desirable that young men should listen to exhortations eight nights successively? I should have thought 30 minutes of oratory was enough for one week. It seems to be a confidence trick, a public demonstration that we are not beaten, and that we are afraid of no one: a by-product, however, of some intrinsic value is the lodging of a Franciscan father here in college during the mission week: and I shall encourage my young men to concentrate on passing him around among their friends. It seems a reasonable thing to demand of the grace of God that this should have some effect. I cannot see what is the good of bishops preaching missions, strange bishops anyhow. A bishop is a pastor in his own diocese, and always for this reason to be received with the expectation of blessing – so indeed is one's archbishop. But if that is what you want, then surely a poor friar or a parish priest of sacrificial zeal or a missionary from Africa is likely to move us more than a prelate borrowed from a neighbouring diocese. [15]

In the event Farrer had high hopes of the college missioner.[9]

The young men have organized endless parties to show him to their friends and he is going to be very thoroughly passed round. The Chaplain is called upon to supply the mechanical part, e.g. the coercing of a servant to ring the chapel bell at impossible hours, and of the stores to supply coffee at even less possible hours: or again at no notice to provide special devotions of an edifying novelty for ten minutes every evening after Evensong. [16]

Shortly after the mission the electors gave Farrer the first refusal of the Nolloth chair, which he declined. He was not ready to abandon pastoral work. But the years of unremitting toil since the war, together with his family anxieties,[10] were now beginning to make themselves felt. In February 1950 he negotiated with the Vicar of Abingdon for two free Sundays in each academic term so that he need never do more than two Sundays consecutively during term at St Nicholas. By August his fatigue was becoming serious. He had five almost sleepless weeks after having a tooth pulled out and treatment for an antrum infection.

> I am told [he wrote to his parents] that I have been suffering from an exhaustion disease . . . I am refusing all undertakings right and left, and I shall have to get rid of my Abingdon commitments wholly during term-time. I admit being tired, but I have suffered no loss in the power of mental decision or found any unusual difficulty in managing my temper, so I have been lucky. I need hardly say that several people and especially Katharine have conspired to make it easy for me. I have finished my book [*A Study in St Mark*] and I do not want to write another for a long time. This is the one I had to write. [17]

However, later in October, recovered but still tired, he had to relinquish all his Abingdon duties on the ground of health. Double duty on Sundays in term, and especially 'the ineluctable necessity of preaching a weekly sermon at Abingdon by virtual extemporization and squeezing of my wits' were too exhausting. In two years he had preached all through St Mark and half through the Epistle to the Romans.

In 1949 he had been again to Cambridge to talk to the Theological Society, a Daniel venturing into a den of lions, and received some unexpected support.

> I had made up my mind not to be put down by their theologians. So I chose a particular and exact thesis about the symbolic treatment of genealogy in Matthew 1, Luke 3 and certain texts of Enoch. They could object nothing but generalities – Did people really think like this? I appealed to the Jews present (Lowe and Daube) and the Jews

sang a heartening duet in my support. Nothing they said would be more natural or better evidenced than the kind of thing I was proposing. [18]

In 1952 he continued his dialogue with Cambridge:

I am to entertain in hall the most violent of my controversial enemies, a Cambridge man called Robert Casey, our common friends having felt it was about time we met. He has written about me with great severity but then *calida in iuventa* [in my hot-blooded youth] I wrote of certain others with equal severity. Violent praise and violent blame are equally embarrassing and useless. My good critics help me bring forth the precious from the vile. I am disappointed when I meet with one who does not even see that I am attempting (however ill) an intelligible task, *but views me with the distance of an* anthropologist studying a Hottentot making rain. [19]

His letters, as we have seen deal mainly with his family, his work, and his friends. On three occasions, though, he spoke his mind forcefully on matters of topical concern. In 1950 his colleague Tony Crosland was standing in the Labour interest in the General Election. He assured Austin that the issues were full employment and justice for the poor. But Austin was sure that the outcome of Labour policy would be *étatisme*, which meant uniformity, corruption, stagnation and tyranny. Anything, even injustice, he said was better.

He felt equally strongly about the current controversy on gambling. Playing games with one's surplus cash, he thought was plainly not a major sin, and if we blocked that outlet then the cinema proprietors would profit. The only useful action would be to provide better outlets for energy, such as playing fields and clubs. He did, however, feel angry about the exploitation of gambling by football pools and wanted them restricted.

When in December 1950 the Allied Forces met with a reverse in Korea he wrote:

There will not be a world war, but the Americans may have learnt their lesson and may institute general military service. And perhaps that is the lesson which Truman meant to teach his countrymen through this whole painful action. If so the general prospect will be vastly brightened and it will be much better than it would have been had Korea been left alone. If you wish to prevent me from dropping in a parachute over Berlin, foaming at the mouth and brandishing a banner inwrought with 666 [the number of the beast in the Apocalypse] and 153 [the Piscatorial Number in St John's Gospel] come here and exhort me to return to divine philosophy. [20]

In March 1951 his mother died at the age of seventy-seven. Farrer, who was with her, was moved by 'a most Christian death'. The letters to his father continued and so did the godliness of Trinity. At the end of the next Michaelmas Term he wrote:

The term's finished. It has been in some ways successful. The religious affairs of the college have been (outwardly) prosperous. Daily Chapel has flourished; instead of almost no one there we have had from ten to sixteen people, and only once too few to sing the hymn. The usually tiresome business of unofficial religious meetings has been happily solved by four excellent people talking about the realities of the Christian life in other countries including Communist countries. The young men are edified and stimulated without being bored. Meanwhile we have got the organ rebuilt to the great assistance of the service and the beautifying of the chapel; I have also made a simple discovery I ought to have made long ago – it is disastrous to elect organ scholars straight from school. They come up mere children and are really no help. The thing to do is to encourage a freshman of character and musical taste to improve his organ playing, and make him organist next year. Then you know what you are getting: he understands how to train singers: he has some authority. [21]

The pressure of work continued and near the end of 1952 he was weary: but whatever the pressure he remained always open to those who needed him.

There are [he writes in October 1952] three streams of humanity always flowing through: every day I entertain a few freshmen, every day some of the older lot bring me some piece of their affairs. Every day, or nearly so, an old student reappears from the great world and calls. There is always teaching, and it seems urgent to me to defend, restate and above all reform my stuff about St Mark.[11] [22]

His energies, in fact, went into his work, his prayers and Trinity College, and he always found meetings and committees tedious, particularly at this stage. One typical meeting he describes:

This afternoon I attended a function advertised as a 'sandwich lunch: sandwiches will be provided'. They were, but mostly gone by the time I got there. It was a well-known type of Oxford fixture – a lot of well-meaning people worrying about the general nature of university education and the duty of the Christian teacher. I came away feeling that there was not much we could any of us do except cultivate the patch we are cultivating with increased zeal: and that we *knew* we ought to do before we went to the sandwich lunch at which sandwiches (though in deficient quantities) were provided. [23]

Tired though he was, the chapel crowded and now restored gladdened him.

I begin to feel like good King Josiah or Simon the son of Onias the High Priest and to rest in the claim that in my days the House was repaired and glorified. I have seen the organ rebuilt the wood repaired and waxed, the cushions replaced, and now all the two hundred William IV quarto prayer books made sound and clean. It remains to clean and whiten the upper walls and ceilings. But it is not expedient for me to boast. [24]

His father died on 21 February 1954 at the age of eighty-two. Austin had written to him without a break for thirty years. Four of the last letters have an interest of their own. He was surprised and moved to find his father present at the Holy Week ceremonies (probably at St Mary Magdalene, Farrer's favourite place of worship).

I was touched that you should come into the very lion's den to hear my sermon, though I trembled for your feelings, especially you not hearing well, for if you have the ceremonies without the words they are intended to set forth, it must seem heathenish indeed. We have not really gone back to the Middle Ages, for our congregation consists of regular communicants and if they come there to adore, it is to adore a mystery of redemption in which at other times they partake. Also – I hope – we balance the boat by preaching the Gospel to them, according to our ability. Do we have no misgivings? Certainly we have misgivings, for all human institutions are abused. But I think it best to abound to all extremes – to give to ceremonies all possible force, to preach out one's whole heart, and to practise a pure spirituality in which not only outward but even inward images are denied – but as you see, I am only transcribing von Hügel. [25]

The speculations on theology and philosophy shared with his father in his earlier years are comparatively rare in the letters written in the last ten years of the elder Farrer's life. Austin mentioned the Introduction which he wrote to the English translation of Leibniz's *Theodicy* (partly reproduced in the SPCK volume *Reflective Faith*), on which he remarked that he needed the money and that the Theodicy is not uninteresting or unprofitable, especially from an historical point of view.

Leibniz is writing at the very end of the great age of Reformation and Counter-Reformation Theology and is on a razor's edge himself between faith and flat rationalism, Christianity and deism. Revealed truth and supernatural faith are both tenderly treated, but no one, you feel, is asking 'What must I do to be saved?' One keeps seeing Butler peeping round the right-hand corner of the book and Kant round the left. [26]

In 1952 he was also asked to write an introduction to *Kerygma and Myth*, the English translation of a series of essays on Bultmann's 'demythologization'.

I have been having a brainstorm – the SPCK sent me a most mischievous collection of papers translated from the German under the title of *Kerygma and Myth* (for which I have besought them to substitute 'Myth and Evangel'). They are by Bultmann and others, and I was to write an English introduction. I refused to do this, but I have written my own contribution to the debate as a terminal essay to the whole. As I had really no time for this, I did it there and then: I spent a day reading the translated German papers and scribbling notes and three days writing my own contribution twice over, and now I will have no more to do with it. [27]

This elegant piece of work is too little known. With gentle politeness it demolishes the presuppositions of the preceding essays almost in one sentence – indeed by anticipation it casts doubt on most of what passed for radical theology ten years later. Farrer argues simply that God speaks to us, conceivably, not only in the proclamation of the Gospel words but in the declaration which consists of divine acts – that the truth may as well be conveyed by miracle as by parable.

The last surviving letter to his father was a comment on a certain type of logical philosopher in the ascendant in Oxford in the 1950s.

> He is an instance of a sort of eccentricity pretty common among academic philosophers whose philosophy is chiefly logical rather than being an attempt to obtain insight into the essence of things. Their intellect becomes absorbed in puzzles about the relation between dream and real experience, about logical identity and inferential validity, about sense and nonsense. The mind having thus gone a-wool-gathering, the rest of their life has to take care of itself, and as the possession of an absorbing intellectual hobby makes for contentment, such men are likely to drop into a virtuous puerility. [28]

A comment not likely ever to be made about Austin or his father.

In the same year Farrer's voice was heard on the schools programme of the BBC. So much so that he can write to his father, 'The religious department of the BBC is entirely staffed with your pupils and my friends, Anglicans and Baptists. By the end of next March I shall have earned £160 in twelve months from the BBC.' The text of six of these talks survives. One on God the Creator, one on Creation Myths, one on The Righteous God (on the argument from morality), one on The Problem of Evil, and one on Revelation and Reason. These were all heard in a series on 'Religion and Philosophy'. In 1956 he also gave the final talk in a series 'Jesus Christ: History, Interpretation and Faith': his topic was Faith and Knowledge. They still make admirable reading.

At the request of his St Edmund Hall student Gordon Phillips, Farrer preached the first London University sermon in Christ Church, Woburn Square, and was a frequent preacher to the students. At the time of Dr Billy Graham's second visit to Britain, Farrer made a courteous but critical reference to Dr Graham (his one-time co-religionist), whereupon a medical student stood up and stamped out in protest. Farrer's puzzled and nervous reaction to this from the pulpit summed up a whole world of theological conflict and tragic misunderstanding, since a Catholic reconstruction of his family faith centred in Bible, baptism, God's Word and the necessity of Church and Spirit was the theme of his whole life's work.

He had to make his influence in London under his own steam, without any of that naming names characteristic of Oxford. No one except a few Oxford graduates had the remotest idea who he was. But London students were highly intelligent, so Farrer's methods of working his way to conclusions by the simple handling of very primary ideas without a mass of indirect literary allusion suited them admirably. At least in those days they seemed to respond to this approach.

In his sermons Farrer insisted time after time that the most evident proof of God is in the lives of saints, and that Heaven is the life of Christ in the company of his saints. In that company some of us would reckon him. Some of his reading reveals his own growth towards maturity.

> When I am in retreat I always (a) read the life of a saint and (b) walk to the top of Shotover Hill, neither of which things I ever do at any other time. This time I read the Curé d'Ars. Merely what he did, his twenty-hours working day, almost without food, was a standing miracle; I also read a good deal of the Lady Julian of Norwich. I should call her above all a theological thinker: it is *l'Augustinisme sensible au coeur*, and very fine at that. And I think she says most of the things that Luther was to say, but not of course the negations. [29]

He also read St Francis de Sales,

> especially because of his repeated teaching that we must be as forgiving to ourselves, and as patient with ourselves as God is, for this is a most healthful doctrine. I have been taught that once anything is confessed and absolved, it is a duty to think of it no more, since we cannot doubt the divine absolution. And though we must weep to be so unworthy of the divine generosity, yet it is in this that mercy is revealed, and mercy is infinite.[30]

Little has been said of the Farrers' home life. Their daughter Caroline was attractive and delightful, and a source of joy to her parents. But as she grew out of infancy she did not seem to learn, and this in Oxford, where an excess of precocious offspring is found, became a matter of concern. Austin and Katharine, both bookish people themselves, had to help Caroline to cultivate goodness and skill in other directions. And how and where was she to learn to read and write? How was the extra money to be found? They took enormous trouble in seeking the right solution. It was finally decided that Caroline must go away to school, and at the age of eight she went to a Rudolph Steiner school in Kent. This was both a painful separation and a triumphant success. When she left school at eighteen Caroline went to a religious community where she was taught embroidery. She has since been able to maintain herself by her own work. But while there was still anxiety about her future, her parents worked to acquire the money for her school fees and to provide for her future. This was why Farrer published some of his smaller works. The matter caused him great anxiety over many years: what it cost him may be seen by the discerning eye which reads *Love Almighty and Ills Unlimited*. Experience, not theory alone, underlies that book.

Any appreciation of Austin Farrer must include his wife and their love for each other. In their earlier years together it was a romantic love expressed by the romantic poetry they read together. Katharine made it very plain in the letters she wrote before her engagement that she was already deeply and emotionally dependent upon him. She was talented and highly strung – one of the few people to whom that overworked term really applied – and from her frequent attacks of bronchitis one may conjecture that she was never physically robust. She was deeply pious, and particularly at home at St Mary Magdalene in Oxford when Colin Stephenson was vicar. (It was he who prepared Caroline for confirmation.) In appearance she had the fragile beauty of porcelain. They must have seemed a singularly unpractical pair: but appearances were deceptive. Kay was an admirable cook who enjoyed entertaining when she was not tired. But she liked what she had cooked to be eaten; her brother remembers signalling urgently to his wife that she must consume all the omelette that Katharine had prepared for her.

Katharine was very much at home with undergraduates, who liked her and confided in her. She could also assume a formality to oil the wheels of grander entertainment. But she was happiest alone with her husband. In conversation she was lively and emphatic, and tended to overstate her case: at which Austin would shoot up his brows with 'Oh, come, come, Kay'. Underneath there may have been some strain in trying to keep up with Austin, which would not be surprising: very few could.

Caroline was a great joy to Katharine as a baby, and a great anxiety when her disabilities were discovered. When Caroline went away to school and it was clear that they would not have another child, Katharine for a time found a satisfying outlet in writing, and of course the writing helped with the fees. Her first published work was a translation of Gabriel Marcel's *Etre et Avoir* (the work from which Farrer drew the distinction between mysteries and problems which he used in the Bampton Lectures). She then discovered a talent for detective novels which were, to her surprise, very successful. She published three, which still make good reading: *The Missing Link* in 1952, *The Cretan Counterfeit* in 1954, which was a Crime Club Choice, and *Gownsman's Gallows*. They were followed by a curiously off-beat novel, *At Odds with Morning*, based on the fantastic career of Father Ignatius of Llanthony – it deals with the founding of an order of Calced Carmelites, an attempt to raise a village girl from the dead, the disillusionment of the only normal member of the community and the effect of these intrusions on a normal country parish.

In his last years at Trinity Austin became very tired. On top of his college duties and teaching, he was in frequent demand as a preacher and lecturer and was working on his most lucid philosophical book, *The Freedom of the Will*.[12] He had never spared himself in the work which he considered his duty whether in his pastoral office or his dedication to the formulation of a Christian philosophy. But now his energies were being eroded by mounting anxiety about Katharine's health. Her bouts of bronchitis recurred; her insomnia was chronic; she had become addicted to alcohol and to the barbiturates prescribed for the insomnia. Austin's struggle to control the addictions led to unhappy scenes at night destroying the sleep of both. As she became more dependent on his constant attention, so he feared to leave her alone. Hence, what was known to his friends and later his colleagues, he would drive enormous distances from outside appointments to be with Katharine at night – and back again next day if he were engaged upon a course. The strain increased as time went on and attempted cures did not work and, while still at Trinity, he wondered whether his pastoral usefulness was coming to an end.

In 1959, amidst all this, Farrer suffered what was at the time a sad disappointment. The Regius Professorship of Divinity was vacant, and his friends were confident that it would be offered to him. No philosophical theologian in England could be compared to him, though many thought his scriptural writings bizarre and unorthodox. However, when the announcement came the choice had fallen on Dr Henry Chadwick[13] of Queens' College, Cambridge, a biblical and patristic scholar. Farrer was deeply disappointed, and it will be enough for the understanding of his mind to quote what he said in a letter to his friend Martyn Skinner. 'The material reasons are that my ecclesiastical opinions are unrepresentative and I have published some wild expositions of scripture: it would be convenient to have more studious leisure and disagreeable to exchange the service of a college for the pomps of a cathedral.'

The disappointment was as much for Katharine as for himself. After eleven years the Gatehouse on St Giles was becoming, with the increasing volume of traffic, almost claustrophobic. Farrer had hoped not only for studious retirement but for a place which would be more peaceful for his wife. The interval between Chadwick's appointment and his own election to Keble in the following year was a bad time, though it never affected the cordiality of his relations with the new Regius Professor. 'What is to become of me?' he once asked. 'One cannot with decency sit in a chaplain–fellowship for twenty-five years.' 'What is to be done for him?' was the question of both the Oxford and the ecclesiastical establishment. On a long-term view, the books were written, the prayers said, the sheep tended: and these were the important things in his life. On his own view the overcoming of disappointment and the care of his home were the simple duty of a Christian. To his friends it was a source of distress to find him, if only for a time, dismayed. It was fortunate that the dilemma was so soon resolved. To Keble it was to be a blessing, and Farrer could say near the end of his life that, his books written and his new college renewed, he could devote his remaining time to trying to be a good man.

Despite some of these sadder moments during the last years at Trinity, much good came Farrer's way too: the continuing affection and support of his college, the comfort and support of his friends, such as Colin Hardie and C. S. Lewis (who dedicated his *Reflections on the Psalms* to him), and his ripening friendship with an old acquaintance of his childhood days, Martyn Skinner, poet and farmer, 'kindest of friends and best of poets' to whom he dedicated his Gifford Lectures. In Farrer's papers in the Bodleian there is a vast collection of Skinner's letters. He seems to have roused Farrer himself to flashes of epistolary brilliance. The letter with which Farrer initiated their correspondence, on 11 May 1952, contains some lines, written in the metre of Skinner's *The Return of Arthur*, describing the Farrers' Gatehouse.

> *Here is the Danzig corridor, the dull edge*
> *Of ease, dividing effort from pretension.*
> *St John's from Balliol: here you must acknowledge*
> *An unsuspected Trinity extension,*
> *Where set between the city and the College*
> *Public conveniences prove an oddity.*
> *We daily feel the private incommodity.* [31]

From Skinner we hear of Farrer's love of the classics, his wide knowledge of traditional writing and his encouragement during Skinner's writing of *The Return of Arthur*. 'He used to put me right over details but was rarely critical of the general progress – Hardy once said of Leslie Stephen that his approval was disapproval minimized – and Austin's disapproval tended to be approval minimized with plenty of enthusiasm thrown in.'

Austin hardly ever mentioned himself or his own books. He rarely brought them into his conversation. This was due to something deeper than modesty – it was that he appeared truly not to be concerned with himself. In one of his books there is a moving prayer which ends, 'Teach me to stand out of my own light and let your daylight shine', and the impression he gave in his letters and conversation, as well as in his books, was that his prayer had been answered.

Another remarkable virtue was the complete absence in Farrer's conversation of any uncharitable reference to others:

> He was witty and amusing enough, but never at other people's expense, friends' or adversaries' . . . And he had the wonderful gift of mitigating one's own acerbities, without appearing in the least what has been called a 'dry blanket' or a 'spoil wit' – somehow he softened the remark with 'Oh, come now . . .' and a disarming smile. Of course where ideas were concerned, no one was firmer in putting nonsense in its place, but with no hint of aggression or attempting to impose his point of view because it was his. [32]

Skinner drew upon Farrer for his priest Matthew Bennet in *The Return of Arthur*, a likeness which the Farrers themselves recognized, though it escaped their friend C. S. Lewis. The key descriptive lines are: 'a kind of rueful joviality, a shine of ruffled mirth, astringently benign'.

In Farrer's correspondence with Skinner after reading C. S. Lewis on Hamlet, and also an article in a 'papistical magazine' by a moral theologian, he speculated ingeniously on Hamlet as a tragedy. Did not Shakespeare live near the end of an age when Christian doctrine was taken for granted? And is not Hamlet a tragic hero, who must then fall by the flaws in his own character? Hamlet had the opportunity to kill Claudius when he was convinced of his guilt by the experiment of the play; but Claudius was at prayer and ready for forgiveness, and Hamlet wants to kill him when his damnation would be certain. So he delays and in the end brings ruin to Polonius, Ophelia his bride, his mother and himself.

Lewis would add that contact with the ghost and thinking about punishment beyond death in torments drove Hamlet mad. But it is at least clear that Hamlet should have been content with justice. His flaw was to desire to keep divine grace from reaching Claudius. Shakespeare is perhaps writing a play inside the traditional Christian scheme.

Farrer continued to write to Skinner in the time of waiting to move from Trinity to Keble. He describes with relish his last invigilation in the Examination Schools. Some, he said, read scripts with furious energy, some laugh, but he could not resist the lure of free stationery and had to write letters. Doing things for the last time was his latest pleasure. The fourteenth of June would be his last invigilation; and on the fifteenth he would cut the Board of the Faculty, having resigned.

He did his homework on John Keble by reading a memoir on him by Coleridge, the poet's nephew, and, going on a pilgrimage to Hursley, preached in the Church. A more tedious occupation was coping with the problems of moving into the Warden's Lodging. He and Katharine walked round the empty rooms and negotiated with the college over decorations or reconstructions. He complained that it was

> beyond the wit of man to treat with the Mind of the College – there should be some sovran person in whom the Leviathan of Keble is constituted. For who knows where the Mind is? Of the Body, one is at Wootton-by-Woodstock, one in Museum Road. The Mind is not,

for certain, in the Head who vainly scratches his ears and wonders whether he will have to fork out £2000 or £500 to make the place habitable. [33]

With all these preoccupations there was still concern for his relations and friends: his aunt, 'deaf and blind' but 'resigned and serene'; C. S Lewis's wife who had just had an operation; reading to Katharine 'whose eyes are not yet good for much, though doing all the doctor asks of them'.

Upon resigning his fellowship at Trinity in February 1960, Farrer wrote to the Vice-President, James Lambert:

My sole motive for accepting [Keble] is that one cannot fairly sit in a chaplain-fellowship until one is sixty-seven. I am now fifty-five and if I don't move now, I shall soon be too old for anyone to want in any capacity. But for this consideration, I would rather stay in Trinity College, as I am, than do any other mortal thing. [34]

He was dismayed when the appointment was put forward from 25 April (St Mark's Day) to 24 February (St Matthias's Day), partly because of the difficulties attached to moving into the Warden's Lodging. He was provoked to this burst of pyrotechnics:

> *On being elected Warden of Keble on St Matthias's Day*
>
> > *Quoth Peter, 'Our economist*
> > *Has burst asunder in the midst.*
> > *Now who can tell if we should trust us*
> > *To good Matthias or to Justus?*
> >
> > *Between the even and the odd*
> > *Seek we the arbitrament of God.*
> > *They cast the die: Heaven ruled the bias*
> > *Up came the odd: and tipped Matthias.*
> > *Though no one could have meant it, he*
> > *Turned out a pure nonentity,*
> > *And simply vanished in the blue*
> > *With Thaddee and Bartholomew.* [35]

The same day more justly stirred Dr E. L. Mascall[14] to composition.

> *When Judas left in ultimate disgrace*
> *Explosively, and went to his own place,*

149

## A Hawk Among Sparrows

*The Eleven solved their problem in a trice*
*And filled the vacancy by casting dice.*
*They hailed Matthias' apostolic reign*
*And no one ever heard of him again.*

*When Keble's Warden[15] with his record clean*
*Reluctantly became Westminster's Dean,*
*The Fellows, huddled in their winter coats,*
*Spent weeks and weeks before they cast their votes.*
*But, patience justified, at last they found*
*One with whose praise all Christendom shall sound.* [36]

# CHAPTER 9

## *Keble College 1960–8*

\*

What could be more appropriate than the translation of the leading philosopher and theologian of the Church in England to the college founded in the nineteenth century as a result of the Oxford Movement and named after the poet and saint who inaugurated that movement? It was no doubt something of a change from the baroque glory of Trinity Chapel and the undergraduates from the major public schools to the polychromatic brickwork of Keble and a more varied population of undergraduates. As his Keble sermons[1] show, Farrer learnt to love his new college and was impressed by its history and its purpose. He wrote in the brochure for the appeal launched in 1967:

> The new Keble College was to be a democratic college. The young men's rooms were to be adequate but equal and unpretentious; and their tutors were to live among them in the apartments distributed round the college. No one was to make a splash or run up bills he could not pay. The success of the project was unquestionable: the new college flourished from the start and fulfilled the need of its day; but that was the least of it. All the ancient colleges have in course of time followed suit and adopted more or less the Keble plan of economic democracy.

The founders had, of course, another purpose. Political reformers were active and the pious feared the total secularization of Oxford university. So the college was to be tied firmly to Church principles. In fact Oxford was not totally secularized – the colleges retained their chaplains and chapels. Keble gradually came into line with other colleges as far as the religious establishment was concerned, except that in Keble (as in Christ Church) the Head of the College was then bound to be a priest of the Church of England. Otherwise there are no credal limitations and no compulsory attendance at chapel.

The foundation was to present problems as the years went

151

by. The college was built by public subscription – thousands of contributions, large and small. All the money went into the buildings. It was the generosity of one family, the Gibbses of Tyntesfield, which paid for the great buildings, the hall, the chapel (which towers so magnificently above the sunken lawn) and the library. It was the poorer benefactors who impressed Farrer – 'all those clerical widows doing without marmalade'. Later gifts provided for scholarships and fellowships and the careful economy of bursars built up a capital for endowment. But Keble was a poor college, and a college needs endowment and some capital in the twentieth century if it is not to become dependent on outside aid. The college opened its gates in 1870; by 1960 when Farrer was elected Warden the buildings were in need of extension and the endowment was still inadequate, though the college was receiving, like other small colleges, £5000 a year from the surplus of the richer colleges.

In the appointment of Warden, Keble had been through a series of phases before it reached its present status as a full college in the university. Originally it had no Fellows, only tutors. The Warden was appointed by the Council and, as Dr B. J. Kidd when Warden once remarked, he appointed and dismissed tutors just as the headmaster of a public school appoints his staff. By 1960 – indeed long before – the college had Fellows. A Warden is nominated by the Visitor (the Archbishop of Canterbury) for election by the Fellows. If the Visitor's nominee does not secure sufficient support, in theory another person should be nominated. In practice the nominator seeks guidance before making a nomination to ensure that his nominee will receive sufficient support for election. Such at any rate was the practice in 1960. Farrer said that the offer came as a complete surprise to him, though the representatives of the Fellows who called on him said that they had never had anyone else in mind. Certainly he was elected on his intellectual powers and standing in the university, in the expectation that he would not be much good at administration. To their surprise the electors found that he took to it like a duck to water.

Farrer came to Keble in the 1960s, a decade which saw the emergence of an 'us and them' mentality among undergraduates – later perhaps at Keble than elsewhere. Some resented the loss of status involved in leaving school where they had been of great consequence and finding themselves of comparatively little account at Oxford. After the golden days at Trinity Farrer found the 'protest' atmosphere of the 1960s irritating. He did not dislike the good-natured but not so bright, and often got on well with them; he could speak very simply, but never commonly. This was liable to irritate the less gifted among the ambitious. To those who symphathized with his Christian convictions his contribution was beyond compare.

Between 1954 and 1964 the governing body trebled in size as new Fellows were appointed who already had university lectureships. Many of these would have little sympathy with the traditions and the Anglican commitment of the college. Amongst them Farrer earned immense respect as by far the most powerful intellect among them. He was a forceful and effective chairman at meetings, brisk without being dictatorial; when everyone was so busy this was well regarded. At the same time he seems to have felt himself in a vulnerable position as the official guardian of orthodox Christianity in a largely non-Christian body. Although Farrer believed in making a job of anything he undertook, at times he found the administration a burden. In November 1960, in his first term in full residence he wrote to Skinner:

> It may be that, however idle, I have never come to the end of my business letters; the nasty feeling that if I take up my pen it must be to deal with these discourages me from even beginning at all. There is a college secretary, of course; but I only bring myself to dictate letters so formal that the girl might just as well invent them herself. And so I have a heap of semi-official letters to write at leisure in my own hand . . . [1]

It was plain that money-raising would be one of his main tasks, and one that was not congenial to him. After years among philosophers he found financial experts something of a strain. He told Skinner that he had just met an old Keble man who claimed to have an American millionaire in tow, and suggested that he should meet him on his next visit to America, 'There is no business' he sighed 'to which noblesse does not oblige; and am I not now a great Lord?'

December 1962 took him to a money-raising meeting of the London Keblish (ex Keble men) where he encountered a superior public relations officer, a clergyman who had brought the combined service of God and Mammon to a fine art – 'it's only a matter of keeping two secretaries'. The rich, they agreed, must be told the truth, and allowed to support projects of which they approved. The poor could be deceived and brought to subscribe to General Endowment without realizing it. Farrer mentioned that he would be in New York in 1964 in the autumn and was told that he would never raise a penny wherever he was. 'I am glad', he said, 'that you realize that; it will save me a lot of useless pain.'

All this was combined with the Oxford round of wining and dining. Farrer ruefully mentions being sick with feasting and even a gouty toe! One evening, dining with the Master of University College, he tripped headlong into a pile of gravel left by some builder's men in Logic Lane. He arrived bleeding and defaced, but the Goodharts proved worthy of their name and patched him up. He sat the party out. 'Quite right,' that venerable peer Lord Saye and Sele said to Katharine, 'if he'd gone home everyone in Oxford would have said he was drunk.'

As well as the constant flow of visitors and preaching engagements, there were other outside commitments – such as the Liturgical Commission.

> The new frivolity is rewriting the liturgy. The Bishop of Southwark is trying to brush up the traditional Holy Week devotions and gave me the blessings of fire and water for the Saturday liturgy to rewrite. I wrote a new literal translation of the Latin from Wimbledon to Streatham, and a contemporary paraphrase from Bermondsey to Balham. It's all very well, but how do you get contemporary about *lighting a candle?* 'Lord, who by the breakdown of electric power dost acquaint us from time to time with the convenience of candles; grant that we may not so wholly trust the more ingenious inventions of our hands as to be caught napping by the failure of material aids, concerning which thou hast warned us, through, etc.'. This is on the side; tomorrow I attend the Liturgical Commission. My gospel for these people will be that when the tumult and the shouting have died, *someone* has got to write the prose. They think that prose can be written in *committee*. It's incredible but true that the New English Bible is a committee effort. No one writes any one paragraph of it. I got this from a chap on the literary panel. So no wonder . . . [2]

Meanwhile he grew busier and more tired.

I've been tired and a bit ill, but now am well again . . . I made one of my famous double engagements – to attend the Liturgical Commission here, and to lecture at Cambridge after lunch, lecturing, holding the floor against questioners for an hour and driving home by nine o'clock, and what is there in that? But I was practically useless for a week after. I've done really nothing – a lot of odds and ends. I wage war on spiders' webs in inaccessible corners of the college and then I suffer defeat. 'No, sir,' says the old head servant, 'it'd take tiptop men to reach them and we can't get them these days, sir, and it's no use thinking it. If I sent these men of mine up those ladders, they'd only be breaking their necks, and what would be the use of that, sir?' So the spiders' webs remain, until the Bursar thinks fit to send for a firm with an adjustable wheeling tower to do all the high roofs together – so I retreat rebuffed, but compensate myself by defeating a covetous tradesman who offers to brighten a rack of old blackened brass in the chapel for fifty pounds. No, I say, I'll go round to the museum and find how they manage with their old brasses. On the way I meet the fellow who teaches engineering. 'Oh,' he says, 'we've got a tub of acid in the Department into which we throw our brass equipment from time to time; let's go and fetch the candlesticks and dip them.' Such are my triumphs and defeats.

Caroline is at home in good form – Katharine has had her annual bronchitis complicated by poisoning with antibiotics which caused much agony, and now is particularly well. Yesterday (or was it the day before?) seven dear old friends in seven separate packets fell into our laps unannounced: which reminds me that Easter is nearly upon us. On Good Friday I shall drive to Malvern, go it for three hours in the Priory Church pulpit, and drive back: well, I must take it gently. [3]

The old pupils continued to see him, one of whom gives us a very illuminating insight of Austin as he now was.

The last time I saw Farrer was some months before he died. I stayed with him in Keble for a weekend because he had invited me to preach at Sunday Evensong in Keble Chapel. During dinner he said with great animation, 'I used to say I was waiting for the encyclical beginning with *Cum grano salis* [with a grain of salt]; but I don't any longer talk like that, not at all. I say now that I am waiting for the encyclical beginning *Quousque* [how much longer].[2] Afterwards in his room we talked at some length about 'Death of God' theology and 'Secular Christianity' and in the course of discussion he said,

'My test is this: do they believe in a future life? If they don't, I say they don't believe in God.' He seemed to me to have changed very little. I could easily have imagined myself back in his room in St Edmund Hall, with him as tutor and myself as pupil. [4]

Again the signs of tiredness reappear.

Of course there is always some fuss going on. The position of a head of college has two consequences – first that being a constitutional monarch he can only achieve his aims by intrigue, which takes a disproportionate amount of doing, second that it being assumed that his time is of no value he has to volunteer for trifling tasks. [5]

The matter of funds also reappears in reference to the Centenary Appeal, which Farrer found more and more preposterous:

So as to sell ourselves to the industrial interests (i.e. the big money) we draw up accounts of our intentions, which, if literally carried out, would turn the college over to engineering and business management, with a little commercial Spanish. The Nat Sci Fellows quickly press their advantage: give them what they want and the money will come in. In the ordinary way it is scarcely considered decent to discuss the balance of studies on its merits – quotas of intake are quietly and marginally modified on special grounds, and so with fellowships or lecturerships. You make out a special case about the difficulty of getting adequate tuition in such-and-such a speciality, and point out that the University is offering a well-paid lecturership in the subject if we will put up a fellowship. Then, having got the fellowship, you point out that the Fellow should have a decent quota of pupils – you see how it goes. But this business of window-dressing for the Appeal has made us self-conscious, and I am making it an excuse for putting the cat among the pigeons. We mustn't, I say, get into a false position by adopting objectives which happen to be money-catching, so we'd better make up our minds what we really want to be. This I trust will have the result that the non-Sci Fellows, who are still a plain majority, will rally round the Ark of the Covenant and lay down a line to hold Nat Sci to 33%. [6]

Signs of weariness did not mean that Farrer did not take the money raising as a necessary – if to him tedious – task. He faced the necessary chores of administration with determination.

The Fellows had elected him as a distinguished scholar, philosopher and theologian to ornament the college with an output of publications from the Warden's lodging. *Faith and Speculation, Saving Belief, A Science of God, Love Almighty and Ills Unlimited* all belong to these years. But he also engaged in routine affairs far more than the Fellows had expected. His involvement was welcomed, but his willingness to do so came as a surprise to the college officers, as perhaps did the wit and dispatch with which he presided.

One of his first problems concerned the occupant of the stall in chapel which might be termed the sub-warden's. The chaplain had occupied it and the sub-warden, Dr G. D. Parkes, a devout Anglican, wished to resume it. 'Who should decide it?' asked Farrer. The Fellows replied. 'It is at your discretion.' 'When I have discretion, I will decide,' replied the Warden, and the decision went in favour of the sub-warden.

The Oxford Historic Building Fund, distributing money under the direction of Lord Bridges, did not include Keble – the College not being old enough to rank as a historic building. Farrer wrote a comical description of Keble's dilemma:

> *A seventh warden reigns where Talbot sat.*
> *Almost a century has lived and died*
> *Since bigot and romanticist allied,*
> *Clothed in the glory of a poet-saint,*
> *Their rose-red college, twice as fresh as paint;*
> *Paint now less fresh; and aged men aver*
> *The very bricks are not the bricks they were.*
> *Dry rot invades the eaves, and damp the floors,*
> *While headless horrors overhang the doors.*
> *Change and decay in all around we smell*
> *And what pollutes the hall no nose can tell.*
> *The Fellows congregate. What can be done?*
> *Silver or gold, like Peter, have we none.*
> *Barritt and Stone with arithmetic ease*
> *Prove heresy and move to raise the fees.*
> *Others more orthodox the shipwreck view*
> *And plan to live by eating up the crew.*
> *First we economize the economist;*
> *The remnant fatten as we lop the list.*
> *Each owns the increment, but fears the pot;*

157

## A Hawk Among Sparrows

*On whom next falls the immolating lot?*
*But hark. We hear an unaccustomed hail*
*And all unite to cry. A sail! A sail!*
*Galleons of gold are riding up the wave*
*Oxford's historic ruins sent to save.*
*Our history respect, our ruin feel,*
*And (great Appeal Fund) honour our Appeal!*
*Slow from the bridge, Lord Bridges makes reply:*
*'Ruined you are: but are you history?'*
*My history ends with George the Third, and North;*
*Or, in appendice, with George the Fourth.*
*I hate to say it, though I have to say,*
*You saw the light when Vicky's hair was grey!'*

As Chairman of the Appeal Committee Farrer approved the proposal to launch a public appeal for £1,000,000. During his last two years they raised about £300,000 and successfully met a challenge from their first large benefactor to match an offer of £50,000 with an equal sum raised by their own efforts. One of the successful activities proposed by Farrer was Dr D. F. Shaw's visit to America in 1968; Farrer had wished to go himself but felt that in view of his health Dr Shaw should go as 'his lieutenant'. Shaw and Farrer worked closely together over a period of several months before the visit and Farrer succeeded in obtaining appointments with three wealthy Americans as a result of personal letters. One of the men who entertained Shaw to dinner in New York said what an honour it had been to receive such a long and interesting letter from the present Warden of his Oxford college, written in his own hand. He was one of those who gave a very substantial sum of money to the college.

It was equally to be expected that Farrer's heart would be in the life of the chapel. He was not slow to take steps to revive interest in corporate worship among undergraduates and Fellows. At the beginning of every term he would write to the Anglican Fellows asking them if they would read a lesson in chapel on a specified Sunday – a practice which used to be observed in many college chapels. He introduced a Corporate Communion once a term to which wives were invited, and the congregation often half-filled the enormous chapel. He also offered joint use of the chapel to the members of St Anne's

College, saying, 'Your college has no chapel and my college has one which is much too big. Would it not be useful if we were to share it?'

The public duties of the Warden were in themselves a strain. Though respected for his learning, Farrer was perhaps better known to the philosophers and theologians than to the other members of the Senior Common Room. The same was often true of his relationship with undergraduates. Those who met him in the tutorial or seminar were devoted to him, but those who knew him only as the Warden were apt sometimes to be puzzled by him. Though unfailingly kind to such people, he could induce a certain uneasiness, a hesitancy in communication on both sides. The ease and confidence he displayed while preaching contrasted with the uneasiness and lack of confidence which appeared when he had to speak on other occasions. In the pulpit he could hold an audience spell-bound, but as an after-dinner speaker he was hopeless – it was often difficult to hear what he was saying and to follow him when he could be heard. His weakness in this capacity sprang primarily from his attempts to talk rather in conversational than in rhetorical idiom. He could be delightful company presiding over his own table in the Warden's Lodgings, but at occasions such as Old Members' Dinners his performance could be embarrassing. He always disliked formality and formal occasions and large assemblies. He abhorred anything even distantly approaching 'heartiness'.

In the management of the college he was most concerned with academic efficiency and achievements. At meetings of the governing bodies when Fellows droned on tediously about matters which he considered to be of no real importance, he did not disguise his boredom or the impatience natural in a man whose mind worked a good deal more quickly than those of the other members.

One episode recounted during his wardenship particularly illustrated this element of impatience in his mind:

Pressure of space in the college library led to a decision to review the contents with the object of achieving a limited 'purge'. Farrer immediately set to work on the theological section and promptly threw out for pulping a considerable number of volumes which he considered to be superfluous. Subsequently it appeared that among

159

them were several of considerable monetary value – one volume, I am told, appeared in a bookseller's catalogue at £600. This to Farrer was irrelevant; all that mattered was that it was no longer, in his view, of academic value as an instrument of learning in a college library. [7]

Keble probably holds the right to present to more benefices than most Oxford colleges – especially to parishes in the Tractarian tradition. Strangely enough Farrer took little part in these appointments. They were left to the sub-warden, Dr G. D. Parkes. One reason may have been that the Fellows of Keble, like their predecessors, the tutors, have always kept their eye on the Warden in ecclesiastical matters. Even Dr Kidd got into serious trouble with the Fellows when he introduced a Sanctus bell into chapel, and was made to dispose of it. In one appointment, however, Farrer did interest himself: he exerted himself to secure the appointment of his old pupil at Trinity, the Reverend Robin Anstey, to St Andrew's, Headington – and it was there that he preached his last sermon, on the morning of 22 December 1968.

A step he took at the suggestion of the Junior Common Room in 1967 happily illuminates the hold he was obtaining on the undergraduate members of the college. In a letter dated 9 January 1967 he wrote:

> I am sending this letter to all Keble men who ever gave me reason to think it might concern them.
>
> In response to JCR suggestions, we are to celebrate the Holy Communion at 6 p.m. on the first Sunday evening of full term (January 15th) in the hope that at such an hour all of you who can fitly do so may be able to communicate together, or at least to be present in chapel. The service is arranged to take forty-five minutes.
>
> We invite the congregation to come straight on to our house for some refreshment before hall dinner. It will give us great pleasure to see you; we have plenty of room and shall be ready for you all. [8]

The undergraduates' attitude to Farrer was much the same as it had been at Trinity. When he resumed his teaching of the New Testament after two or three years' break, he embarrassed his successor at Trinity, J. L. Houlden, as the latter relates: 'I was much embarrassed when, a green new Fellow of Trinity, one morning at 8.45 the Warden of Keble phoned and asked for an immediate interview. He insisted on coming to me. Within five minutes he came into my room, sat down and said, "Now tell me what one must read about the New Testament".'

He applied himself conscientiously to the needs of his new pupils. He listened carefully, commented helpfully and took pains to avoid merely selling his own theories. He was perhaps unusual in being ready to give very long tutorials, sometimes in two halves. He was aware, perhaps more so than at Trinity, that his pupils had examinations to pass. He was sometimes restless, on one occasion occupying every chair in his study in turn, and on another taking every piece of paper out of his wastepaper basket, unscrewing it, reading it and returning it.

Farrer as pastor was not submerged in Farrer the Warden. While some of his pupils were keenly conscious of the intellectual gulf between them, they knew too that he was kind to moral failings. He visited the sick assiduously. He knew all the members of the college, not only the chapel congregation, and prayed for them daily in his half-hour of prayers after the daily Eucharist. When the perplexed brought their problems to him he had, they said, an uncanny ability to see through their problems to the root of the trouble and to shorten their ramblings with a sentence.

He still gave the impression of diffidence. Once he asked the choir to use a particular setting. The organ scholar, after some fruitless discussion, said 'Well, you are the boss, Warden'. He spun round and walked slowly out of the chapel, touching the furniture in a dazed sort of way and repeating, 'Yes, well, I suppose I am the boss.' It was as near as he could get to giving an order.

Yet with this diffidence was combined a determination to do his job: when he had all the freshmen to sherry he knew their names and faces. There was in him a streak of donnish good humour, as when he accepted an invitation to a 'sherry and smarties' party, or replied in verse to an invitation to visit a farewell party at St Gregory and St Macrina's House in Canterbury Road:

> *Next Wednesday will fill up the measure*
> *Of cheer and of sociable leisure;*
> *A sup and a crack*
> *At St Greg and St Mac*
> *The Warden embraces with pleasure.*

He was, in fact, game for anything. Though he seemed fragile he claimed to be able to climb the back gate at a run and a jump in one go. A bold undergraduate astonished him by asking him one day to come down to the river and encourage the college boat in Eights Week. The idea had plainly never occurred to him. 'What', he said, 'can I do?' 'Warden, you can run,' was the reply. He knew his undergraduates even when he seemed to be unforthcoming. He kept, indeed, a delightful list of the religious affiliations of Keble men. There were 'practising Anglicans', 'Anglicans of another sort', various other denominations, and finally 'Saracens'.

As Warden his greatest contribution was in chapel. The sermons of his Keble period (many reprinted in *The Brink of Mystery* and *The End of Man*) have a note all of their own. They have all the ingenuity and brilliance of the earlier sermons; but they move directly, if possible, to the simpler duties of the Christian undergraduate, to work, to care for his parents, to live the life of heaven on earth. His delivery was not good in Keble Chapel, which needs an enormous voice to fill it, though some improvement was made when chairs were rearranged in the choir to bring the congregation nearer. But the man and his conviction came through. He preached as if beyond the veil, communicating a sense of the eternal.

The daily services in chapel continued as at Trinity. The weekday Evensongs were like those at Trinity. He selected suitable psalms, chose lessons on the basis of reading one gospel each term with typological lessons from the Old Testament to fit, and himself wrote superb collects; he could extemporize in Prayer Book English with extraordinary facility. The weekday morning services were a compromise arrangement. Matins might be tedious, with the server (for the Mass which followed) reading the lessons from the ordinary lectionary. Thus only alternate Old Testament lessons in the lectionary were read, since Evensong had its own set, a highly unsatisfactory arrangement. Mass made no concession to the college at all, being always (even after Series II) the 'Interim Rite', with large *sotto voce* additions in Latin from the Tridentine Mass. The atmosphere was good, but its appeal even in Keble was very limited. Evangelicals on the whole distrusted and sometimes even disliked Farrer, and he certainly treated them with little respect. The Sunday services worked on the whole but were somewhat gloomy, partly because Farrer never felt that he had a free hand, and partly because of the size of Keble Chapel. His sermons were recognized as masterpieces, and the common conviction of his personal holiness made people want to go and pray with him. Feeling that the chapel suited him, the congregation let it suit them.

Farrer appeared at his best in dealing with candidates for confirmation – a rather unusual role for the head of a house. He would, with some diffidence, offer his help if it seemed to be needed. One candidate who believed deeply in God but was perplexed by Christian doctrine was approached by the Warden with a note which ended 'Don't worry'. After an interview Farrer offered to prepare him. 'The Warden', he writes, 'never imposed his views on me, but listened with patience and treated me as an equal, though he did find it hard to begin or end a conversation.' Another, who must have been his last candidate, was noticed by Farrer for his regularity in attendance in chapel, though he did not communicate. Farrer again offered his services in preparation and talked to him from February to September 1968.

> I was very awed [he says] at the idea of a solo confirmation class with a theologian of such standing. He sent me *Saving Belief* with a typical self-effacing letter. The first couple of discussions we had were about the book, but it was very clear throughout my confirmation preparation that the ideas set out in *Saving Belief* were the very heart of his own thinking. He was always very reserved during these discussions and I am afraid that I was equally shy. Luckily he understood this and even made a joke of it sometimes, as when discussing Quoist's *Prayers of Life* he observed that neither he nor I would ever have the nerve to write such a book! . . . He talked of suffering, judgement, and salvation with such clarity that he bolstered my faith tremendously. He explained that 'He shall come to judge the quick and the dead' meant to him that when he died he would see clearly how far short he had fallen of the standard God required, and how utterly he had failed to fulfil all the potential for goodness that was within him. He was convinced . . . that God's mercy extended to everyone, although he was not prepared to say that it was impossible to put oneself beyond redemption. [9]

The letter to this candidate, accompanying the gift of *Saving Belief* and dated 8 March 1968, survives:

There are many better books, but then it is only of one's own books that one has free copies to give away. And at least if you ask me questions about this one, I shall be able to answer out of the mouth of the author. The first chapter is, maybe, both the most difficult and the least satisfactory. If it bothers you, don't let it deter you. Indeed the whole book may be off the mark; if so, let me know and we'll try something more sensible. [10]

It is possible to guess the high and affectionate regard in which many undergraduates held him from the names they gave him – 'the Happy Wanderer', when he sometimes lost his place in the order of service, or 'the White Rabbit' – a not inept description of him as he hurried on his way to chapel. There were those too who, looking more deeply, could say that he resembled St Francis de Sales, for whom indeed he had a profound admiration, in his air of calm sanctity.

There were, inevitably, those who did not think so highly of him as Warden – who thought of him as a square peg in a round hole. They did not doubt that he was a good and kind man and that he was intellectually outstanding. But at the time when the college was emerging into full status, they felt that he was not the man for the job. He would try to do things himself without waiting, as when he removed those books from the library. The truth was that Farrer always wanted to 'make a job' of whatever he was doing – it is a favourite theme in his sermons, especially in his Keble sermons; so it was that he became so improbable a scoutmaster in his Dewsbury days. His interpretation of the Warden's function may not always have coincided with the general view, particularly that of the older Fellows, who may well have wished for more consultation.

It is indeed astonishing that in the last eight years of Farrer's life, despite the pressure of academic and administrative business, domestic worries and the strain of increasing age, he conquered a new world, not only geographically but also philosophically. With Katharine he visited the USA three times to lecture, carrying on what he had begun in the central section of *Finite and Infinite* and in his Gifford Lectures *The Freedom of the Will* – the purging of the Aristotelian leaven, as he put it, of his earlier work, and the continuation of his voluntaristic metaphysic using the self as the clue to rational theology. These

American trips produced some of his best and most fruitful work.

In 1961, in a cold spring, he delivered lectures at Yale (published as *Love Almighty and Ills Unlimited*), and a remarkable commemorative address on Bishop Berkeley. He also went to Middletown, Connecticut, to New York University and to Drew University, Madison, New Jersey. In 1964 he delivered the Deems Lectures in New York, which form the central section of *Faith and Speculation*. He also preached at the General Seminary in New York and went on to Chicago. His third visit was in 1966, when, at the Perkins School of Divinity of the Southern Methodist University, Dallas, and at Louisiana State University, Baton Rouge, he delivered one of the most brilliant of his shorter papers, 'The Prior Actuality of God[3]' – a deep criticism of process theology and a masterly restatement of his own views.

Farrer had known Americans before. His books had been read in some American universities, not so completely enclosed by the positivists and their successors as their English counterparts. Also American research students at Oxford had come to his lectures, or, as candidates for higher degrees, had him as supervisor. Over them he exercised the same charm and fascination as over his British pupils.

As philosopher and theologian, Farrer was introduced to the world of American philosophical theology by the Faculty of Yale Divinity School and in particular by Professor Julian Hartt of the University of Virginia, who was at Yale for twenty-five years. Hartt knew Farrer personally and supervised several dissertations on him, or inspired by him, of which perhaps the most prominent was that of Ray Hart published in a revised form as *Unfinished Man and the Imagination* (Herder and Herder).

On his first visit to Yale, Farrer delivered a lecture on the theory of images under the auspices of the Department of Religious Studies, not the Divinity School. It became clear early in his reading of it that he was not happy with his own argument. Hartt recalls the episode:

He looked up from his manuscript and said (more or less) 'I can't believe that anybody here is interested in what I am doing, and I am anything but happy with it myself. So why don't we call it off and go to dinner?' American academic audiences are not prepared for this sort of unsparing honesty from distinguished – or, for that matter, undistinguished – lecturers. A ripple of appreciative amusement ran across the lecture hall, but no one moved at all; I rose to dismiss the meeting. At dinner he asked whether he had made a real gaffe. I was happy to tell him that on the contrary his chances of being heard gladly on another occasion must have been considerably improved. He was wonderfully amused by the whole business, as were we all. [11]

Professor Ray L. Hart of the University of Montana, editor of the *Journal of the American Academy of Religion*, entertained the Farrers on their first visit to the States and they became fast friends. Hart's dissertation on 'The Role of the Imagination in Man's Knowledge of God' was the first dissertation done on Farrer in the United States. He secured an invitation for Farrer to give a series of lectures at Drew University in the spring of 1961; the subject was to be theology and the imagination. Hart reports Farrer's own introduction:

> Some time ago I received a dissertation from Professor Hart which dealt with Austin Farrer's doctrine of the imagination. I personally know that Mr Farrer did not have a doctrine of the imagination. So Mr Farrer was well advised to go away and get himself one. When he got a doctrine of the imagination in hand, he was embarrassed not a little to find that it was identical with what Professor Hart said it was. Mr Farrer reports that he has nothing to add and will not entertain questions on the subject. [12]

This was typical of his sense of humour.

Both Hart and Farrer were amateur woodworkers, house restorers, and furniture refinishers.

> We talked little theology directly: he had vast contempt for the prevailing winds in contemporary theology, and often chided me for having wasted so much of my life reading all those German Bs (Barth, Brunner, Bonhoeffer *et al*): he remarked to me once that American theologians were insanely preoccupied with *talking* theology. 'I should have thought if one believed in Christ, one wouldn't have to talk about it so much – one could get on with sand-papering or gardening.' [13]

The lectures at the Yale Divinity School on Theodicy in 1961 were sparsely attended after the first one or two, partly because the book[4] had actually preceded them and was available in the bookstore at the same time as the lectures were being delivered. However, during his stay at Yale, Farrer and his wife spent a memorable evening in discussion with graduate students. Most of those who came had been through *Finite and Infinite* but were unacquainted with anything he had done since then. They pressed a number of critical objections to the argument of that book, which Farrer attempted to answer – frequently by appeal to something he had said in *The Freedom of the Will*. Yet he was obviously uncomfortable with the line of questioning. Finally, after about an hour of this, he said that he felt like a doctoral candidate at Oxford called up to defend his dissertation, except that in his case it was a dissertation he had written twenty years earlier, and he added, 'I am not in the habit of rereading my own work.' 'Yet', he went on to say, 'it is coming back to me.' This was typical of his disinclination simply to restate old ideas. He might say the same thing many times over, yet somehow he managed to do so in a way that always seemed fresh and original – as though he were thinking of it for the first time.

In 1966, at the Louisiana State University at Baton Rouge where he delivered his paper on 'The Prior Actuality of God', Farrer met Edward Henderson, who was to prove an acute interpreter of Farrer's works. There is a delightful picture of Farrer on that last visit:

> Finally, personally, Farrer was warmly received by all who met him here. A fine person who made one feel entirely at home. No arrogance, no condescension – even in the shadows of our disreputable 'professional' football field here at LSU (we Americans support collegiate athletics more passionately than academics, I'm afraid). Katharine Farrer was also a delight. None of us here knew that Mrs Farrer was a writer of detective stories. When Charles and Anita Bigger were fetching the Farrers to Baton Rouge from the airport in New Orleans, it was necessary to drive through the rather large swamp between these cities. After the English landscape, to drive down that road makes one feel in an absolute jungle. It is lush and wild. Well, Mrs Farrer was looking at this wilderness and pondering it passing by, when suddenly she turned to Anita and said, 'What a lovely place to hide a body!' That was a shock. Not until later did we find out about the mystery stories. [14]

It was good for the Farrers to get out of Oxford into an

atmosphere where Austin's enterprises were regarded as possible for an intelligent man. Though there were those in Oxford who did appreciate his philosophy and many more who appreciated his sermons, the general tide was against him; and his biblical work had always seemed, undeservedly, eccentric. It was good for him to rethink his philosophical position in the light of his American friends' criticisms. Essentially his position remained the same but, as he wrote in the second edition of *Finite and Infinite*, he was moved to purge out the Aristotelian leaven. The works of his last eight years are among his most valuable. But it is remarkable how little they were read – including the Gifford Lectures,[5] though these were published ten years before his death.

Back at Keble after the 1966 trip to Dallas and Baton Rouge, the pressures of work and anxiety took increasing toll. In the summer of 1967 he complained about headaches and growing old age, and of being unable to concentrate or think of things easily. When he went to Mirfield in July 1967 to deliver the addresses at the community retreat, he collapsed with hypertension, but insisted on delivering the addresses. He had to be driven back to Oxford by a member of the community.

Griefs during these final years were the death of C. S. Lewis's wife when her cancer recurred, and later the death of C. S. Lewis himself. Farrer was in time to give Lewis the sacraments. Their friendship had been close. (The death of Lewis is movingly recounted in Walter Hooper's biography of him.)

For some time after his 'black-out' at Mirfield Austin was very subdued and lost his usual fluency. He was chronically very tired and could not get enough sleep because of Katharine, who was now even more restless and demanding at nights. His heart was a cause for concern, and he may have felt that his life was ending. This was perhaps the time when he said that he had written all the books he had to write, though not all he could. He must spend what remained of his life trying to be a good man. About a month before his death, probably in Advent 1968, he visited Kelham and on his return he had to crawl upstairs on his hands and knees. He recovered sufficiently to preach in St Andrew's, Headington, on the morning of 22 December, a sermon which went out on BBC radio – appropriately enough on 'The Ultimate Hope'. It is reprinted in *A*

*Celebration of Faith* and deals in his superb style with our hopes of heaven.

The Farrers had a quiet and leisurely Christmas, and on Saturday evening Austin went to bed early with a stomach upset. At some time in the night Katharine got up, fell in the bathroom and broke her arm. She managed to rouse Austin but nothing could be done till Sunday about 9 a.m. The doctor came and first looked at Austin, examined his heart and was not alarmed. Katharine was taken off to the Radcliffe Infirmary and Austin returned to bed. Before her return he died of a coronary thrombosis and Katharine and Caroline found him dead on Katharine's return early in the afternoon. The funeral was on 1 January 1969. The Bishop of Oxford (H. J. Carpenter) celebrated the Requiem Mass and Farrer was buried in St Cross churchyard near the house where he and Katharine had lived in Manor Road. On 1 February there was a memorial service in Keble Chapel, at which Basil Mitchell delivered the remarkable address which is published as the introduction to the collection of Farrer's sermons in *A Celebration of Faith*.

Katharine Farrer stayed on in the Warden's Lodging until the summer of 1969, greatly assisted by her daughter; the grief and new responsibility gave Caroline a remarkable maturity. Katharine then moved to 71 Lonsdale Road, Summertown. Much of their furniture had to be sold and Austin's library was dispersed. But Katharine managed to express her personality in her new home and happily entertained many of their old friends there.

Although much care was arranged for her, she continued to take drugs for her insomnia. On Palm Sunday, 26 March 1972, she died after falling in the night against a piece of furniture near her bed.

# CHAPTER 10

## *Farrer the Philosopher*

\*

'Scripture and metaphysics are equally my study, and poetry is my pleasure. These three things rubbing against one another in my mind seem to kindle one another . . . ' So wrote Farrer in the Preface to his Bampton Lectures.[1] In these characteristically modest words he sets out the elements which it was his life's work to attempt to combine. He taught theology and philosophy for twenty-nine years; he wrote books on metaphysics and scripture; not only did he preach regularly in his college chapel but, as we have seen, he was in demand in many other places; his poetic gift is manifest in the prose of his sermons, and, indeed, wherever in his works he returned to his central theme: how we may know the Triune God.

Metaphysics and scripture were *equally* his study in his labour to know God and show him to others in teaching, writing and preaching. He himself set out the purpose of his gospel studies in his Hulsean Sermon of 1948.[2] In metaphysics he set out to produce a Christian philosophy for our time, as he and Hodges had proposed to themselves at Balliol, or, as he later described it, a rational theology. Few of his contemporaries, in Britain at least, appreciated his work in either field. The biblical theologians did not understand his philosophy and were scandalized by his unconventional biblical opinions; very few of the philosophers were concerned with the philosophical problems of divine revelation. As his friend, Professor Edward Henderson of Louisiana State University, says, 'The difficulty of appreciating Farrer fully is due to his having been so philosophical a theologian, and so theological a philosopher.'[3]

Farrer's philosophical learning was enormous. He had studied the philosophers from Plato and Aristotle through Aquinas and the Schoolmen to Descartes, Spinoza, Leibniz Kant and Croce, and the English empiricists Berkeley, Locke and Hume. He grew up in an Oxford still partly dominated by the idealists and worked among colleagues absorbing the ideas

170

of Russell, Whitehead, Moore and the Viennese circle headed by Wittgenstein. He was familiar with it all. He wrote for the philosophers around him, but he paid more attention to them than they to him. Few could understand what he was trying to do, most did not care.

Admittedly Farrer's philosophical works are difficult to read, even for those with some knowledge of metaphysics. His literary style is elegant and clear but he assumed too much of his reader. His arguments are condensed, he spurns repetition, references and footnotes. His method of exposition is often dialectic but he refrains from naming his antagonist or even the philosophical tradition he is assumed to represent. It requires both scholarship and patience to follow him fully.

His first book was *Finite and Infinite*, published in 1943, when the first phase of logical positivism still held the stage with a certain arrogant confidence. Metaphysics and theology had been dismissed into a limbo of meaningless propositions. The later work of Wittgenstein was little known outside Cambridge, and English theology was dispirited and lacking in backbone. William Temple's *Nature, Man, and God* had been written too much under the influence of the older Oxford idealists to speak relevantly to a new generation of philosophers. Indeed to most English scholars theology meant the discussion of the Fathers and the Scriptures. Those who wrote on questions of theology as such tended either to repeat what St Thomas Aquinas had once said, insisting on the possibility of inescapable demonstration and writing with a curious aridity, or, if they avoided St Thomas, to philosophize naively, ignoring the analogical nature of theological terms. There were those who argued that to speak of a personal God was to speak of a God with plans that needed to be fulfilled, and moved from this shaky ground to argue that God was passible and needed his creation for his fulfilment. Barth's disciples eschewed rational theology but exercised their rationality in tidying up the deliverances of revelation. Into this situation *Finite and Infinite* arrived setting out a rational theology, on the one hand rigorous and taking account of the difficulties of talking about God, and on the other hand presenting a God who was the God of Christian tradition and not a modification of idealism.

Some twenty years before they became topical Farrer had already, with wit, clarity and brevity, disposed of two themes which attracted attention in the 1960s. The first was the superstition that traditional theology thinks of God as a being among other beings, the second the equally unfounded assertion that theological arguments rest on filling gaps in scientific explanations.

> We promised also to renounce dramatic order. By this is meant an order which produces the rabbit of proof from the hat of impartial cosmology. It is indeed traditional to use several hats indifferently, in order, one must suppose, to underline the fact that between hat and rabbit there is no connection whatever. So sometimes it is impartial cosmology, sometimes impartial ethics, sometimes epistemology or even aesthetics that plays the part: no doubt one could think of others. We work up an insoluble antithesis, fence around a lacuna of explanation; bang goes the pistol and therefore, we say, God.[4]

Farrer begins, not by showing what sense-experience or introspection would verify or falsify theological statements, but by an analysis of theological statements and the way in which they are used, so anticipating what was soon to be the common phrase of philosophers: 'Never mind the meanings: show us the use.' How *do* people think who use the term 'God' seriously? Having examined their pattern of thought one can then look at its presuppositions and test their soundness. We know that the paths of traditional theology regarded as arguments are not demonstrative arguments, since no one can get out of an argument more than he has put in. By argument we may make plain what we normally think confusedly or find what our thoughts entail. Theistic arguments operate with phenomena and their aspects regarded as finite – change, motion, contingency, degrees of perfection, appearances of order. To call them finite prejudges the question: as indeed to talk of 'effects' prejudges. We are faced with the appearance of causal relations, as we are faced with degrees of freedom and goodness, and we leap from the intra-finite scale and extrapolate. Such a leap is not demonstration: it is clarified apprehension. Demonstration is hypothetical – *if* A is the case, then B can (or cannot) be shown to follow. But in asserting the cosmological relation – the relation of finite to infinite being – we are clarifying what we already know in a confused way. Descartes in his *Meditations* saw God as a clear and distinct idea involved in his thinking. Farrer saw God in the experience of finitude: in knowing the finite we grasp the infinite as the fullness of being. God and the world in the cosmological relation are grasped together.

The language of 'cosmological relation' refers to a unique relation and a unique existent: if it is to be used, the possibility of talking about relations between the finite and infinite in terms drawn from the finite scale must be explored. The value and the limitations of analogy must be examined. With patient care we are shown the traps into which each kind of analogy may lead if it is not corrected. Take, for example, the two most obvious inter-finite metaphysical relations:

1. agency and interior effect, when one state of my action gives rise to another, as when I am writing this chapter;
2. agency and external effect, as when I trample the daisies.

The first will suggest the unique relation of creation, but the creation will be an immanent phase of my actions. The second will give us the independence of God and the reality of the creatures – but it will not give us the one-sided dependence of the creature and it makes divine action external to its creatures. In what light can those analogies be corrected? In the light of our apprehension of the scale of being and the scale of goodness. This is central to the whole argument. To see finite activity is to see a finite mode of existence qualified by this or that essence; and we rise from qualified and therefore limited activity to activity which is unlimited, of which the essence is the existence. This, of course, involves seeing the world of finites in a particular way: seeing it in fact as a world of interacting finite substances, not casually occurring sense phenomena but substances with characteristics of their own out of which their behaviour flows, as the sulky tug of the grayling sinking to the bottom can never be taken for the flash and lightning of the trout. It is a world of substances in action since ESSE is OPERARI and not PERCIPI, and it is a world of *finite* substances, not simply finite in the sense that a trout is not a grayling, one thing not another, but finite in the sense of dependent being. We are to see the scale of being as the splintered image of the fullness of being. If there is to be God and a creation which has its own existence (derived but genuine), if we are not to be pantheists, God exists in and of himself and the world of finites always poses the question, 'Why this existence in this mode?' Such, at any rate, is the mechanism of the cosmological intuition: if it is to be supported, we must assert the metaphysical relations of the finite and the real actions of finite substances, knowing them on the scale of being and aware above all of the scale of human voluntary action as we move from fixed habit to freely chosen, fully conscious projects. Our pattern of finite substance is to be found in ourselves. We do not know what it is to be an electron and can scarcely conjecture what feline existence may be, but we do know what it is to be human.

The second part of the book is a defence of a doctrine of finite substance. The materials with which it works are not religious experiences, mystical intuitions or moral claims. They are simply what may be known in the life of any human agent, but viewed in a light which may open our eyes and make us say: that is what really happens. It is in fact a general metaphysical discussion. We look for finite substantial being where we have all along found it, in the active self and the unity of the act of will. Here are limited yet real degrees of the ESSE which is OPERARI, here we see what it is to be not simply a string of contiguous parts: we have a past and a present; we have our habits, our dispositions, our abilities, which in us are a fixed pattern. I cannot dissociate myself from my consciously acquired abilities nor my unconsciously formed aversions, nor am I their victim, since they are I and I they: but as I move into the future there are my projects, some of them freely chosen, a free super-pattern in the luminous apex of my being, and I know myself to move up and down the scale from mere habit to conscious choice. To realize this scale is to accept a doctrine of finite substance with genuine causal relations – my acts do really flow from me, from what I am and what I will. The activity so seen is the basis of our talk about God in terms of will, intellect, and goodness. If we apply these terms to a unique existent, it is because, in the coexistence of elements in our finite life, we are confronted with the source of our splintered being. In applying the terms of our analogy we strike out any imperfections in the hope that what remains is relevant, or we criticize them, knowing that our existence is qualified and limited, but with some insight into what ceaselessly energizing activity would be. We exercise our will often heavily and sadly, in duty and not delight and rarely with joy and love: but we can faintly see from what is positive and negative in us what it would be to energize tirelessly in love. We bet in fact on the scale being genuine and on our extrapolation being in the right direction.

The last forty pages of *Finite and Infinite* are occupied with a discussion of the traditional proofs, in the terms mainly of the distinction between essence and existence, which Farrer later played down as part of the 'Aristotelian leaven' which must be purged. The book ends with words which suggest that his mind was turning to the biblical topics on which he was to write in the next fifteen years.

As I wrote this, the German armies were occupying Paris after a campaign prodigal of blood and human distress. Rational theology will not tell us whether this has or has not been an unqualified and irretrievable disaster to mankind and especially to the men who died. It is another matter if we believe that God Incarnate also died and rose from the dead. But rational theology knows only that whether Paris stands or falls, whether men die or live, God is God, and so long as any spiritual creature survives, God is to be adored.

In the preface to the second edition of *Finite and Infinite* (1959) Farrer described his discomfort with the Aristotelian method of analysis as conveyed through St Thomas Aquinas.

We can [he wrote] make an analysis of finite being or finite process which will reveal its existential insufficiency. Of all the philosophies which have attempted such an analysis Thomism may strike us as the most searching. [The Thomist] brings to bear a battery of categories, potency and act, matter, form, essence and existence, categories which have their home in an abstract account of our descriptive speech . . .

Eighteen to sixteen years ago I sat down and wrote this book because I was possessed by the Thomist vision and could not think it false. The core of the doctrine must somehow be sound, only it must be freed from the period trash in which it was embedded: it must be rescued from dependence on the breath-taking naïveté of old linguistic realism. I told myself that I had to reconstruct the doctrine of substance; by which I meant that I could not be content to derive the structure of being from the grammar of description. I must unearth it where it could be genuinely apprehended. And where was that? Initially, anyhow, in myself, self-disclosed as the subject of my acts.

My starting point was correct . . . but my methodology was ill-considered. What was I doing in fact but finding a certain abstract, artificial and diagrammatic account of my active being applicable or luminous? What right had I to claim that any such account was *the* account? The fatal gap between language and reality yawns again, and unless we can close it nothing like a metaphysical argument in the traditional manner can be attempted.

Never mind, for the gap can be closed, and at the place where I proposed to close it. For language is otherwise related to our acts than it is to anything else. Speech is the very form of our linguistic activity and linguistic activity a type of intentional action in general. A grammar of being is not a chimerical project where the being in question is our own. Every grammar is a grammar of speech, but speech is human being, and uniquely revelatory of the rest of it. And as I trust I was able to show in this book, we both do and must think of the being of all things through an extension of our self-understanding.

In his Deems Lectures for 1964[5] Farrer offered a further criticism of himself.[6] He revised the arguments of twenty years earlier, inspired by his American friends and well aware of the trends of American process theology. He restates basically the central section of *Finite and Infinite* while abandoning the Thomist descriptive system. We begin with a modified verification principle. We can say nothing about any reality with which we cannot be engaged. But we do not wish to deny that the existence of a God with whom we have to do is indicated for us by a contemplation of finite being. What conception of God arises from the venerable argument, *a contingentia mundi*? 'I have the strongest motive in the desire to stamp out the traces of my youthful errors. In a book called *Finite and Infinite* I compromised between voluntarism and formalism in a way which now seems to me to have been perverse.'[7]

The argument, he continues, was about being. The ancients were right when they said that the normal use of 'be' entails existence. Statements like 'mermaids are fish-tailed girls' are sophistications. Simply saying 'Giraffes are the longest-necked animals' need not be replaced by 'Giraffes are the longest-necked mammals *and there are giraffes'*. Where the ancients went wrong was in giving the copula a unique status. Most verbs express action and their primary sense involves an equally plain affirmation of existence. Our fellow creatures are in and as the activity they exercise – though normally such words as 'hit', 'take' and so on do not express the systematic continuity of that action and so of the subject's existence. Descartes was right to derive 'I am' from 'I think' – his error was to restrict the modes of his existence to the phases of his thought.

In *Finite and Infinite* Farrer had asserted that the theist is the man who does justice to the question 'Why is it so?' about any fact of finite existence, following it from brute proximate causes to brute general rules. If we can meaningfully ask that question, we can distinguish an 'it' and a quality which might not, but does, characterize it. 'Why should it, being an actuality, have the mode of actuality we found it to have?' We take activity to be the character basic to all existence we can meaningfully conceive, and we conceive activity in general and experience it in ourselves as capable of varying in its mode. Confronted with any manifestation of active existence we naturally ask why it is what it is or does what it does – the question to which we find no final answer in the natural world.

Now we reach the crucial point. What sort of explanation do we seek? If the attachment of the mode to the existential act appears arbitrary, what attachment of the one to the other would satisfy us? Why not say (as atheists do) that we are simply faced with brute facts? There are two answers, the formalist and the voluntarist. In *Finite and Infinite* we have the formalist answer. If 'it' puzzles us by being so rather than otherwise, it is because we contrast it with an 'it' exempt from such arbitrary determinations, an active existence, full, absolute, entire, having all the 'suchness' or modality worth having. Such a Being is not the addition of all the positive beings and doings there are. Absolute Being must be the existent Act of maximum richness and elevation.

I fought, and will fight to the last ditch, for the contention that active existence is thought of by us, and rightly thought of, as having levels of elevation and degrees of richness. But it is not clear that we are under any obligation to think of the 'scale of being' as running up to a determinate maximum. We can persuade ourselves to think so by concentrating on certain analogies, such as a series of decreasing defects approaching a norm. But it is not obvious that analogies of that sort are the right analogies to take . . . [there is no] general assent for the formula, 'The levels and modalities of all being which is thus or thus are graded by us as measures of Being just being itself'.[8]

He saw the difficulty but had defended the formalist doctrine by suggesting that, because we feel the force of the question 'Why is it so?', we acknowledge the vitality of the motive which prompts the question, and that motive lies in the idea of sheer Being. In the question pressed upon us by the contemplation of finite existence, the finitizing Infinite Cause makes his determinative act felt in the finite effect.

In *Faith and Speculation* Farrer suggested that, if an alternative account of the concealed motive is open, we can still take the question seriously, while rejecting the formalist doctrine.

'The Infinite Cause makes his determinative act felt in the finite effect' – but, he asks, what is felt in the finite effect? A determining act; an act which (to escape an unending regress) must be purely originative, or sovereignly free. Need we then accept the formalist account of 'Why is it so?'

> If we see something arbitrary, betraying external appointment, about an active existence in a particular mode, why should we not be contrasting it with an existence which should clothe itself (its action, that is) with no form but the form it freely chooses? And thus . . . we may reach the God who is all he wills to be; and wills to be all he is: for his act is himself, and his act is free. And that is what we called the voluntarist solution. So . . . there is no discord between our pragmatic theology and the argument *a contingentia mundi*, if it is allowed its proper logic. Both come to rest in the Unconditioned Will.[9]

The tracking down of God in the path of Absolute Being is then to be regarded as a misleading trail. It is the point where Aristotelian causal theory misled the theologians through the ages. God creating the universe is not like a carpenter imposing form on wood.[10]

One reason why Farrer changed his mind was the apparently speculative character of the formalist solution – does an impar-

tial examination of the world yield the notion of God independently of any active relation with God? To put the question like
this seems to bypass the aspiration of the self which makes
theological argument plausible at all. *Finite and Infinite* defines
God neither by what he is nor by how he acts, but purely by the
functional position of his Being as supreme term in a speculative scale – and so it offends the new empirical principle that we
can think about no reality about which we can do nothing but
think. If metaphysical knowledge of God is possible, it is because
we are, whether we appreciate it or not, related to the sovereign
creative will, with which we may engage ourselves.

However, all knowledge of God is analogical. We cannot
conceive an unlimited will: it lies beyond the highest point of
aspiration as we know it. Yet the aspiration of our voluntary
being carries us in its direction – we strain to be quit of our
limitations, and our thoughts are carried in the direction of a
will not so fettered. We have gained by a conception of God
which is concrete and personal: and we have come upon a new
problem. Is the divine will disembodied and therefore removed
from the context where we can understand the operation of a
voluntary act? Has not modern philosophy shown that the
notion of incorporeal spirit is unintelligible?[11]

> My own act, of which I am myself the voluntary author, is my
> standing example of activity; and I become aware of environmental
> activities or forces in so far as they engage with mine. I am bound to
> think of the activities with which I engage as being in some sense *in
> pari materia* with my own; even though I am obliged to make a
> discount of uncertain amount in transferring my conception of my
> own action to the credit of natural forces or agents. They are not
> conscious, they are not voluntary, and yet they act; their act is their
> existence and they have a place somewhere in that scale of agency
> which spans creation and, in its upward reach, points on through
> man towards God.[12]

The complexity of operation attains consciousness in will, in
the unity of activity which is the self: but the self's rationality is
not so pure as to mark it off completely from bodily operations,
which make the self's higher operations possible.

Our mental activities are carried by acts (e.g. speech) and
those acts are employments of bodily powers, however subtle,
however refined. So how can we conceive of God as pure

undetermined Act, independent of the physical universe? The relation between acts and bodily processes raises doubts about the intelligibility of the notion of a transcendent will. Some theists therefore seek refuge in the notion of the universe as God's body.[13] Creative will, they maintain, subsists in the physical world it creates, so that 'God is that Agent who does not exist otherwise than in freely creating'. This implies that God has always been creatively engaged upon material realities, roughly the view of Hartshorne and his disciples, with whom Farrer totally disagreed.[14] Farrer does not propose to make the being of God mere mind: he proposes to acknowledge in him sheer act. We are prejudiced against disembodied act because 'body' is taken by sense to be sheer crass material. But the bottom of substance is ceaseless act. Our personal action arises out of the world; it is not, like God's, that out of which the world arises. His action, being prior and creative is free and simple; to believe in God is to believe this. What we cannot conceive is action *in vacuo*, that is, action without interplay.

> But to Christians at least it has not appeared that the Godhead self-disclosed to them exhibits so desolating and inconceivable a solitude. They believe Trinity of Persons in Unity of Substance . . .
>
> The God of Professor Hartshorne . . . must be human enough to have a natural need of his creatures. It is apparently a matter of no concern that he should be divine enough to save their souls alive. Here is a rival doctrine about that divine charity which is the heart of our religion.[15]

Farrer never abandoned his insistence on the reality of the scale of being known in human act, the scale of intellect, goodness, freedom; he never abandoned the identification of existence with activity; and he never ceased to throw light on the nature of humanity as at once free and limited, which is the clue to understanding the completely Free Act which is God. Farrer was always unmoved on the crucial point that God's freedom is his transcendence.

*The Freedom of the Will* (the Gifford Lectures for 1957) is a book appreciated by professional philosophers and has recently been republished in the United States of America. The interpretation of *Finite and Infinite* depended on a doctrine of finite substance – found in the unity of the self concentrated in the act of will. From this followed the intuition of finite selves as real yet derived, and the scale of being from which we dare speak of God and his qualities – a scale of freedom rising from mere habit to fully conscious choice. So in this work, which is almost purely philosophical, Farrer examined the doctrine of the will: will is *ex hypothesi* free – no freedom, no will – and without a will his doctrine about finite selves cannot be maintained, although there are those who doubt whether the word 'will' now performs any useful philosophical function.

This book is perhaps the most lucidly written of all his works as he arms himself against a Proteus who can assume many forms. The Proteus is determinism, the doctrine that what we choose is prefigured in what we are or what happened to us and so our choices are in principle predictable, though not by us. The most obvious form that this belief would take is to say that we are well acquainted with the studies of neurophysiology – with the minute events in the nervous system of men and animals and the electrical activity of the cerebral cortex. If all action could be reduced to these terms then a clear physical determinism would be established. Many philosophers would have been content to find arguments of a logical kind to show this to be absurd; Farrer, ingenious and vigorous, undertakes more – to give us a credible and possible alternative account of the relation between our conscious actions and the minute events which scientists study. Any action of which we are conscious is a large-scale pattern of physical functioning, an action-pattern which, like all higher forms of organization, has 'a real power to bewitch the lower forms and lead them a new dance'. The putting into effect of one action-pattern rather than another is not to be explained by any purely physical laws; it is what we intend. The action-patterns provide the directing framework for physical regularities. If our actions were decided for us by physical law, consciousness would be denied any natural utility and the physiological determinist would have to account for how it came into being.

The rest of the book pursues determinism to other lairs: we may be offered as determining causes of action wishes, motives, interests, and the fatal biographies discovered by the psychiatrist in the unconscious of his patients. The fighting goes on over varied ground. Two topics of particular interest are raised. There is an illuminating discussion of the relation between human will and the causal regularity of the physical world in which it is shown that the one needs the other. You cannot play croquet if the mallets turn out to be flamingoes uncurling as they swing and the balls turn into hedgehogs. We can play croquet or indeed perform any physical act because we can rely on the results which are intended in our actions. We do not deny that much of our life is not intended. I do not plan how to walk or breathe. I am given or I grow into a fixed pattern. But I may impose my own super-pattern on my materials and my knowledge of this freedom is that which is most luminous to me. Here is the second topic. In the light of my freedom I can interpret my neighbour and face his claims, since the freedom I have is freedom to choose: but the claims which confront me I do not choose. I can choose to ignore them, but not without triviality can I claim to make up my life, like a poem, as I go along. ('I detest', Farrer once wrote to a friend, 'the spirit of existentialism in general, and deplore its licentious use of language, but no one can help feeling the force of the position.')

The 1960s saw the publication of *Love Almighty and Ills Unlimited* (lectures delivered at Yale in 1961), *Saving Belief* (lectures to undergraduates at Oxford in 1963) and *A Science of God?*, the Bishop of London's Lent Book for 1966. We have already discussed the change from a formalistic to a voluntarist position between 1940 and 1967. Other changes appear in these later books. There is a greater awareness of the methods and discoveries of modern science and a more direct approach, as if his mind and thought were simplified (by which I do not mean made easy – it is more like the simplification of the life of the good man). In the first edition of *Finite and Infinite* he had said, 'Rational theology leads us to the knowledge of existent perfection conceived through the analogy of spirit, and the knowledge that this Being is the creator of all finite existence. But no sound reason for a belief in Providence is deducible from these premises'.[16] In the second edition of 1959 he adds, in the Preface, 'unless a general and sovereign Providence makes sense, the link is cut between life and creationist belief, and the investigation of that belief appears superfluous' (prophetic of his later principle that we can think of no reality about which we can do nothing but think). Between 1944 and 1959 he was occupied with revelation and the will: to discuss whether the God of rational theology acts in the world by grace we must turn to the field of particular contingent events. Only at the end of *The Freedom of the Will* does he turn to the wider theological questions raised by determinism: the theologian has his own problem, the relation between creative and creaturely wills. For 'omnipotence not only can dispense with, but even seems to exclude, additional or subsidiary agencies. But then, on the other side, the pattern of physical forces fills all the time and space there is.' The relation between creator and creature is opaque to us: the closest analogy is where we experience the relation of our embracing or co-operating with the divine will.

*Love Almighty and Ills Unlimited* is subtitled 'An Essay on Providence and Evil'. It is a work of both philosophy and theology – without confusion or separation. First there is the general argument about the necessity of conflicting systems, and therefore of accident and loss. And there is the theology of the saving incarnation which particularly illuminates God's working in the world. Farrer uncompromisingly rejects the view that evil can be ascribed to the Devil. The Devil is not God: if he exists he is a created spirit and the puzzle of how a created will can be perverse is no more odd than how our created world can be: except that if he be a fallen angel, it is even more perverse to fall from a good clearly known. What is plain is that talk of the Devil has no explanatory power.

The world, he argues, is not to be thought of as a single quasi-robotic system which runs like a well-oiled machine. The calling of creatures into existence means the interaction of many systems, built up in a hierarchy out of the elementary energies, each working according to its nature so that, while the end product is an ordered world, there are inevitable clashes when different systems come into conflict. A genuinely physical universe cannot be conceived otherwise. If we ask, 'Why does God create a physical universe?' we are told, in a parable, that there must be such a screen between finite and infinite if the former is to have an independent existence over against the Creator.

At first this looks like deism: God creates a field of forces acting on their own principles. But the fact that they produce a world of life – ultimately men able to respond to their creator – shows that creation is continuous and moulded in a particular direction. *But* 'the hand of God is perfectly hidden'. Imperceptibly God works through multitudes of individual

183

creatures to bring about the evolution of new species. The process itself shows how God is God to his creatures.

Above this natural providence God saves the individual man; uniquely in the incarnation God becomes a brother creature to us. This requires the Christian hope of resurrection to meet the objection of maimed and truncated lives. In this life we do not escape from the natural order. The higher orders of God's providence do not destroy the lower. But his infinite contrivance draws some good out of every cross accident, though he has not arranged the accident for the resultant good. Farrer's view of the world is comprehensive. He does full justice to the laws of nature, but he insists too that a mechanical view does no justice to human reason and will. The hidden hand of God is apprehensible not only in the evolution of reasonable species, but also in particular events, especially in the history of salvation; and yet again in individual lives – so far as we can detect a pattern embodying God's purpose for us and experience in our own lives what it means to co-operate with his grace. The natural world is not a closed system but open to the contrivance of the divine will, bringing to reality particular purposes. Not all God's purposes are realized here and now: eternal life is the postulate of the only ultimate theodicy. It is Farrer's basic position that no gap in scientific explanation will ever be found, and equally that the natural systems are plastic to the divine moulding in general and in particular.

The second and third chapters of *Saving Belief* continue the problem of particular providences. Nature is created to act on her own – 'Running one's own way is the same thing as existing: but all that are are the means used by God for purposes both general and particular.' The metaphors used are instructive: the divine Goodness *radiates* upon his creation; God *superimposes* higher levels of organization; the divine will in evolution is an imperceptible *persuasion* on the chaos of natural forces. God steered many sequences of cause, many lines of influence to their meeting place in you and me. The words he will not have are words like 'violation', 'leading-strings', 'manipulation', yet new things are drawn out of existing states of affairs.

It would be infantile to think that God would disregard the interests of his creatures to arrange things for us. 'The difficulty of the criss-cross of forces in a world of creatures is not a difficulty for God, but it is still a limitation since it is a finite limited world that he has created.' God makes the creature make itself in its own way. This applies both to evolution in general and to particular lives. This we see most plainly in the life of Jesus. There is a line leading to him through the spiritual history of Israel with a providential clarity; nowhere else is the goal of God's purpose so clear. Equally God has made us what we are. The eye of faith sees two levels of action – the creature making itself and God making it make itself; and at different levels of creation there are diverse modes of divine action. In the case of physical causes where there is mutual externality we can call God's action a cause; in the case of men with intellect and will there is penetration: the divine working on the human is inspiration and the human will responds by co-operation. In the person of Christ the interpenetration is so complete that we can talk of personal identity.

He mentions miracle only to say that it is an exception to his general idea of providence. The gospel miracles cannot be ruled out since criteria drawn from a survey of ordinary humanity cannot be applied to the unique case of Jesus. Farrer is essaying a doctrine of providence which neither leaves the world to mechanism or pure chance, nor relies universally on the direct miraculous action of God. When he talks of miracle he talks of the enhancement of natural powers. The resurrection is a case neither of providence nor of miracle: it is a unique manifestation in the world of the transition God makes for us from this way of being into another. Even this is not a violation of nature since it is the ultimate destiny of all nature – but being so, we cannot make it the standard of our own experience of God's providence in the world.

These later works are designed not to establish providence but to say what can be said about the manner of God's action in the world. The typical divine actions which reveal God to us take place in purely human affairs – just as Christ's message was conveyed with the mental furniture acquired from his village rabbi.

*A Science of God?* (1966) makes the same points with even greater clarity and force. We must not guess what God's designs in nature are nor think that his purposes are what ours would be. He does not impose an order against the grain of things – nor does he over-rule. He does not let natural forces work only till their nature would conflict with the welfare of men, nor does he at such a point substitute miracle for nature. Yet disasters, while they are disasters indeed, are nevertheless worked into God's providence, which cannot finally be defeated. God raises the dead. Our acting and willing are the clearest way into God's actions. If we can feel the attraction of the divine will, we can co-operate with it and hasten the creative process. Prayer is the sincere seeking of the divine will. The deepening of faith is the only experimental test of religion. 'To realize a union with our Creator we need not scale heaven or strip the veil from ultimate mystery: for God descends into his creature and acts humanly in mankind.'[17] Philosophy trembles on the verge of theology.

And so, out of chronological order, we come back to the Bampton Lectures[18] given in 1948 in the Church of St Mary the Virgin, Oxford, which, according to Basil Mitchell, had surely heard nothing like it since John Henry Newman occupied that pulpit.

God brings good out of evil, and we are assured of that by particular contingent events – the acts of Christ. Christians have commonly supposed that the sentences of the New Testament have some relation to what they take to be a divine activity in the acts of Christ and the life of the Church. Writing the lectures in 1948 Farrer had his eye on the controversies of the time. Christians perhaps once thought – some still do – that the Holy Spirit is the true author of the scriptures, dictating inerrantly what we need to know, leading us into truth and avoiding all error, so that sentence by sentence we are instructed and rightly instructed. Revelation in fact was given in the form of propositions. A century of critical study made this view seem untenable: and so we were bidden instead to say that God's revelation is his saving activity, the events, and the scriptures are the evidence for and the comment of the Church on that activity: it is in the coincidence of event and interpretation that revelation is to be found. If sometimes the interpretation is in terms natural perhaps to a Jew on the fringe of Rabbinic learning we can discard this temporary husk and rewrite the interpretation in our own terms. So we can abandon the words and keep the original substance. But can we? This is the problem of the book.

Suppose, since we are talking as Christians, that there is

revelation, yet it will still be talk about God, since neither apostles nor theologians are – mercifully – going to be struck dumb, and if they were, nothing would stop them writing, and so here we are back again. What will talk about God be? We know part of the answer to that from *Finite and Infinite*, and the reader who found that hard going will find the same themes more easily expounded in chapters 4 and 5 of the Bampton Lectures. Even the most devoted Barthian must write in words, and if these convey sense it will be in terms of our knowledge of the world, ourselves, our nature, and our history. The metaphysician, as he faces the natural mysteries of the human self and looks at them from his own point of view, finds his own analogies and presses those that seem most fruitful and illuminating. If he must use analogy to describe finite experience he can, like the poet, know both his mystery and his analogy, and out of his knowledge find new analogies to correct his first choice. If 'the winter of our discontent is made glorious summer by this Sun of York' we know winter, summer, discontent, and the Sun of York and we may revise our estimate of him. The theologian, on the other hand, writing of God's particular activity uses what words he can find in scripture or make for himself, and yet can hardly claim a direct inspection of his two terms.

We talked of contingent events. Perhaps we shall get some light if we go back to those contingent events. Whether we care for propositions or not, we shall all agree that the primary revelation is Christ: and we will go further. What we have at the heart of the New Testament is not apostolic comment on Christ, it is Christ's interpretation of himself. Christ performed the primary action and spoke the primary words. The history of Israel looked forward to the Kingdom and the New Covenant. Christ called round him the Twelve, instituted the covenant for many, named himself the Son of Man, died and rose. What had been images on the clouds was manifest in the flesh. To be a Galilean carpenter, to die and perhaps indeed to rise, is not revelation, though it is surprising. A Socrates may die and die movingly. But to die as a Son of David, a martyred Israel, and a Lamb of Sacrifice, this is revelation. 'Christ clothed himself in the archetypal images and then began to do and to suffer.' The meaning is in the images which convey the supernatural action and, in setting them down, the apostolic authors – if they were apostolic – are setting down what is signified by the images. Throw away the images and there is no revelation: those who wrote with pens in their hands are writing as parts of the body of which Christ is the head, and writing also as themselves, as the kind of men they were. The natural is not the contradictory of the supernatural.

What, then, are we saying? Certainly not that the whole of the New Testament is on the same level. St Paul sharply distinguished his own speculations from the tradition of the Lord. We say there is a central core of meaning which is the self-interpretation of Christ in the primary images, and that the revelation is in the images, and that they are not old clothes to be discarded, but the means to understanding. We will also say what Farrer did not say in these lectures but certainly believed: that the crux – how does the theologian trust his analogies, in this case his revealed images? – depends for its answer on his belief in the resurrection and – to say an even more scandalous thing – on those stories of the empty tomb which anchor talk of the resurrection to the world of fact and, like incarnation, distinguish images from platonizing myth. For if the images do not and did not convey their meaning in the world of flesh, what is left but piety and morals?

C. G. Stead,[19] who was Farrer's colleague at Keble as chaplain, has some judicious words to say about Farrer's philosophical work:

> As a philosopher I think his position was a little like Collingwood's in his day: his brilliance was undeniable, but he was too far removed from the main current to be effective at the centre of influence. I think this was a pity, and in the last resort avoidable: if he had chosen he could . . . have shown much more sympathy with logical empiricism, which was already becoming much less uncompromising and less uniformly hostile to religion and to metaphysics. Part of the difficulty was that where others were content to swim with (use, develop) the philosophical current while making room for a few basic theological commonplaces, Austin wanted a philosophical position which gave a place to Christian theology and devotion in depth. But also at this period his highly distinctive style of writing wasn't entirely helpful; it brought him deservedly a band of admirers and (later) students, but it isolated him from many of his intellectual equals. He could talk with

Mitchell and Crombie and Hare, but not, I think, to any profit with
Berlin or Hampshire or Strawson, I think in fact he was rather
insensitive to their technical competence, and the same goes even
more for J. L. Austin. [1]

Against this I would say that Strawson reviewed Farrer's
Gifford Lectures warmly: that the real snag was that *Finite and
Infinite* appeared during the war, and that from 1943 to 1957,
when the Giffords were delivered, most of his published work
was biblical; but I agree that he wanted a philosophical position
which gave a place to Christian devotion in depth: is not this,
after all, the verification principle of the Deems Lectures? 'We
can neither think nor talk about any reality about which we
can do nothing else.' But I would agree that, like Collingwood,
he felt that he had a battle to fight.

He summed up what he had to say and what he was in two
letters to America written towards the end of his life. The first
was to Ray Hart:

Now about this wretched *Finite and Infinite*. I went through the
exercise of reinterpreting the scholastic distinction between Form
and Essence to see what would happen to it. I am fairly sure that the
relation of active existence to its characterizing form, as I then
conceived it, was not to be located in the 'no man's land' lying
between form and essence, but that my account of this debatable
region was a mere scholastic translation of a formal doctrine on
that relation. What I say is that active existence as we know it can
only work from a characterizing form which makes it the existent it
is, but that it exists by implementing, defining, extending, enriching
and modifying this form, so far as the form allows. I concede to John
Glasse that the God for a world of beings thus conceived is that
active existence which takes all the form that it wills to take, and
wills to take all the form that it has. I do not concede to the
process-theorists that God is what he is by his action in the
*creatures*, for that appears to me to be the overthrow of all sound
metaphysical reasoning.

About Whitehead: it seems to me to be a point of small
importance whether his actual occasions or primary entities have
some duration or none. Whitehead sinned against the light by
saying that a personal existence in its continuity over time is a
society of entities: for our standard example of an entity is a
perduring person: it is silly to say that a man is a lot of little men.

Whitehead was misled by the logical atomism of his youth: and in his age he called on God to put together what he and Russell had put asunder. I don't see how a metaphysical system can ever go right which starts so wrong. [2]

The second letter, to Edward Henderson, is on a more personal note, in answer to a question about the comparative neglect of his philosophical work. He replied in March 1966;

You ask about my position in the philosophical world. I am disregarded because I am an orthodox professional theologian, and because I do not keep up with the philosophical game. I do not attend philosophical conferences. I do not write for the philosophical periodicals. If anyone bothers to criticize me, I don't answer them. And why? My attention is hopelessly distracted. I am interested in scripture, especially the gospels. I have this college of which I am what you'd call President. I am also in charge of the chapel: I am an expositor of doctrine in our terribly weak Church and do what I can by preaching and pious working to crumble the bread of Truth for the people. [3]

Professor Henderson himself sums up his feelings about Farrer like this:

Austin Farrer was a philosopher and theologian of the highest order. He represented the best tradition of metaphysics in the line of Aristotle, Aquinas, Spinoza, Leibniz, Kant and Whitehead: yet he was an unabashed spokesman for orthodox Christianity and used his philosophy to support his faith. Now the effort to support any orthodox faith with original philosophy is dangerous. It all too easily either makes philosophizing into rationalizing or orthodoxy into heresy. I shall not be so rash as to say that Farrer perfectly resolved the tension between faith and reason, but he did manage to wed the two without sacrificing either to the other. 'The Prior Actuality of God'[20] shows in fact that this is Farrer's distinctive achievement. He has developed a rigorous and contemporary analysis of the being of finite entities, taking into account the main modern criticism of metaphysics: and on the basis of it has argued the essentially Christian understanding of reality as opposed to alternatives which variously depart from it (including the Scholastic). Whether his metaphysics and his arguments from it to theological conclusions are true is a different matter. In Farrer' work is a truly Christian philosophical understanding. *Credo ut intelligam.*[21]

It is time to sum up. The core of Farrer's philosophical work in his three major books is the assertion of the reality of finite substances experienced as activity – but as continuing activity. It is most clearly evident to us in the unity of the willing self. And those activities we meet are experienced as having 'levels of elevation and degrees of richness'. For this Farrer said, 'I will fight to the last ditch' – and rightly so: do we not hear rumours that some philosophic sects are ready to 'abandon the concept of will as useless lumber'? Because there are spiritual beings and degrees of goodness, the will to which we are led as the Creative Will is one which moulds the world, bringing new goodness continually out of the ordered energies. This is the answer to those who saw in Farrer's new emphasis on God's will a bare emphasis on the divine fiat. It is a *good* will.

Farrer wrote about C. S. Lewis as an apologist words which may well be used to define his own work. 'The apologist's eye is on the point of attack: he is a frontiersman; there are frontiersmen and frontiersmen, of course. There is what may be called the Munich School, who will always sell the pass in the belief that their position can more happily be defended from foothills to the rear.' Farrer's position was in the front line.

# CHAPTER 11

## *Farrer the Biblical Scholar*
### (by Michael Goulder)

*

Farrer remarked to me about *Faith and Speculation*, 'When I have finished it, I shall have rewritten all my books.' The remark was near enough to the truth to be witty, but the wistful suggestion of wasted labour was wide of the mark. Farrer was for ever thinking radically new thoughts, and radical novelty is rarely convincing at first breath. He wrote books about two of the New Testament *biblia*, Mark and Revelation, and he rewrote them both. *A Rebirth of Images* came out in 1949, and his Commentary on *The Revelation of St John the Divine* in 1964; in between came *A Study in St Mark* (1951), followed by *St Matthew and St Mark* (1954). In both cases the argument and the presentation were simplified in the second book: one more easily sees the wood from the trees. The riddle of the New Testament in fact never left him. He tells us that he began to seek an explanation of the Apocalypse in 1941. We can see him at work on St Mark in his Bampton Lectures, *The Glass of Vision* (1948), and he is already revising his first solution to the symbolism of the numbers in the feeding stories in the *Journal of Theological Studies* in 1953. In 1955 came his brilliant and controversial article, 'On Dispensing with Q', in the R. H. Lightfoot memorial volume. After nearly a decade in which his attention was largely given to the problems of freedom and evil and the problem of Dr John Robinson, he returned to the first two Gospels with his intriguing and profound Lent Book, *The Triple Victory* (1965) and a revised edition of *St Matthew and St Mark* (1966). He was writing about St Mark still when he died: there were eighty pages of manuscript entitled 'St Mark's Materials', some of which Dr Conti has published.[1] Part of this was written on the back of the sermon which he preached the Sunday before his death.

It has been widely felt that Farrer is in one way to be compared to Isaac Newton. Both men had priceless insights to communicate, Newton on the foundations of physics, Farrer in philosophical theology: both men were distracted from their calling and frittered their genius in empty speculation on the Book of Revelation and other texts. Bishops wished that Farrer would leave the Bible alone and return to philosophy where he was a redoubtable defender of the faith: cycles and paracycles and numerology in the Gospels could only serve to undercut the historicity of Jesus. New Testament scholars were quick to agree with them. Patterns in Mark were subjective imaginings unknown to the ruling orthodoxy of form-criticism, pictures in the fire.

It must be confessed that a part of Farrer's failure to convince the learned world was his own fault. It is an elementary precaution when assaulting the established critical positions of a century to show that you have read their leading expositors and to provide some critique of their work. Farrer contemned the footnote. He wrote with authority and not as the scribes, and the scribes did not appreciate this. But he did in fact read the standard English and some German commentaries on Mark, although he did not make this plain. Nor did his style commend itself to the serious. In all his writings he adopted the brilliant scarlet of epigram in place of the sober subfusc of word-counts and references. He used sometimes to refer to a practice as being typical of the rabbis, and I have no doubt that he had consulted the texts; but verifying such details can be a headache.

However, such faults are perhaps trivial, the price of his soaring mind's continual quest for the truth. In his New Testament work his consistent aim was to enter the mind and intention of the author and so to reveal the literary, artistic and dramatic structure of the text as well as its theological unity and coherence.[2] In the course of this attempt he produced many original and sparkling suggestions: but what we want to know is how much is there of permanent value in them? Was Farrer's biblical enterprise sheerly misguided, as is today's common opinion, or was it in some ways at least seminal, or even right? I should wish to take the latter option, and in the matter that follows I shall consider three of his main ideas, each of which seems to me to be either illuminating or in part correct. In the nature of the case I cannot avoid being both highly selective and completely personal. We have not leisure for more than a fraction of the things Farrer said, and you cannot hope to meet a critic of Farrer more biased in his favour than I. But although prejudiced, you will not find me, I hope, undiscriminating, and I shall try, even in my piety, to sift wheat from chaff.

The first topic that I wish to take is Farrer's attack on Q, which is limited to his essay in the Lightfoot volume. The radical nature of this attack may be seen from the fact that a source common to Matthew and Luke, called at first the Logia and later Q, goes back at least to Schleiermacher in 1832 and had been an accepted part of source-criticism since Holtzmann in the 1860s. No reputable scholar apart from Schlatter had doubted it, and the final problems had been laid to rest by Streeter in *The Four Gospels* (1924) and J. Schmid in *Matthäus und Lukas* (1930). It was not until 1951 that Q was challenged again in a serious work, B. C. Butler's *The Originality of St Matthew*; and by this time Farrer had already worked out the argument of 'On Dispensing with Q'.

Farrer saw that Q is methodologically a second-best hypothesis. The non-Marcan matter common to Matthew and Luke, which comprises about 200 verses, could be plausibly explained by two theories: either Luke knew Matthew or they both knew a lost source, Q. But the two theories do not compete on a par. Lucan knowledge of Matthew is the more economical hypothesis and makes a natural reading of Luke's words, 'Inasmuch as many have undertaken to compile a narrative . . .' It would be easy to understand Luke's selection of the most 'Luke-pleasing' texts from Matthew and his omission of such matters as controversies with the Pharisees. Nor is Luke's ordering of his material any difficulty. Luke has taken Mark for his basis, being the older-established and more historical text. He has inserted into Mark's outline up to Luke 9 only those Matthaean paragraphs which the context required – the baptism and temptations, at the beginning, the Galilean matter of the mountain sermon, the centurion's boy and John's question from prison in Luke 6–7. He then calls a halt at 9.51, and gathers in a compendium those Matthaean paragraphs which he values, forming them into a journey-narrative. In all this we are on firm ground, interpreting two texts which we have before us.

The Q hypothesis *per contra* is nebulous as well as unnecessary. There is no agreement as to what paragraphs were in Q, nor is there any definite flavour to its core which we can distinguish from that of Matthew and Luke. It is not just a body of logia for it contains a considerable element of narrative; and furthermore the narrative forms in part a symbolic series, the baptism, temptations and mountain sermon corresponding to Israel's experience at the Red Sea, in the desert and on Sinai – the very symbolism which we find worked out in Matthew! There is no proper parallel for such a postulated document as Q in the ancient world – Isaiah, for example, with its call narrative and predominance of prophecies, does not answer because God's seal on Jesus was not the baptism but the resurrection. Q further labours under the difficulty that there is a considerable number of 'minor agreements', places where all three Gospels tell the story, and Luke, while following Mark in the main, agrees with Matthew on small points. Streeter had divided these into groups, explaining them on the basis of assimilations in the manuscripts; but his explanations are only successful in so far as he multiplies hypotheses. Q gained force because in Streeter's time, and before, the Gospels were taken to be scissors-and-paste compilations of tradition. We see the evangelists to have exercised some freedom of handling as well as of ordering tradition, and it falls to the ground. Farrer gives an example of how he takes Luke to have rehandled Matthew in Luke 11. He answers the objection that the Lucan form of some logia seems to be prior to the Matthaean by pointing to the naivety of the criteria used. Matthew is often taken to have amended Luke's 'Blessed are you poor', for example, in an ecclesiastical sense, adding 'poor *in spirit*'; but then Luke's antithesis with 'you rich' would require 'you poor' *tout court*, and Luke elsewhere adopts the Old Testament equation of poor = godly.

All this sounds extremely convincing: how far has the learned world been convinced? Well, not very far; partly from bad reasons, and partly from less bad. Parallels to Q have been cited in the Pirke Aboth and the Gospel of Thomas, for example, so Q would be a collection of 'Sayings of the Wise'; but neither of these collections has Q's narrative framework, nor does the Q collection think highly of 'the wise and understanding'. Several editions of Q have been proposed, beginning from sheer logia and ending with a proto-Gospel; but no internal grounds can be offered to support such speculations. Attempts are made to find a Wisdom-christology in Q, distinct from the Matthaean redaction; but the evidence is virtually limited to two texts, in both of which 'Wisdom' can be a periphrasis for 'God', and one of which has the word in only the Lucan version (11.49). Besides, Matthew himself has something like a Wisdom-christology at Matthew 11.28–30.

More interesting are the objections which led Streeter and others to prefer Q in the first place: (1) Can the Lucan form *always* be shown to be secondary? and (2) Can any justification be provided for Luke's scattering of the ordered Matthaean material? Farrer was certainly over-confident in feeling that his methodological point would cause Q to collapse. The fact that his theory was more economical counted for nothing. Q held the field, and would not be shifted without high explosives. Furthermore, it is not clear that it could be shifted even with high explosives. Suppose it were shown that the Lucan form of the Q logia was always secondary to the Matthaean form, would this result in Q being withdrawn? Farrer showed that the Lucan form was interpretable as secondary in a number of crucial instances like the Beatitudes, and I have argued my way through every Q passage to the same conclusion in my *Midrash and Lection in Matthew*.[3] But when I announced my intention of doing this during my Speaker's Lectures at Oxford, a Professor present remarked, 'First he must disprove Q'! Nor would a conclusive instance the other way demolish Farrer's theory, for, as he says himself of the Lord's Prayer, Luke might have read Matthew and still have preferred his own version of any logion. So it is not clear that *any* amount of argument would settle the matter.

On the question of Luke's scattering of the Matthaean order, Farrer himself bedevilled the discussion with his brilliant but perverse suggestion that both evangelists were following a Hexateuchal pattern. Bacon[4] had pointed to five discourses in Matthew, each signed off with a formula, and had said it might be a kind of Pentateuch. Farrer saw the Genealogy, with its opening 'The book of genesis of Jesus Christ . . .' as evidence of a Matthaean Genesis; and this left the Baptism, Temptations and Sermon on the Mount as the Matthaean Exodus: the evidence was thick, and the idea euphoric. But what a thin Leviticus, the missionary discourse to the Twelve, the so-called priests of the new Israel! And no sign of Numbers at all in the grain and fishes harvested in Matthew 13! A bit of Deuteronomy, and a Joshua almost limited to Jesus passing through Jericho. No one was much convinced by this and still less by the even more scanty traces of the same pattern in Luke. With the enormous *vis inertiae* of an accepted solution to the Synoptic Problem with a hundred years' standing, Farrer was not going to move Q like that.

What then are we to make of 'On Dispensing with Q'? It was a vision, but the vision is for many days. Q is not going to collapse: it has the highest vested interest of any New Testament hypothesis in that virtually every scholar has written a book assuming its truth. It will have to be hunted from the field, and this can only be done by disproving it, not dispensing with it. A moment's reflection will show how difficult a task this is, for Q is so set up as to be almost non-falsifiable. Take a pericope of a hundred words and suppose it to be a difficult one for Q – say the storm-stilling, where Luke has 31 of the Marcan words and 15 in which he agrees with Matthew against Mark. Then Professor Frans Neirynck of Leuven, the international champion of Q, will make it his business to explain the Lucan words as being Luke's natural vocabulary – we find him using this word three times in the Gospel, and that one in Acts. But of course he does: on Farrer's hypothesis you would also expect Luke to take from Matthew those words which he uses naturally. And if by chance there are some difficulties which cannot be solved plausibly, if *per impossibile* we discovered fifteen more 'minor agreements', should we have disproved Q then? Not on your life: the insoluble agreements would be taken as evidence that Q also had a version of the storm-stilling and that Matthew and Luke were following this in addition to Mark. We should be congratulated on all hands for extending our knowledge of Q!

Is Q then incapable of disproof? Not quite. We need to look for passages common to the three Gospels in which there are agreements of Luke with Matthew against Mark which satisfy two conditions. First the words must be in some way characteristic of Matthew: then we are not liable to the reply that before they were in Matthew they were in Ur-Markus, or Deutero-Markus, or some *Nebenquelle* – we must walk delicately, for our way is full of mines. Second, the words must be in some way *un*characteristic of Luke; and this, as I have hinted, is no easy condition – Luke has far the biggest vocabulary of the evangelists, he has written two books, he has both a natural style and a good Septuagint pastiche, and he has an alarming way of varying his synonyms. Nonetheless, there are, I believe, more than fifty words in the Gospel in some twenty passages, especially in the Passion, which fulfil these conditions. I have presented twelve of these passages in an article in *New Testament Studies* 24 – 'On Putting Q to the Test' – and it will be interesting to see whether it is possible to make a convincing reply to them. If this is not forthcoming, some competent person will have to write a commentary on Luke showing how the evangelist has ordered his Matthaean material. I am confident that this can be done, and that Farrer's attack upon Q will be shown not merely to have been brilliant but in the main brilliantly right: but until Q is brought a little lower, nobody will attend to such a book. In the meantime Farrer's achievement is the not inconsiderable one of reducing Q from a fact to a hypothesis.

I do not need to observe that Farrer would not have been content with so negative an assessment. He was an exegete of rarely paralleled sensitivity with both the learning and the empathy to follow the direction of thinking of writers two millennia ago; and it is this that makes his biblical works so intoxicating to read, even when we feel sure that much of them is wrong. They are emphatically not dry-as-dust commentaries; they are insights into how the imaginations of sacred writers may have worked, and they convey, as good nineteenth-century commentaries used to convey, a sense of urgency that the inspired writing should be understood, and followed. He writes, for example,

> If St John were to return to us now, he might say, 'I warned you that the day would come when for the folly and sin of man fire would fall upon them from the sky. Well, it has fallen. You complain that it was vindictive of me to give you the warning . . . I advise you to look into your consciences.' Such was the mind of the whole apostolic Church. But we evade the evidence where we can, and hate the book in which the evidence cannot be evaded.[5]

I say 'may have worked' because Farrer was a great reviser; and many of the interpretations of *A Rebirth of Images* are ploughed under in his *Revelation*. He tells us that he was excited by the early work he did on the Apocalypse, and it is a heady book to read. Pattern is piled upon pattern. The Apocalypse is a week of weeks, a series of six groups of seven visions apiece, each culminating in a scene of sabbath-worship, and the whole looking forward to an ultimate Sabbath. But the six weeks are each also quarters of a Jewish-Christian year, running from Dedication, symbolized by the seven lamps in chapter 1; to Passover/Pentecost in chapters 4–5, where the lamb, symbol of Passover, opens the seals of the scroll, representing Pentecost; thence to the seven trumpets, symbols of New Year; to the wilderness, tabernacling and harvest/vintage visions symbolizing Tabernacles; to the vials representing Dedication again; to the Bride of Christ, antitype of Esther at Purim; and so round to a final Passover and Pentecost in the final visions. So the six sevens are also six quarters, a year and a half. But the calendrical thread on which the visions hang is not a straight line of cotton. It is caught up into loops, so that now and again St John runs through a whole subsidiary year, like a kind of epicycle in Ptolemaic astronomy. When we have reached the end of this exposition, we note with alarm that there is nearly as much still to come. The movement of the Apocalypse is also governed by the order of worship in the Temple on a single Jewish day; and it is also a year and a half's march round the foursquare city whose gates are the twelve apostles, the twelve tribes and the twelve stones on the high-priests' breastplate. When we have finished, we are in chastened mood: here is inspiration indeed.

It was two weeks of years before *A Rebirth* was succeeded by the Commentary; and in fourteen years much exuberant growth may be pruned away. There are changes, but the essence of the previous book is still there, distilled and purified. St John is no longer the common author of both Apocalypse and Gospel, as he was in *A Rebirth*, but now the evangelist is a fellow-Asian and pupil of the Seer. The weeks pattern is changed. The six weeks of visions in *A Rebirth* were in fact four counted weeks and two uncounted weeks. John himself says that there were seven messages to the churches, seven seals, seven trumpets and seven vials; the seven beast-visions in chapters 12–14, and the seven last things at the end of the book, are not counted by him, but were obtained by counting the phrases 'And I saw'/'And there was seen'. In the Commentary Farrer withdrew his six-week format and replaced it with a four-week format. The beast-visions are taken as subsidiary parts of the seventh trumpet, and the last things as subsidiary parts of the seventh vial, and good reasons are adduced for this interpretation. So we have half a week of weeks, a time and times and half a time, the great final week of tribulation which God shortened for the sake of the elect.

This amended structure has a new and important corollary. What is to become of the six-part week of the New Creation, ramified into the six-quarter, year-and-a-half circuit of the Jewish year and foursquare city? This was the core and glory of the former book, but now we have but a four-day week. Farrer follows his former logic and turns his six quarters into a year; the extravagances of his former calendar fall away, and he is left with a single annual cycle of festivals backed up by a cycle of zodiacal symbolism. He divides the four weeks of the visions between the four living creatures of the throne in chapter 4: the lion, bull, man and eagle. The bull is the middle sign of the three spring signs (Aries, *Taurus*, Gemini), the lion of the three summer signs (Cancer, *Leo*, Virgo), the eagle is a constellation rising at the same time as Scorpio, the middle autumn sign, and the man with the waterpot is the middle winter sign (Capricorn, *Aquarius*, Pisces). So the lion of the tribe of Judah comes forward to open the seals in summer; the eagle cries 'Woe, Woe, Woe,' at the end of the trumpets in autumn; the man pouring water is transmuted into the angels pouring fire from the vials in winter; there is no bull, but the ram/lamb for Aries at Passover. The supernumerary Jewish festivals are withdrawn. If anything, the vision in chapter 1 is more like Easter than Dedication. The candlestick is merely familiar to Jews from the latter; the great whore and the bride may be formed on the types of Vashti and Esther at Purim, but need not be. Farrer somewhat surprisingly stresses his zodiacal matter rather than the festivals. The titles of the four chapters of the book are 'The Lord's Day', 'The Lion of Judah', 'The Woes of the Eagle' and 'The Heavenly Man'.

Such an exercise may leave us exhausted and depressed. We had felt exhilarated, now we feel conned. Our heads have spun to no purpose; if it turns out that the first revelation, in *A Rebirth*, was in part misconceived, what credence are we to place in the second? Perhaps we had better go back to R. H. Charles, and theories of interpolations and second editions. I don't think so: I think that Farrer has found the key to understanding the Apocalypse, but that he has not turned it firmly enough in the lock. He has too many keys that will not open the door of its mysteries, but one that will. If we will have patience, and endure to the end, sorting the persuasive from the implausible in his 500 pages of argument, we shall enter through the door and see the vision of truth.

First, then, the year and a half and the epicycles of *A Rebirth* are not at all convincing once Farrer's golden eloquence is removed; and the Zodiac seems absurd as a *basis* for the book, even if it is a subsidiary feature. The bull is not mentioned in the first quarter, nor is there any *water*-pouring in the fourth; and John can have scorpions, not eagles, when he feels like it. Nor is it easy to credit the half-week of weeks: for there are four weeks, not three and a half, and it would seem as if St John would have limited himself to four vials if this had been his intention. On the other hand, parts of the calendrical scheme are very persuasive. Chapters 4 and 5 *are* a tissue of Pentecostal texts, Exodus 19 and Ezekiel 1, of which the latter is in the Talmud and the former is evidenced BC, and both are in use today. The thunders, lightnings and trumpet-call, the summons to come up, the priesthood and kingship of God's people, all are in Exodus 19; while Ezekiel 1 describes the one seated upon the throne, with the rainbow round about, and the four living creatures. Moses then receives God's word written on stone; written on stone but read to Israel from a scroll, and it is as a scroll that Ezekiel receives it in chapter 2 and St John in Revelation 5. New Year *is* the feast of trumpets, and trumpets are traditionally sounded in the weeks preceding the feast, as in Revelation 8–9; and the events following the seventh trumpet are New Year themes, especially the coming of God's eternal kingdom. Tabernacles *was* the traditional celebration of Yahweh's victories over Rahab and Leviathan, who reappear as the dragon and the beasts from the sea in Revelation 12–13; it *was* the occasion of the standing of all Israel on Zion, and the ingathering of corn and vintage (cf. Revelation 14). The lesson of Dedication *is* Numbers 7, the dedication of the vials and dishes of the Temple, for the pouring of libations; and in Revelation 15–16 the vials of the heavenly Temple are used to pour out God's wrath. All these references follow the central themes of the festivals and they fall in order. Surely they are impressive.

The two weak links in Farrer's first chain of festal references were the whore/bride, Vashti/Esther scheme for Purim, which lacks any verbal basis (as he knew); and the unhappy equivalence of the seven candlesticks in Revelation 1 with the candlestick of Numbers 8 and Zechariah 4, the Dedication lessons, a blind alley from which he escaped in the Commentary. In fact the opening vision is repeatedly associated with Easter, rather than Dedication. Jesus is the firstborn of the dead . . . who has freed us from our sins by his blood (being our Passover sacrifice); every eye will see him, everyone who pierced him; his first words are: 'Fear not, I am the first and the last, and the living one; I died, and behold I am alive for evermore, and I have the keys of Death and Hades' (Rev. 1.18). John sees the vision 'on the dominical day'; which may mean Easter Day – and if not, it is by virtue of the resurrection that every Sunday is dominical. So we have in fact a much stronger and clearer opening to the festal year; an Easter vision, followed by seven messages for the seven weeks to Pentecost, and then a Pentecostal vision in chapter 4. Furthermore, we do not lack evidence that both Christians and Jews expected their redemption to come at Passover; so we have an encouraging suggestion at the end of the book for the repeated emphasis on prayers for the Lord to come: 'The Spirit and the Bride say, "Come." And let him who hears say, "Come." . . . He who testifies to these things says, "Surely I am coming soon." Amen, come, Lord Jesus!' The Apocalypse opens with an Easter vision and closes with this pre-paschal prayer.

I think, then, that Farrer was right in *A Rebirth* when he saw the central thread of the book as the Jewish festal cycle, and that he was right in the Commentary when he saw the cycle as covering a year and not eighteen months. I think further that we can probabilify his theory in a number of ways, two of which I give here, both direct developments of his own suggestions. First, Farrer always saw Revelation as a poem; he gives some detailed account of the manner of inspiration with which he credits the Seer and it is a reflection, pen in hand, on Jesus's prophecies in Matthew 24 crossed with the words of God through Ezekiel, Zechariah, Isaiah, Exodus, etc. But if we take seriously the constant refrain, 'And I saw', coupled with the calendrical series, we have something much more down-to-earth and probable. The Apocalypse is a series of Sunday

visions round the year, one for each Sunday, starting with
Easter and ending before Easter. The messages take us to
Pentecost; there are two supplementary scenes in chapter 5 and
seven unsealing visions for the nine weeks between Pentecost
and 9th Ab (a fast day in the Jewish calendar); and then seven
trumpet visions for the seven weeks leading up to New Year;
New Year and the Tabernacles visions follow, and then the
seven vials with the seventh in Dedication week; and there are
then sufficient visions to take us round to the second week in
Nisan at the end of the book. St John will have set himself to
meditate each Lord's Day, with the general pattern of vision
governed by the advance of the coming drama in Matthew 24
and 1 Corinthians 15: preliminary trials, the persecution of the
saints, the fall of Jerusalem, the Great Tribulation under
Antichrist, the coming of the Son of Man, the Millennium, the
Kingdom of God. But these topics are considered under the
influence of the advancing liturgical year, so that, for example,
the archangel's trumpet is developed with New Year symbolism, or the Son of Man's reaping with Tabernacles themes. It
would be natural to think that St John not only wrote the
Apocalypse so, but expected the Asian churches to read it so: he
writes, 'Blessed is he who reads aloud the words of this
prophecy, and blessed are those who hear' – a public reading in
church is assumed, and we can hardly think he would be
satisfied with a single reading. As Farrer says, 'He did not think
it was going to be read once to the congregations and then used
to wrap up fish, like a pastoral letter.'[6] What more straightforward than that the local preacher should first read a few verses
from the Saint and then expound the matter in his sermon? The
Apocalypse has not lacked full-bodied expositions through later
Christian history.

We find an impressive confirmation of this view by developing a remark of Farrer's early in *A Rebirth*. At first, he tells us, he
thought the Apocalypse to be a development of Ezekiel,
Zechariah and Daniel taken in order, but was forced to give up
this hypothesis in favour of the Festal Year view. But in fact the
two hypotheses are not incompatible. Farrer was misled by the
unfortunate theory of a three-year cycle of lessons proposed by
Büchler in the 1890s; but in fact the triennial cycle cannot be
traced earlier than the end of the second century AD, and even
then it only partly replaced an earlier annual cycle of readings.

In the earlier period we have evidence of an annual cycle, most clearly in Philo; and the prophets are likely to have been known to the laity through being read as five cycles, the Histories, Isaiah, Jeremiah, Ezekiel and the Twelve, read round the year whether together or in different years. In an article in *New Testament Studies* 27, I have set out the possibility that Farrer's early hunch was in part justified. I have divided the text of the Apocalypse to give the calendrical sequence outlined above, and put the forty-eight chapters of Ezekiel alongside. It can then be seen that in no less than twelve of the fifty visions one can see the Seer as drawing inspiration from the Ezekiel chapter read that day: the throne-vision in Ezekiel 1, the scroll-vision in Ezekiel 2–3, its prophecy of famine in Ezekiel 4 (with pestilence and sword in Ezekiel 5); the slain by the altars follow in Ezekiel 6, the loosing of wrath on the four corners of the earth in Ezekiel 7, the sealing of the foreheads of the faithful in Ezekiel 8–9, the scattering of burning coals and of fire from heaven in Ezekiel 10; the resurrection in Ezekiel 37, the war of Gog and Magog in Ezekiel 38, the mountain-vision of the walls of the new Temple in Ezekiel 40, the divine presence like the sound of many waters in Ezekiel 43, and the name of the city in Ezekiel 48, the last verse of the book. It is not hard to suggest reasons why other Ezekiel chapters (the sealing of the saints, the eating of the scroll, the laments of the mariners etc.) have been taken out of order; but our twelve passages that fit the sub-division of the book and the general parallelism of development from the throne-vision to the New City vision in the two works cannot fail to strike us as remarkable. So Farrer's work on Revelation seems to me to be seminal from beginning to end: his discarded continuous Ezekiel theory no less than his festal calendar theory and his final zodiacal year theory. There is truth in them all.

It was no accident that *A Study in St Mark* followed hard on the heels of *A Rebirth of Images*. The development of symbolism in the Apocalypse suggested the same possibility for Mark, and Farrer's ideas for the Gospel were formed within a year of his publication on Revelation. *A Study in St Mark* was in fact written at an enormous rate. He began it soon after the Korean War broke out in the autumn of 1950, and he finished it in a little over three months, in February 1951. It was 398 pages in the edition which Dacre Press produced, almost faultlessly, in the same year. Although he recanted some of the formal parallels he drew in the *Study*, and changed the details of his exposition of the feeding stories and other matters, his central approach to Mark was unchanged in the two editions of *St Matthew and St Mark*; and his posthumous *St Mark's Materials* resumes some of the positions of the *Study*, for example the tribal symbolism. He had little cause to repent his haste.

In 1950 Mark was widely viewed as a simple transcriber of tradition. The flood-tide of form criticism, having washed away the nineteenth-century illusion of a chronologically ordered biography of Jesus, seemed to leave the gospel paragraphs as so many independent rocks strewn by natural force along the shore. Mark as an evangelist was of little interest; he had merely taken the rocks as he had found them and linked them together in his crude style. Farrer remarked with justice that Mark's style was no indication of simplicity of mind and that the absence of chronological ordering did not preclude some other kind of ordering. There seemed to be some sort of symbolic ordering in Daniel and the Pseudepigrapha, and this was a plausible model for Mark; if it seemed to be there, then the study of the parts must wait on the study of the whole. What one must do with Mark was what one did with the late biblical and post-biblical works, count.

Farrer saw as basic to Marcan thinking the symbol of the twelve tribes of Israel to whom Christ was sent with a thirteenth, the gentiles, to whom God's grace had extended the mission. Mark described two or three general scenes of healing, but there were twelve individual Israelites healed in the Gospel, together with one Gentile, the Syro-Phoenician woman's daughter. The twelve Israelites ended, as many had seen, with a kind of symbolic climax: a deaf stammerer and a blind man at Bethsaida, both healed in private, both with spittle, both gradually; then a deaf-and-dumb boy and blind Bartimaeus, both healed publicly, immediately and with a word. Farrer noted that Mark began with a string of healings: a demoniac in a synagogue, Simon's mother-in-law, a leper, a paralytic, soon succeeded by a man with a withered hand. Then after two chapters there was a further series of healings which seemed to echo the first group: a demoniac in the tombs, shouting out almost the same words as the demoniac in the synagogue; Jairus's daughter raised from death, following Simon's mother-in-law raised from her sickbed; a woman with sexual flux, as described in Leviticus 15, following the leper to whom Christ cited the law in Leviticus 14. So Mark's twelve Israelites do not look like a casual string whose total might or might not be significant: they seem to be a carefully ordered series, two fives and an extra two: demoniac, sick woman, leper, paralytic, withered hand; demoniac, girl in deathbed, unclean flux, deaf-and-dumb, blind; deaf-and-dumb, blind. The last two members of the first series, the paralytic and the withered hand, are afflicted in the two organs of action, legs and hand; and legs and hand form a climax with the two later healings of the two organs of sense, ears and eyes. Mark himself gives the climax elsewhere: 'If thine hand offend thee . . . If thy foot . . . If thine eye . . .' When the twelfth Israelite, Bartimaeus, is healed at the end of Mark 10, the Evangelist brings Jesus into Jerusalem for his Passion (11–16). The series of healings occupies the whole of the pre-Jerusalem ministry from the scene in the synagogue in chapter 1.

Mark has chosen twelve healings out of a larger stock, to symbolize Christ's coming to heal the whole of Israel. They are representative. But Jesus showed that he had in mind to bring all Israel to salvation also by choosing twelve Apostles, whom he called. Mark begins the Gospel by taking the healings step by step alongside the callings. After his baptism and temptation Jesus calls two pairs of brothers, Peter and Andrew, James and John (1.16–20): then he heals two pairs of sufferers, the demoniac and Simon's mother-in-law on the same day; then, after a brief intermission, the leper and the paralytic. Then he calls a fifth man, Levi the son of Alphaeus; and then he heals a fifth man, the one with the withered hand. It would be pedantic and unhistorical to string out all the callings in this way, but the Twelve are called and named after the first succession of healings, in chapter 3, and they are sent on mission after the second succession of healings in chapter 6. Furthermore, Mark has again given us a twelve-plus-one pattern, for Levi is called exactly like the first four, but he is not one of the Twelve. Just as there were twelve sons of Jacob but thirteen tribes (because Joseph subdivided into Ephraim and Manasseh), twelve landed tribes and the priestly tribe of Levi; so has Christ called twelve apostles and a supernumerary Levi. Mark stresses the equivalence of healings and callings at the scene in Levi's house

'Those who are well have no need of a physician, but those who are *sick*; I came not to *call* the righteous but sinners.'

The twelve-plus-one symbolism recurs a third time in the numbers of the feeding miracles; these seem to be stressed in the conversation in the boat in Mark 8, when Jesus recalls them to the Twelve and then asks 'Do you not yet understand?' At the first feeding there were five loaves broken, at the second seven, so twelve loaves in all are distributed among the thousands of Israel. Between the two feedings the gentile woman's daughter is healed, and the healing is compared by Christ to bread: 'It is not right to take the children's bread and throw it to dogs.' But she replies that the dogs eat the crumbs from the children's table; so the recurrence of bread and baskets full of crumbs in the next chapter seems to imply some symbolizing of the feeding of the gentiles with the bread of the Eucharist, no less than their calling to salvation. Farrer always thought that the two feedings in some way symbolized the feeding of Israel and the gentiles with the bread of Christ's body. In the *Study* he thought that the first feeding, on the west side of the lake, stood for Israel, only partly fed now, but with twelve creels of crumbs for the future; while the second feeding, apparently in Decapolis, stood for the gentiles. However, since Mark's symbolism, if there, is not at all clear from his geography, Farrer took a more complex view in *St Matthew and St Mark*: the gentiles' bread is there seen as being partly represented in the one loaf which the disciples had with them in the boat, and partly in the difference between the creel (*kophinos*), which he took to be a large basket, and the *spyris*, which he took to be a smaller basket. There were five thousand in the first feeding because they went with five loaves, and the five loaves were drawn from David's taking five loaves of the twelve shewbread loaves in 1 Samuel 21; there were four thousand in the second feeding because there had been five healings in the first group and then four of the second five up to the time of the four thousand. The four thousand still seemed to lack a convincing solution, and at the end of his life Farrer moved over to the idea that four was the better half of seven – the measure you give is the measure you get, and more: after the first five thousand there are still seven thousand to be fed – only half come, but the divine bounty feeds them with the seven loaves provided, and seven basketfuls of crumbs besides.

The reviews of the *Study* varied from Noel Davey's mildly

enthusiastic reception in *Journal of Theological Studies* to a contemptuous dismissal by R. P. Casey in *Theology*, but the general tone was sceptical. Farrer turned to ask whether Matthew, in his reshaping of Mark, might show any sign of familiarity with the symbolic schemes he had outlined. If Matthew simply ignored the schemes the evidence would be against them, for Matthew was Mark's first interpreter and more likely to have understood him than Farrer. If Matthew simply copied Mark's order, there would be no indication either way. But in fact Matthew does rewrite Mark's arrangement and in such a way that Farrer was able to claim that he had understood, and reproduced in variant form, the symbolism of the healings. Matthew's characteristic editorial function is to collect similar material together in a kind of tractate, and in place of the healings strung out over the length of Mark 1–10 we find them concentrated in Matthew 8–9; ten Israelites and one gentile healed; with two additional Israelites after the sending of the Apostles and the Rejection discourse in Matthew 12. The healings in chapters 8–9 are themselves divided into two groups separated by the call of Matthew; and the two groups each comprise five Israelites in a parallel series, just as in Mark. Matthew's first group opens with the leper, his second with the woman with flux (Mark's pair of Levitically unclean sufferers); then comes Simon's mother-in-law, paired with Jairus's daughter, two females raised from bed; then two demoniacs shouting in the tombs, paired with two blind men shouting in the road. The paralytic closes the first five, a dumb demoniac the second: both healings, unlike the earlier ones, raise hostile criticism and so look forward to the withered hand and the deaf, dumb, blind demoniac, the two most controversial healings of all in chapter 12. Matthew thus has twelve Israelites and the centurion's boy healed in his 'healing section', with the sending of the Twelve to the lost sheep of the house of Israel between. There are three further healings which are anchored to later Gospel situations, the Canaanite woman's daughter, the possessed boy after the transfiguration, and the blind man at Jericho; but although this brings the total of healed people to seventeen in all, Matthew has so arranged matters that several of them are healed two at a time. In all there remain twelve *healings* of specified Israelites and two healings of gentiles, the centurion's son and the Canaanite's daughter.

What are we to make of this mass of highly attractive patterning? Well, the first thing must be to confess that much of it is quite implausible. When we say that in reading books like Daniel and Enoch we need to count, two quite different things may be meant. In the Son of Man vision in Daniel 7, or the apocalypse of weeks in Enoch 93, we do need to count, and the counting is done for us in the text so that we do not miss it. When, however, Farrer does the counting in Daniel and produces a neat analysis of the book in dreams and visions, this may or may not be right and it must suffice to show that it is not obviously right, that no one has ever made his analysis before. But Mark does not do the counting for us, and in Mark also the analysis is Farrer's original finding. So the apocalyptic writings do not really provide the parallel we need for saying that it was natural for ancient Jews to count such features as healings as they read a sacred book. Perhaps a better analogy might be the miracles of Elijah and Elisha which are confessedly the model for a number of the evangelists' healing stories: it has been credibly argued that Kings ascribes seven wonders to Elijah and fourteen to Elisha who inherited a double portion of his master's spirit.

Secondly, Farrer drew far too black-and-white a division between the standard picture of Mark as editor and his own view of Mark as author. Ancient authors were more tied by tradition than modern ones, and ancient editors (*darshanim*) more free than modern ones. This comes out clearly in the discussion of the feeding numbers which tied him in such knots: for where there are many theories and none satisfy, the likelihood is that the assumption is wrong – here the assumption that Mark is the complete master of his material to write *kophinoi* or *spyrides*, four or seven, as he thought fit. Perhaps a midway view should be ventured to illustrate that both Farrer and the older view have some share of the truth. Space limits me to a single example. The feeding stories have both been shaped to some considerable degree by the tale of Elisha multiplying twenty barley loaves and cakes (*palathas* in the Greek) at Gilgal (2 Kings 4.41–4 in the Septuagint/LXX version, which Mark is using): a dependence well known to Farrer. Elisha said, 'Give to the people and let them eat'; with the five thousand Jesus said, 'You give them something to eat': with the four thousand Jesus had compassion on the crowd because they had been with him three days and had nothing to eat, and he hints that the disciples feed them. Elisha's servant replies, 'Why should I set this before a hundred men?'; with the five thousand Jesus's disciples reply, 'Shall we go and buy two-hundred-denarii-worth of bread and give it to them to eat?'; with the four thousand they say, 'How can one feed these men with bread here in the desert?' Elisha continues, 'Give to the people and let them eat, for thus says the Lord, They shall eat and leave' – and they ate and left. In both the Gospel stories Jesus prays and the bread provided by his disciples is multiplied and the disciples set it before the people, and the crumbs left are taken up and counted.

Should we not look here first for the numbers as well as so many other details? Jesus was remembered as preaching to large crowds, more than a hundred: but rabbinic exegesis was often done *au pied de la lettre*. How many pieces of food did Elisha have? It says 'twenty loaves and cakes'. We should say, 'You cannot tell – twenty loaves and some cakes.' But if you wanted a number you could say, 'Perhaps it is like six knives and forks, or six eggs and bacon, or the dinner lady might tell the cook at a school, "Twenty meat and pudding".' So if one wanted a number in the Kings story one might say: 'Twenty loaves and twenty cakes, forty in all.' And how many men were there there? We should reply again, 'A hundred'. But it doesn't say so. It says that Gehazi said, 'Why should I set this (*touto*) before a hundred men?' He saith not 'these', as of many, but 'this' as of one. Gehazi plainly held up a loaf and said to Elisha, 'Why should I set this before a hundred men?' So there were a hundred times forty men, four thousand.

Could we solve the five thousand in a similar way? Well, as Farrer also remarks, there are two miraculous multipliers of food in Kings, Elijah as well as Elisha. Elijah only multiplies meal and oil for a widow and her son (1 Kings 17), but we are told that during the famine in Elijah's time Obadiah took a hundred prophets and hid them by fifties in a cave and fed them with bread; and it looks very much as if Mark's five thousand has been 'discovered' here. For Mark tells us that they sat down in groups, in hundreds and in fifties, and if one is on the look-out for a large crowd, fifty times a hundred is five thousand.

What does all this tell us? Well, it suggests that there are two feeding stories in the Gospel because there were two in Kings;

and this is confirmed by the presence of other stories in Mark close by that are plainly influenced by the Elijah saga – John's death like Elijah, as Herod's courtiers hint at 6.14f, Jesus passing by the disciples in the boat like God passing by Elijah at Horeb, the woman of Syrophoenicia and her child like Elijah's widow of Zarephath and her son, the transfiguration with Moses and Elijah. Second, it suggests that the story of the four thousand was composed first, on the model of Elisha's feeding, and that of the five thousand second, as assimilation of the four thousand to the famine feeding. We note that the five thousand story is verbally closer both to Gehazi's words and to the story of the Eucharist in Mark, both signs of further development, and perhaps by Mark himself. So in part the Form Critics will be right: the stories are doublets, and at least the four thousand will have come to Mark in the tradition. But Farrer is also right in seeing the typological nature of the development and surely, in part, over the numbers and the meaning of the symbolism too. Once you have two feedings with five thousand and four thousand, it is a short step to number the loaves as in 2 Kings 4. Five loaves sounds right for five thousands and the crumbs will symbolize what remains ultimately in eucharistic bread for the twelve tribes of God's Israel, the Church, twelve basketfuls. Five loaves out of the traditional twelve shewbread loaves leaves seven for the second feeding, and seven baskets seem natural from seven loaves. So the standard view is partly right, and Farrer is much more right in his use of the typological Elisha story, the shewbread reference, in seeing that the numbers are significant and in getting the main drift of the symbolism right.

Was he right also about the twelve-plus-one healings and callings? I do not know. Other explanations have been proposed since his death which would account for many of the phenomena; but parts of his scheme seem to me to remain the best available, for example the changed order of the Matthaean healings. Overall it can be said that the pattern he proposed remains very impressive and that if it is wrong it is a massive coincidence. But in the long run what is important is not whether a new theory is right in its details but whether it has within it the seeds of truth; and for this it is needful that the work be done not only with integrity, the scholar's foundation, and learning, a sometimes over-valued virtue, but with sympathy and imagination, uncommon gifts which Farrer possessed to an uncommon degree. I have tried in this essay to give some instances in which I think his work was right, for example over Q, and the calendrical basis of the Apocalypse. There are many more for which there has not been space, like his analysis of the Sermon on the Mount. But even when I must think that he was wrong, I almost always find him illuminating. His integrity was rock-solid; his knowledge of the Greek texts of the Bible was redoubtable; and he had the sensitivity and imagination to feel his way into how first-century men may have thought. Like St Paul, he looked into the glass of vision and some of what he saw he saw darkly; but in part also he understood, and the knowledge he gained, like his charity, will not pass away.

# CHAPTER 12

## *The Doctor of Divinity*

\*

'I am', said Farrer, 'distracted; a philosopher, a student of the gospels; an expositor of doctrine in our terribly weak Church; and I do what I can by preaching and pious working to crumble the bread of Truth for the people.'[1] He wrote no systematic treatise on theology apart from the brief but superb statement in *Saving Belief* (1964). The main source is his sermons, collected in *Said or Sung* (1960), *A Celebration of Faith* (1970), *The End of Man* (1973) and *The Brink of Mystery* (1976). In these sources, as indeed in his other writings, four great themes stand out as central to Farrer's theological thinking and teaching: four cardinal doctrines of his Catholic faith, the Trinity, Incarnation, Redemption and Resurrection. Trinitarian religion was the heart of Farrer's devotion. At the end of every sermon – more particularly the Bampton Lectures – there is the mounting excitement of waiting to see how eloquently the final words of praise to the Triune God will be phrased. His own statement of his trinitarian belief is most simply expressed in *Saving Belief* (pp. 63–8), which may be summarized thus:

To believe that there are in God truly loving relations, independent of God's relation to his creation, is vital to a true belief in the trancendence of God: otherwise we shall find ourselves saying that God's love needs the world to find an object of love, possibly even that the loving nature of God is enhanced by having a world to love: and then God's creation will be no more a matter of grace but of need and there will be an end of sound theology. He suggests that we have used, all along, our personal being as the clue to God's being and that our personal being is that of persons in society, thinking and loving. This discourse between persons is the only clue we have: 'If God is to be God, the Godhead must be at once more perfectly one than any one of us (for we are mutually external) and also allow a mutual love more outgoing that is found in any two of us.' We might have reached this concluson: in fact it took the impact of the Divine Son to make us acknowledge the Father and Son in spiritual relations. The trinitarian doctrine is essential if God is to be God.

We would give much to have from his pen a treatise on the incarnation of God in Christ. Instead we have superb and scattered sentences like, 'He began to do divine things humanly'. But again we can find a brief expression of his thought in *Saving Belief* (pp. 78–82). In one of his sermons he had remarked how those called Sons of God in the Graeco-Roman world, like the deified Roman emperors, were held to be great in their own right, as Augustus who by his wisdom inaugurated a Golden Age restoring peace and so earned heaven, whereas the divinity of Christ lies in his working of his Father's will. He has nothing but what the Father gives and does nothing but what the Father wills. In writing of the incarnation the year before the Deems Lectures he uses this basic theme.

The action of Jesus is at once human and divine. All created energies make their own patterns and are sustained by God: Christ is the pre-eminent instance, since in him the personality of God shines as it does not in the electron and the tree.

> Christ like the sun, casts light on every part. As we know in personal life, the nearest image of God in the created world, that God does not remove but enhances the freedom of his creatures, so we believe that Jesus is both more human and more fully himself than any man: Who more spontaneous in his compassion, more frank in his indignation and more immediate in his decision. We have scarcely any record of his inner thoughts: we do not need it: inner and outer with him are one.

The entire humanity of Jesus means that his life story, if we could fill the gaps, would be a piece of historical biography: we would see him as a man of his time.

> It is often said that the traditional interpretation of Christ's person was distorted by pagan Greek philosophy. This is so little true as to be on balance misleading and virtually false. The ancient and medieval conception of Christ's person was not poisoned by philosophy; it was starved by a lack of historical sense. Those ages saw him too much in the colourless abstraction of a man-in-general

. . . We see him as a Galilean villager of the first century. The tools of his thinking came from the local stock, only he made a divinely perfect use of them. The Jewish ideas he inherited, broken and reshaped in the course of his life, served him for mental coinage in the traffic of his unique sonship to his Father, and his assertion of God's Kingdom over mankind. He had what he needed to be the Son of God; as for defining the divine sonship, that was a task for other hands, using other tools; the Apostles began a theology of his person and the Fathers continued it.[2]

The third theme is redemption – what would be normally called the Doctrine of the Atonement.[3] Our wills are in opposition to the Divine Will: how is our reconciliation achieved? Theologians will say that the work achieved by Christ's death is a mystery for which the scriptures offer parables, none of which is adequate; we must take what we can from them, and so learn it. But

in the saving Incarnation God came all lengths to meet us, and dealt humanly with human creatures. If ever he made his ways plain, it was there. The variety of parables express the love that went into the redemption, or the blessings that flow from it. They are not needed to state that thing that was done. What, then, did God do for his people's redemption? He came among them, bringing his Kingdom, and he let events take their human course. He set the divine life in human neighbourhood. Men discovered it in struggling with it and were captured by it in crucifying it. What could be simpler? And what more divine?[4]

Christ's work began from this parable of kingship. Those who heard him hoped that, as Persians, Greeks, and Romans had successively held the empire of the world, the people of God would hold it. 'The hope was crucified at Calvary, it rose transfigured from the Easter sepulchre.' If men can be partakers of a kingdom, they can more literally be associated with the Godhead; we have in us that which allows us to hope such a blessing. For the true marks of a man, to love and to think, are in a manner both divine and infinite. Thought can hope to think things as they are, not as they affect the thinker. Love can care for God's creation as God made it to be, not for personal interest or attachment. We cannot think God's thoughts or have God's love as God. But if he descends to think his thoughts

215

and love his loves as man, in the human form, through word, image and feeling, then we can be associated with divine activity. The parable will be fulfilled; we shall be made sharers in the divine kingship. The divine life is of its nature communicable. In the blessed Trinity is already the society of his own life and there is the love of the Father and the Son into which the Son may bring us by living as man, and making us the partners of his life.

Farrer goes on to consider those modes of speech about the Atonement which are commonly used among Evangelicals, in each case extracting the pearl of truth from the conclusions drawn from it which he considered misleading because the parabolic nature of the concepts is taken not only seriously but also literally. What then is to be said of those accounts of the matter which have scriptural authority and are particularly dear to hymn writers? For example, those who say that Christ paid the price of sin. Are we in debt to the law of justice? Is our debt infinite so that we can never clear it? Did the Divine Son therefore take our place, undergo our punishment, and pay our score? These are parables – taken literally they become monstrous. There is no Heavenly Bank of Justice and if we personify the Bank as God we turn metaphor into blasphemy. Nor will debt do – we do not in that sense owe anything to God – for before he made us we were not here to borrow: we owe our existence to God in the sense that he gave it to us. But the parables are good parables: the great merit of parables is to convey passion or lay on moral colour.

What truth then do the parables contain? 'There was no other good enough to pay the price of sin.' We do not commonly think there is anything more costly than death; not anyhow for a man in the early prime of his life. It must be admitted that what he won, he won *at* a price, not *by* a price – no payment is made to anyone: nothing is in that sense owed: but the mountain rescuer risks his life on the hills to bring in those who stray foolishly. Is there a sense in which the redeemer stands in for the person he redeems? The prisoner owes the debt: his deliverer pays it. In a human quarrel the offended party may make the first approaches. The father may persevere against arrogance until his son repents: has he not stood in for his son and done what the lad ought to have done? The Gospel story indeed outruns the parable; the divine Son's approach was not only rejected but he was killed by those who said that they represented God's justice. Well then, 'to pay the price of sin' – what does it cost to reconcile sinners with their creator's will? 'Not the serving of a sentence in some supernatural Dartmoor', but the abandonment of our pride and folly, and those costs are not remitted to us: we have them to do; only Christ's initiative sets us in motion.

But there is still more in the parable of the debt paid. The blood-shedding of Jesus was the price of our forgiveness. What do we make of that without the theory of a debt to the Bank of Justice? If there is no score to be cleared before God can forgive, surely he forgives in any case without needing to send Christ? God does not make mere gestures. God does not scratch out entries in a ledger. He acts. He has no grudges to set aside. In a man, forgiving is an attitude; reconciling is the subsequent action. In God action and attitude are one. He comes among us and forgives in reconciling. Christ's death is the price of forgiveness as it is the expression of forgiveness. And still there is no need for the Bank of Justice. Even those who are not yet reconciled to the will of God are forgiven. God's act is the whole purpose working through Christ, through the Spirit and the Church, to the reconciliation of the reconciled in this world or in a world to come. And of this Christ's blood is the cost – in the sense that the divine action reaches its peak in the death and continues from there. But we do not read the story of the cross to make theological deductions. We work out our theology that we may rightly read the story of the cross.

The fourth major theme is that of heaven and hell and the resurrection of Christ and men. 'We will not try', Farrer characteristically observed, 'to vindicate divine providence without reference to the hope of eternal life.'

In chapter 6 of *Saving Belief* he sums up a dialogue about heaven in four 'principles',

1. To hope for heaven is not selfish. No one ever thought he could keep heaven for himself.

2. Heaven is not a cash payment for walking with God: it is where the road goes.

3. Heaven is not an optional extra; our belief is nonsense without it.

217

4. Our reason for believing it is not that nature points to it, but that it leads us to itself; it is a new creation.

Therefore the Christian need not try to isolate a piece of himself called soul, naturally endowed to outlast the body's collapse. Our immortality is the new gift of God, not the survival of our old nature. It was the Greeks who thought the human soul a detached fragment of the Godhead. God alone can give us a future. Belief in resurrection is belief in God who raises us. *It is the acid test of belief in God.* 'A God who raises the dead is a real power: not just a fanciful name for the order of nature, physical or moral. A God so identified with the natural order that he adds nothing to it is difficult to distinguish from the world he makes or from the laws which govern it.'

There is a second consequence; if the heavenly is what God bestows, not what nature produces, our ideas of heaven are bound to be ideas of a relation to God, but cannot only be that: the citizens of heaven must have some way of being which is proper to them, only we do not know what it is. Our future self must bear some relation to our present self or it will not be ours and we may speculate from what we now experience as a foretaste. It is not silly to say, 'Every now and then I manage to be at the disposal of God's will. How marvellous to be in heaven. I shall live in it all the time.' Nor is it silly to say, 'From time to time I think I catch a glimpse of what God is doing. How marvellous to be in heaven! I shall see his purposes in everything as clearly as I read my friends' purposes in their faces.' Nor is it silly to say, 'Every now and then I see a bit of what God has put into the people round me: how marvellous to be in heaven. I shall see it all.' Nor is it silly to say, 'I acknowledge Christ by faith and bless him in words for being very God and very man. How marvellous to be in heaven: I shall be familiar with the man in whom Godhead is.' These speculations are based on joys of which we have a foretaste in this life: they are joys which arise from a relation with realities, with God and his children. They are joys which might be actualized under a variety of states of being. 'Our faith in heaven is a confidence in the pattern of perfect relations: as for the state of being we can leave it to God.'

We often say that heaven is the presence of God – which is true if we mean that the presence of God makes heaven heavenly; and nonsense if it means that the presence of God defines a region or condition. There is no God-space and no God-state where God is and other things can lodge. God is his own world of being: nothing else exists unless God creates its level, not in his world nor on his level. So if heaven exists, it exists by God's creation and he upholds the real beings of whom heaven is made, and he ordains the pattern of their relations. For God is everywhere by his activity and will. Nothing would be if he were not with it, willing and upholding it. Sometimes, indeed, he works more richly and revealingly: we could say he is more present in man than in beasts, in saints than in Laodiceans, in heaven than on earth. Heaven then is a created sphere where God bestows his presence by action: but can we sensibly ask where it is? If it is non-spatial, we feel the heavenly life would be featureless – a shapeless ecstasy – and if it has any spatial dimension it falls somewhere in the field of space: an astronaut might reach it; it is part of the perishable universe.

So we feel if our physics is Newton's. But try Einstein. Then space is not an infinite area where lots of matter floats about. It is a web of interaction between energies which form a system by their interacting. Unless the energies of heaven are such as to interact physically with the energies of our physical world, heaven can be as dimensional as it likes without getting pulled into our spatial field. There may indeed be non-physical contacts between earthly and heavenly minds: but that's another story.

So whatever we think of heavenly dimensions, heaven is a sphere of created being where God bestows his presence by a more visible providence, making the whole order the evident expression of goodness, by a more abundant grace making the hearts of his people more open to his love, and by an incarnate presence in the glorified man, Jesus Christ. We come to Farrer's most solemn words, 'Christ in glory is the heart of heaven,' and it is difficult to see how those Christians who leave the life to come an open question can be Christians at all. If Christ is not now in glory, then this is a Christless world and God is a Christless God and we are Christless men. 'Those who say heaven is nothing to us now, but an optional hope, may say the same of Christ.'

By communion with the risen Christ even in this world we begin to share in his spiritual state. This annexing of an earthly fellowship, like an outlying province to the heavenly state, was begun when Christ visited his surviving friends. Nothing like it has happened again or can happen: that the heart of heavenly being should visit earth to leave on earthly senses the stamp of heavenly substance. The resurrection can be classed with no other event, as God can be classed with no other being.

So with great originality Farrer avoided platitude and stated this powerful doctrine. Why, we may ask, though, should any one believe in the life to come? Because God has promised it, is the reply. The promise is not a matter of finding texts: it is a rope of several strands which belong together, mutually supporting one another – if we believe in God. First there is the promise which lies in our nature: what can a creator mean by bringing into existence a creature capable of immortal hope and of a voluntary attachment to his creator? The second strand is the teaching of Christ: he did not only make his own the hope of a future life beginning to dawn in Israel. He wagered his existence on it and accepted an early death as the gate to a Kingdom where he would rule God's people. The third strand is the evidence that his hope was fulfilled: the resurrection. His body was not found: his friends could not use it as a relic, nor his enemies use it to disprove the Gospel. By his visitation he convinced his disciples that he had laid the cornerstone of heaven. The fourth strand is the possibility which Christians find of relation to a living Christ in sacraments and prayer. The fifth strand is the direction of such life in the Spirit as God gives us. If it is real, how can the end be unreal to which it tends . . . ?

The strands belong together. The Gospel facts would not convince us if they found no echo in our present experience. Experience would not convince us if it found no foundation in the created nature of man.

A difficulty remains. Christ spoke with the mental furniture of a Galilean rabbi. Some would distinguish the core of the teaching from the period trappings. Where, on which side of the line does the teaching about the eternal hope lie? Was not the essential the proclamation of the Kingdom to be embodied in a fellowship beyond national boundaries? He did indeed teach a life to come like the Pharisees of his day: but their idea was connected with historical prediction not visibly fulfilled.

We say that the line is artificial. The mission depends on the opening of God's kingdom. How is the Father's will to be done s that his creatures attain their true happiness? The offer of the Kingdom is a present offer, its achievement is to be future, brought about by a change divine and mysterious. The road to the future is spoken of under ancient Jewish symbols; but it is opened up by the death and resurrection. The disciples had still to learn what their path would be: Jerusalem fell and yet the age did not end. The road runs on, 'but none who walk it have far to go before they meet their saviour and their judge'.

And what of those who reject the Kingdom? Perhaps no persuasion of divine love will reconcile the rebel. He will not have everlasting bliss. But may he not be dropped out of existence? We can at least say that the teaching of Christ and the nature of our free will all suggest that the loss of heaven is a real danger. Christ teaches that men whose moral misery is hidden from them by comfort and pride will be a prey to that flame 'which can surely be nothing but the scorching truth'. He speaks of the flame as everlasting: 'but cannot everlasting mercy save from everlasting fire?'

> Looking to myself and the hopes a Christian dares entertain I find conscience and moral reason join forces with Catholic teaching and forbid me to claim exemption from the burning of that flame. Perhaps before we suffer it, we may be assured of mercy: perhaps the light of mercy will make the torment when we see what a God we have and how we have served him; what wounds we have inflicted on the souls of our fellows by our egotism and neglect.

Finally Farrer argued the reasonableness of this belief. What is the relation between Christian discipleship in this world and salvation hereafter? Heaven cannot be for Christians only: and their position there cannot be one of privilege. But if 'the Christian road is not the beaten track to heaven, we make the whole Christian effort an irrelevance'. No doubt those who never knew Christ are reconciled by Christ in glory; the parable of the sheep and the goats shows Christ receiving into bliss those who in succouring the wretched did not know that they were ministering to Christ. Yet what then is the Church for if men can be saved without a knowledge of Christ in this life? The mercy of God desires to redeem as many souls as may be redeemed in this present existence. The divine society must really be built upon earth out of earthly materials. If it exists it can welcome multitudes from outside; otherwise there would be no communion into which they might go, since heaven is essentially its citizens, not its pavements or its bulwarks: heaven without Christ would not be heaven: but the Christ without his friends would not be heaven either. Christ's continued life is a life in relation with those he left on earth, from whom the mystical body is built up to welcome all. Then the moving concluding sentence, 'If those who know Christ in this life begin to complain because multitudes, who do not, will one day be made equal to them, we know what Christ thinks of their attitude: it was one of his themes when he walked in Galilee and taught his companions by his parables.'

Farrer began life as a Baptist and ended as a Catholic of the Anglican sort: and between the two he saw no opposition that was basic. It is fitting to end this section with some words from *Saving Belief* in which he explodes the common supposition that the Catholic and Reformed positions are eternally divided and opposed.

> It is often said that there is a tension, if not a contradiction between two expressions of our faith, one in terms of incorporation with Christ's body, the other in terms of reconciliation through his death. The incorporation theology is Catholic and sacramental, the reconciliation theology is Protestant and personal. That Catholics and Protestants have quarrelled is as undeniable as it is tragic. But so far from there being a natural tension between incorporation and atonement, each needs the other and without the other neither makes sense. Christ did not come to get himself killed: he was not a suicide, he came to associate his people with divine life, and they killed him for doing this. By so dying he reconciled sinful wills to God, and made their incorporation in his mystical body a real possibility.[5]

Before he went to Keble there was a tentative suggestion that Farrer might be appointed to the Chair of Moral Theology (see chapter 8). Yet he did not write often about moral theology as such. The most moving and direct statements about Christian duty and virtue are to be found throughout his sermons, particularly in *The End of Man* where it seems as if maturity had simplified his mind and his approach and the voice of duty and love is heard with compelling force. On two occasions he wrote more formally on the topic, possibly in response to specific requests because, though well worth reading, the pieces somehow lack the sparkle and imaginative power of his other writings. One is an article, 'The Christian Doctrine of Man', in volume 2 of the collected volumes of the 1937 Oxford Conference on Church, Community and State.[6] The other is an article on 'The Theology of Morals' in the May 1939 issue of *Theology* – again part of a series on the theological task, which marked the beginning of Vidler's editorship.

The discussion in *Theology* has some prophetic overtones, dealing as it does with themes that would later come into prominence. Moral theology professes to repose on what human nature is, and we must ask first if this is a valid concept. Is man in any sense a separate species, or does an endlessly changing biological process so mould him that what was once true no longer applies? If that were so, if it were a case of man today and superman tomorrow there would be no work for moral theology to do. In fact we know that the biological process produces relatively static types: the theme of human nature is constant, though the variations are endless. It becomes then a task to distinguish what belongs to true mankind, and what changes are due to the legitimate variation of cultures. Paul's views on women are those of a Jew of his time: but what of the institution of the family? Is that an institution we have outgrown or a permanent pattern of good? How in fact are we to realize the true humanity restored by grace: do we consult the scriptures alone or the human conscience alone? If Christ restores the moral sense or reason, our only authority can be the conscience brought into harmony with the mind of Christ.

The task of knowing the truth is co-operative: we look for it in the Body of Christ, since Christ promised the Spirit's leading. We may need to make interim decisions; we may make mistakes. Christ has promised that his Church shall not fail and that the Spirit shall lead her into the full truth, but we do not find that he has guaranteed her against falling into false conclusions on the way or promised oracular certainty on every question as soon as it is raised. Where there is a settled tradition, it is a Christian duty to obey: it is not a duty to stop thinking until a surer conclusion is reached.

So as circumstances change we have to ask if duties change: has warfare so changed since medieval times that it is now an unthinkable evil? What is it our duty to think about contracep-

tion in an over-populated world, not to mention an over-populated island? There is the danger of Pharisaism in clinging to the
detailed settlements of the past, and the danger in reaction of a
fetishistic attachment to the text of scripture.

Moral theology gives us rules and precepts, and principles for
their application. The Pharisees were wrong, not in trying to
work out the application of these principles, but in allowing a
detailed system to make them moral pedants, obscuring the real
situation instead of illuminating it. We are now strong in
principles of application but weak in positive law. Some positive
precepts belong to man as man: about this there is no perplexity
in Christian minds. But we are baffled by the duties of man in a
changing environment – whether the case of contraception
has altered since St Thomas pronounced against *venena
sterilitatis* – whether we say so much the worse for his maxim
or so much the worse for our culture: and how are Christians to
behave in this culture till it can be amended? When is
capitalism not the sin of usury? What is a reasonable standard
of life and where does criminal luxury begin?

In the sermons, some twenty years later than the *Theology*
discussion, the commands for the Christian life are derived
straight from the completeness of his theology and the
language is sharp and compelling. The moral philosophers of
the time were writing about the use of language, mostly
propounding the view that moral words suggest our attitudes
to proposed courses of action – attitudes of approval or disapproval, but never quite clear about the grounds of such
approval. In general they would vote for kindness and against
cruelty, but quite how good differed from evil somehow escaped
them and 'sin', being a theological word, was not in their
vocabulary. For Farrer the moral word is 'claim'. He sees duty
founded on fact, on the claims of the neighbour who calls to us
by being there and by being there as the representative of
Christ. So over and over again he comes back to his favourite
example. There is Dives the rich man and there is Lazarus
sitting at his gate. There is good leading to eternal joy and evil
leading to eternal loss. As he grew older, his sermons grew
simpler. There is stronger emphasis on the neglected and
unpopular duties – the duty of the undergraduate to work, to
write to his parents, to help his friends, to stick to his Christian
discipline in the dark days. And over and over again there are

the brilliant sketches of his life, his parents, his friends, to illuminate the Christian duties of all. There is, too, the devastating dismissal of the casual propaganda of the sixties – which dismissed moral rules and considered the 'situation'. All moral philosophers knew that rules have exceptions: that sometimes we can only choose the least evil: should Joseph have refused Potiphar's wife and left the poor woman a prey to her inhibitions and frustrations? Such speculations, said Farrer, had better be published in Latin or some other learned language, so that the youth of our ancient universities might not be led astray. Behind all his ethical teaching there lay the strong conviction of man's eternal destiny and he would not dream of discussing God's providence or indeed of giving moral precepts if he did not see man as destined to inherit God's Kingdom.

# CHAPTER 13

# *Conclusion*[1]

\*

Farrer came into Anglicanism in the years when Oxford liberal high Anglicanism (*Essays Catholic and Critical*) was in the ascendant. It was a generation which took thinking seriously. They were more like Frenchmen than Germans: they admired and were influenced by the clarity of French Catholic thought with Dominicans, like Sertillanges and Garrigou-Lagrange, at the head and lay philosophers like Maritain and Gilson, re-establishing the respectability of scholastic thought. Farrer was sometimes described as a 'neo-scholastic'. The title is only true in the sense that he believed in the importance of the intellect as well as the will and the affections. This did not mean academic sterility, simply that intelligence had pride of place.

By 1927 idealism was waning, and in Oxford logical positivism was still in the future. The Oxford thinker from whom he derived much inspiration was R. G. Collingwood, like Farrer very much a 'lone wolf'. Both were against the fashionable thinking of their day and both felt that they had a cause to defend. They were both fighters: in the end, Collingwood tells us in his autobiography, he felt that the logical positivism of his later years entailed ethical anarchy; Farrer felt that he was the defender of the metaphysical tradition interpreted in his own way. His points of difference with the popular orthodoxy both in philosophy and in theology are stated with a remarkable clarity in his concluding essay to the English translation of *Kerygma and Myth*.[2] After complimenting the essayists, he goes on to suggest their weaknesses, highlighting weaknesses which have haunted English theology ever since.

> We may usefully make certain distinctions between the refusals of the modern mind. We will classify them as necessary, accidental, lamentable, and factitious.
>
> 1. The established, or vitually established, positions of science and history give rise to *necessary* refusals, as when we refuse to

believe that the world was created eight thousand years ago, or that the sun stood physically still for Joshua.

2. The things which modern men happen not to pay attention to give rise to *accidental* refusals, in the case (for example) of industrial workers who have a blind eye for imagery based on the procedures of pre-scientific agriculture.

3. Accidental refusals become *lamentable* when they involve the atrophy of a spiritual function, for example, the sense for poetry.

4. *Factitious* refusals are those that arise from a philosophy or attitude that men either embrace or swallow – Communism, physical materialism, or economic utilitarianism . . .

   Our respect for factitious refusals is the respect of a physician for a disease: if he respects the fact, it is that he may overcome it. Lamentable refusals are likewise to be cured, so far as they admit of cure, by the cultivation of the atrophied function. Accidental refusals can be overcome by the imparting of information. About necessary refusals nothing can be done or ought to be done. They must be accepted . . . Angels above the blue and devils underground fitly frame the setting of man in the spiritual hierarchy, but execration will not reach the one or aeronautics the other.

He draws upon his own experience of prayer to speak of the true demythologizing:

When we proceed to live the promise out, the images are crucified by the reality, slowly and progressively, never completely and not always without pain. Yet the reality is better than the images. Jesus Christ clothed himself in all the images of the messianic promise, and in living them out crucified them. But the crucified reality is better than all the figures of prophecy. This is very God and life eternal, whereby the children of God are delivered from idols.

The essay in *Kerygma and Myth* was in fact a very powerful argument against the kind of loose thinking that says, 'Modern thought will not accept . . .' In his discussion of C. S. Lewis as an apologist he discloses also what his own task was:

It is commonly said that if rational argument is so seldom the cause of conviction, philosophical apologists must largely be wasting their shot. The premise is true but the conclusion does not follow. For though argument does not create conviction, the lack of it destroys belief. What seems to be proved may not be embraced; but what no one shows the ability to defend is quickly abandoned. Rational argument does not create belief; but it maintains a climate in which belief may flourish. Why even Butler's *Analogy* opened polished ears to the message of the Gospel. Yet no one can call the *Analogy* theophanic. There are no chinks in that unremitting continuity of prose through which celestial light shines!

After the first blast of his trumpet in *Finite and Infinite* he did not spend much time trying to talk with positivists. On the difficult frontier of philosophical theology he declined to do battle on his adversaries' ground; he built up his case using the most simple concepts of personal existence and decision in his own way.

Gordon Phillips has some interesting comments on the resemblance he detects between the earlier Wittgenstein and Farrer:

> My own enthusiasm for the early Wittgenstein and my conviction, long before it became so fashionable as to be almost unbearable, that what he said had important bearings on theology, was contemporary with my first meetings with Farrer. It would be hard to see at the outset any similarity between an Austrian engineer of mathematical bent working in the Cambridge of Moore and Russell and the witty classicist of Balliol. Yet in the last analysis, remove all the environmental differences and there is a remarkable similarity between them. There is the same quest for simplicity, the same distrust for books about books, a similar dialectical approach to truth, a common attraction to the questions which lie behind questions, a family likeness in respect for the mysterious nature of fundamental simplicities, a tendency on the part of both of them to tremble even in their most philosophical moments into what the world calls mysticism.
>
> Both were ready to correct the positions they first held in the light of further interior debate. Wittgenstein wrestled, alone sometimes, and occasionally with a handful of kindred spirits whom he deemed capable of understanding, with his puzzlements at ordinary language; Farrer conducted most of his debates with his own *alter ego* – that elusive man who is always there to say, 'Ah, you will say . . .,' so that we who read him are flattered to find ourselves endowed with so much wit and intelligence, to be credited with such remarkably able objections, or so much acumen as to agree with the resolution of the difficulty when proposed.
>
> The method is that of St Thomas Aquinas who in the *Summa*,

when he squares himself to tackle some terrible profundity, about the eternity of the world for instance, states his thesis, then lists all the objections to it he can think of (and quite a number no one but he could have thought of), then sets out his own position, marshals his authorities, and quietly disposes of the objectors in the light of the general position he has established. Austin was not in the strict sense a Thomist. He knew his way round the *Summa* and some of his best friends were Oxford Dominicans. But for him the Thomist tradition was just something in the mainstream of the history of that rational theology to which he dedicated his life: he did not use Thomist writings as a text from which to cull a Christian rabbinic lore. He operated on the same basic questions which exercised St Thomas as they must exercise any Christian intellectual and always as one who shared the same Christian thought-world as that great mediaeval writer. But it was the abiding Christian thought-world, not its Aristotelian or mediaeval setting which generated his philosophic zest.

(I'm not sure about Farrer's 'alter ego'. When he wrote in running dialogue form he was disputing opinions actually held, especially in *The Freedom of the Will*, though in characteristic fashion he does not name them. The same is true of St Thomas.)

'I am engaged', Farrer once said, while composing his Gifford Lectures, 'in the work of philosophy – combating sophistry with platitude': which perhaps gives us the final way of looking at his work. For by platitude he means looking and looking deeply at the realities of our human existence and building from them – the reality of the self, the reality of its aspirations, its possibility of attaining freedom and love. Platitudinous indeed, and therefore overlooked and therefore in need of continual restatement so that our vision may be refreshed.

The refreshment came partly from the style of the writing, the style which was the man: the man who was so concerned with the realities about which he wrote, that he did not consciously aim at style at all. It is the reflection of a mind which is not over-concerned with the topical which is the ephemeral, but is absorbed in what is really present when time and the eternal meet. The writer whom the critics accuse of over-subtlety achieves simplicity at a cost – the cost of the life-long work of thought and prayer. As C. S. Lewis said in a review, 'To talk to us thus Dr Farrer makes himself almost nothing, almost nobody; to be sure in the event his personality stands out from the pages as clearly as any author – but this is one of heaven's jokes – nothing makes a man so noticeable as vanishing!'

Now I must try to sum up this amazing man. There was in him a remarkable quality of simplicity and directness, varied sometimes by a strain of impishness. Someone said of his sense of humour compared with that of his friend Gregory Dix: 'Gregory could be waspish, but Austin was simply mischievous like a nice child.' What he could not stand was the kind of jargon and pomposity that goes with conferences. 'The Bishop of Woolwich' he said, 'has summoned me to a conference to write hymns for our generation. I excused myself.' Then there was the great lack of self-consciousness when faced with a problem. He went straight to the solution. Finding the vestry door at St Mary Magdalene locked he simply climbed the partition. This directness was part of the simplification of his thought in his later years. His brother-in-law, Arthur Newton, described how he would sit in silence and think for perhaps an hour neither moving nor writing. Then he would take up his pen and write, knowing what he wanted to say.

The important things have been said already, the constant willingness to be at the disposal of those who sought him (his shyness was a form of not forcing God on people), the care with which he answered all the letters he received with all the force of his mind, the titanic work in philosophy and scripture so often ignored or misrepresented by those who have not read it, the service of his college and university; his devotion to his daughter and the long days and nights of unremitting care for his wife which never distracted him from his duties, exhausted though he was; and behind all this and beneath, the prayers, the communions, the confessions, the preparation for the life of heaven which was for him the undoubted reality. There are still the sermons and the books; we can still catch the echoes of that beloved voice.

I would wish to make my own the felicitous words of Gordon Phillips at the end of his second Gresham Lecture:

'I regard him as one of the most remarkable men I have ever known. He combined so many excellences. He was a scholar, a wit, a saint, a philosopher, and a man of prayer. Few men have given more freely of their talents to the service of a Church. Yet in the life of his friends and of his pupils his influence will continue and others will perhaps turn to his books in times when the theological and intellectual climate will once again pay more attention to learning, spirituality and style than it does at the moment. When we read his letters we shall also find that there too is one in whom the lost art still survived. He was a hawk among sparrows and it was an honour and grace to have known him.'

Martyn Skinner went to his funeral. 'It was biting cold, a strong east wind, ice on the pavements, and in the quad in Keble a pipe had burst and formed a cascade of ice from the eaves to the ground on one wall. But I quoted to myself a sentence from one of Austin's books which has often been in my mind since, "to grow up is good, but to die is better – provided we die right".' He had surely done that.

# APPENDIX I

# A University Sermon

*

*(The Hulsean Sermon preached in Great St Mary's Church on Sunday, 14 November, 1948, by the Rev. A. M. Farrer, DD (Oxford), Chaplain and Fellow of Trinity College, Oxford)*

'We have the mind of Christ.' (1 Cor. 2.16)

The Word became flesh, and invisible God was made visible. Therefore the Christian faith is grounded in plain history. The conditions of this sermon allow the evidences of Christianity to be the preacher's subject, and it is of historical evidences that I propose to speak. I propose to speak of them more in general than in particular. As to the particular points of historical fact which together establish Christian origins, the students of positive theology sift them with learned care, and it is the especial pride and just glory of your theological faculty here, that it has devoted itself to the plain historical and positive method of inquiry. Suppose we desire to know what part of the Christian gospel came from the lips of Christ himself, and what part was supplied by the Spirit of Pentecost speaking in the Apostles; suppose we are concerned to establish the legal and political facts of our Redeemer's condemnation and crucifixion, or the supernatural fact of his resurrection: then we must submit to the rigours of long and exact historical study; there are no short cuts, and nothing which I could summarize here in half an hour would be of any solid use. But even in half an hour we can reflect profitably on the true nature of historical inquiry and of its particular bearing on the New Testament.

A man's philosophy of history increases in practical importance in proportion as his field of historical study is more obscure. If the field of study is straightforward and well documented – if, for example, the subject is mundane and intelligible, say the biography of a hard-headed politician; and if the period is recent and readily imaginable, say the reign of Queen Victoria; and if the evidences are sufficient, the official

232

papers, the private letters, the garrulous diaries, and the columns of *The Times*: under such conditions as these the capable historian will make a tolerable job of his undertaking, whatever his doctrine of historical method may be. And if we treat cases of this sort as typical, we shall be likely to conclude that the question of historical method is academic. It may amuse the wits of the philosophers, but it will not affect the practice of the historians.

But we need only choose different instances, and we shall form a different estimate. If we turn from the hard calculations of worldly statecraft to the delicately balanced psychology of religious exaltation; if we leave the English politician for the Jewish saint, and the comfortable familiarity of Victorian London for the twilight strangeness of a Galilean religious underworld, where lost sects and forgotten racial groups touched in the shadow of the synagogue; if we exchange official minutes and dated letters for scraps of sacred legend, and pages of liturgical recitation: faced with materials of this kind, a context of this kind, and questions of this kind, we shall soon be invoking whatever aid and guidance the theory of historic method can bestow.

If there is any historian to whom the theory of his art is of crucial importance, it is the New Testament historian, because his subject-matter is pre-eminently difficult. Yet we do not find that historical theologians have been forward to study the theory of history at a philosophical level. What we do find is that they have been the frequent victims of philosophical propaganda, and the fervent advocates of ready-made methodological recipes. If theologians are specially liable to such intellectual disorders, it will be the effect of the special difficulties inherent in their study. Theologians grasp at a method, as a drowning man grasps at a straw.

When I was a lad we were devoted to the method of documentary analysis; we divided our ancient books into an infinite number of distinct constituents; and the masterpiece of skill was to discover six sources, in a paragraph where others had detected only three. When I was a young man, we had thought of something else: we shifted our attention from the documents to the supposed underlying oral traditions, and these we subjected to examination by the somewhat fitful light of a general concept of folk-tradition and of its evolution. And now that I have finished growing up, I hear it said that there is a newer and shorter way with the evangelists, called the typological method; but I cannot find out clearly what it is supposed to be, nor who are the authors and protagonists of it.

The first principle of true historical method is to have no method at all, that is, no set and ready-made method. The subject-matter of history is human action, and human action is not, in the last account, studied by a method: it is the object of direct personal understanding. I say 'in the last account', because set methods offer us assistance in coming to grips with our objective; empirical psychology, for example, and speculative economics may have their parts to play. But ultimate historical reality is human action, and human action can in the end be understood by nothing but personal understanding. As we understand our friend by the direct and sympathetic interpretation of the intention which his words and acts express, so in the end we have got to understand the mind of the characters in our history, or we have understood nothing. From their expressive acts, however indirectly reported to us, we have got to seize *them*. There are, indeed, regions of history in which we get no further than generalization, we talk about fictions like 'nation' and 'policy-trend', and never reach the individual at all. But whichever those regions of historical study may be, the study of Christian origins is not among them. We do not want to know statistical averages, we want to know Christ.

The historian is not concerned with the living individuality of single figures taken one by one and in isolation. How simple his task would be if he were! History does not deal with a staccato series of Robinson Crusoes, each living out his life in a human vacuum; it deals with a pattern of lives interacting upon one another. The point at which the pattern touches us, its would-be historians, is in the existences of our writing authorities. As a student of Christian origins I do not touch Christ, though as a Christian who receives the sacraments, I may. As a student, I touch Paul, Mark, and John. When I have learnt to know them, I may hope to perceive what, in them, is reaction to Christ and to his saving acts; and so I may come to perceive what manner of Christ it is to whom they react.

I should here like to pause, and to express regret and indignation at a manner of interpreting the evangelists which neglects, and attempts to destroy, their living individuality.

234

That St Paul is a man, nobody doubts, nor that we have to understand him if we are to understand the Christ who stands behind him. But when we turn to St Mark, it is another matter: our oldest and best narrative authority is treated as individually negligible, a piecer together of traditions, a hack editor. We make haste to shoulder him out of the way, that we may lay our hands upon an impersonal and disjointed mass of tradition, which he is supposed to have had in his desk, or in his memory. We pull the Marcan mosaic to bits, and then it is amazing how free we find ourselves to reconstruct the ikon of Christ according to enlightened principles, whether it be scientific probability or transcendental neo-Calvinism that lies most near our hearts.

But you may say, it is no use pouring the vials of indignation here. For it happens to be a fact that whereas we have abundant data for reconstructing the personality of St Paul, for reconstructing St Mark's we have virtually none. True, but irrelevant. For we are not concerned to reconstruct St Mark as a missionary priest or a husband and father, or as anything save the author of a gospel. The only Mark we want is the Mark who became, for an unknown number of days and hours, the inspired act of meditating and writing this book. We want nothing but his mental life, and of his mental life no more than is enclosed between the first verse of his first chapter and the eighth of his sixteenth. If this is a whole, living, personal and continuous mental act, and I can touch it, then I can touch a vital and significant part of that web of life which made up the substance of Christian origins; and from it my thought can spread to other and connected parts of the web, and ultimately to the centre, which is Christ himself.

No efforts, then, can be too great to spend on the recovery of St Mark's mind, of a process of thought moving continuously through his book. If we cannot arrive at living by sympathy in his mental life, nothing can compensate us for our failure: and if we fail many times, it will still be better for us to try again, obstinately imputing our defeat to our own proved incomprehension, not to St Mark's supposed incoherence.

Our first historical task is to understand the men who give us the writings, and who, in the writings, give us themselves. But neither the men nor their writings can be understood in isolation. We cannot understand them unless we understand to

235

what they are reacting. And that means, above all, that we must understand Christ. Put in general, like that, what I have just said sounds commonplace enough. Of course the aim of our New Testament history is to understand Christ; who disputes it? But what I want to say is something far more alarming. What I want to say is, that according to the canons of a sound historical procedure, we cannot establish what happened, we cannot establish the bare historical facts, without a personal understanding of Christ.

It would seem so much more comforting – it has seemed to many so much more comforting – to proceed by separate stages. First we will determine what the evangelists think and mean. When we have done that, we will compare their accounts and check them by general probabilities and by our knowledge of the period, and so arrive at a decision of what were the facts of Christ's teaching and life. Having fixed the facts, we will take the third step, and advance to the interpretation of them. With humble diffidence we will conjecture what the mind of Christ may have been, if it expressed itself in words and actions such as these.

How comforting such a dividing-up of our work would be! We need not, in that case, imperil the historical facts by the terrible and thought-destroying task of understanding Christ, of moving in the mind which, according to our credal profession, made us and all the world, before it abased itself and stooped to pass the narrow door of Mary's womb. Into the abyss of that wisdom, into the heart of that devouring fire we need not plunge, until we have safely first established the historical facts. Vain evasion! Even if our faith permitted us to write a Christless history of Christ, the mere requirements of history-writing would not allow it. There is no establishing of the historic facts without an understanding of Christ.

We have not, to begin with, got the facts; we have only got second-hand reports of them. What we have to do is to find the causes which gave rise to these reports. How much was contributed by the devout theologizing of the evangelist, how much by the credulity of the eye-witness, how much by the real action of Christ? It is obvious that these three factors, the credulity of eye-witnesses, the theological formalizing of evangelists, the action of Christ, cannot be estimated in independence of one another. If we could safely reduce the other two

236

factors to zero, then we could confidently attribute the whole effect to the sole action of Christ, that is, we could simply believe the narratives about him as they stand. But we cannot confidently discount either the theologizing evangelist or the credulous witness. Nor yet can we allow just so much for credulity and theology, subtract that, and attribute the remainder to Christ's naked action. No rules, forms, or principles of historical procedure can see us through such a task, or enable us to estimate the contributions of credulity and theological stylization, independently of our estimate of what we can see Jesus of Nazareth to do.

Any example will suffice. Did Jesus ride into Jerusalem on an ass, with the circumstances of an arranged triumph? Well, Zechariah had prophesied that Sion's king should come to her riding on an ass. This being so, it is very possible that theological stylization has exaggerated the chance ride of a footsore man into a messianic triumph, and that credulity has added the miraculous provision of a mount, the vision which saw an ass tethered on the further side of the hill, and the command which sent disciples to fetch it. On the other hand, such preternatural vision is well evidenced in the lives of spiritual men; and Christ may have deliberately wished to fulfil Zechariah's oracle. But did he? Can we see him do it? Is it a proper part of his life and action; especially of his final invasion of Jerusalem? Only as we answer this question, shall we decide whether he sent for the ass and headed the triumph, or not.

There is no history of the things concerning Jesus (to use scriptural phrase) without an understanding of Jesus, any more than with any other biographical passage – it cannot be written without the understanding of the principal person concerned. Without understanding Jesus – but Jesus, what was Jesus? The secularist historians think they know, but their hypotheses produce no agreement, even among themselves, but wildly various travesties of what seems historical probability to Christians. But we – how can we understand, for as the apostle says in words borrowed from the prophet, 'Who has known the mind of the Lord, that he might be of his counsel?' Understanding goes by sympathy: history is possible, because it studies men, and the historian is a man himself. But Christ is not simply man, he is God-as-man, and mere natural human sympathy will not avail to know the mind of the Lord. If we lay

237

down the dogma that gospel history is just like any other history, we are committing ourselves to the proposition that Christ is just like any other man, or anyhow that his humanity is cut off from his deity and holds no communion with it. 'Who hath known the mind of the Lord,' says St Paul, 'that he might be of his counsel?' 'But, as for us,' he continues, 'we have the mind of Christ'; and this, as he shows plainly in the context, is no natural sympathy with a human figure in his mere humanity but a supernatural gift, by which we penetrate the abyss of wisdom and move with the mind that moves the world.

The New Testament writers are perfectly clear, and perfectly realistic about this. The natural mind could not understand Jesus in his historical existence, not even the natural mind of his immediate companions. Nothing but the supernatural overflow of the mind of Jesus into them created that affinity whereby they could begin to understand him. Only God can understand God, even when God is incarnate. But God is in us by the Holy Ghost, and therefore we can know incarnate God. This is as true of us in our historical study, as it is of us at our prayers. We cannot know Christ in the history about him except by the Holy Ghost. The historical understanding of Christ began in St Peter and the other recipients of the Pentecostal Gift. It continued in those who received both the historical testimony of St Peter's lips, and the gift of the Holy Ghost through the benediction of St Peter's hands. Later generations have received the historical testimony from the Church, the Church using the written scriptures as her norm of teaching; they have also received through the Church the Holy Ghost.

In one sense, then, Gospel history is just history, and its procedure is the same as any history's. It is the interpretation by sympathetic understanding of a web of interacting minds; with some of which, the evangelists, we are in immediate contact with others, Christ and the Twelve, Caiaphas and Pilate, in a contact not in the same way immediate. So far Gospel history is like any other history. It is different, because one of the minds, Christ's, is not merely a natural mind, and can only be understood, therefore, by a supernatural gift. There is, therefore, no neutral history of Christ common to unbelievers and believers. We either accept, or do not accept, the witness of the Holy Ghost. We understand the Christ who proclaimed himself the Son of God, because we understand, though but partly what it is for Christ to be the Son of God. And we understand what it is for Christ to be the Son of God, because we perceive ourselves to be, in him, partakers of divinity. The God incarnate is not to us an unintelligible enigma, because our existence in Grace hangs upon the fringes of his incarnation. We know, on our knees, and in the depth of our heart, what Christ is, by knowing what he has made us: and we know that he has made us, by knowing what he is.

# APPENDIX II

## *(i) Hymnus de Sancto Edmundo*
### (Composed by Austin Farrer at the request of Dr A. B. Emden)

\*

*Haec est dies quam nobili*
*Christus sacravit gaudio,*
*Edmunde, te fortissimum*
*Donans corona militum.*

*Tu sorte natus diviti*
*Pauper bearis spiritu.*
*Tu supplicanti porrigis*
*Dextram sinistra nescia.*

*Tu parvulos contemnere*
*Caves amore sedulo*
*Quibus ministrans frigidae*
*Potum minister fis Deo.*

*Doctor sapis caelestia*
*Sanctae columbae numine:*
*Praesul gubernas Israel*
*Saccum tegente purpura.*

*Pacem tyranno dicere*
*Pax nulla cum sit abnuis:*
*Ad Sempiternum cor levans*
*Mali sagittas neglegis.*

*Das exsul ossa Franciae,*
*Aulam paras Oxoniae!*
*Quae te patrono gaudeat*
*Virtute florens perpeti.*

*Praestet Pater piissimus*
*Patrique compar Unicus*
*Cum Spiritu Paraclito*
*Regnans in omne saeculum.*

## *(ii) Wenceslaus*

(Recently discovered Goliardic verses, perhaps the originals of a
well-known ditty. Supplied by Mr Steven Willinck.)

\*

*Wenceslaus prospicit Stephani in festo:*
*Firma plana plurima nix ubique praesto*
*Saeviente frigore, splendet luna tamen:*
*Lignum legit rusticus, hiemis solamen.*

*Veni puer, adsta mi; si quid noris, ede*
*Quis sit ille rusticus quave fixus sede.*
*Silvae, rex, in finibus ad Agnetis fontem*
*Tribus abhinc milibus tangit casa montem.*

*Vinum fer cum carnibus, necnon pinum sectam:*
*Comedi videbimus coenam ibi vectam.*
*Prodiere dominus simul et minister*
*Ululat dum Boreas et gelatur Ister.*

*Here, nox tenebricat, ventus aggravatur,*
*Mire tristor, amplius progredi non datur.*
*Quin meis vestigiis insta, puer bone.*
*Sanguis quo concreverit minus Aquilone.*

*Passibus dominicis puer insistebat*
*Sanctus quam calcaverat ipsa nix calebat!*
*Ergo scite, creduli, quibus venter satur,*
*Qui beavit inopes invicem beatur.*

# APPENDIX III

# *Examples of Farrer's Correspondence*

\*

These two letters are to the Reverend R. J. Vaughan of Harrow. He had been an enthusiastic pupil of Austin's at St Edmund Hall and I publish them for their intrinsic theological interest and also to illustrate the care and kindness with which he answered the questions or discussed the work of those who wrote to him, even when he was most busy and most tired. Mr Vaughan had sent him an article he had written for the *Modern Churchman* on the virgin birth, in which he suggested that Mary and Joseph came together in an ecstasy, being inspired by the Holy Ghost. The conception was in the physical way normal, but the paradigm is the transfiguration and the guiding idea the supernaturalization of the natural. To this Austin wrote twice from Keble, and at one of the busiest times of his life.

You have made the transfiguration your paradigm for the formula, 'Supernaturalization of the natural'. And you propose a total Christology along these lines. And so you think that Joseph and Mary might have come together in a sort of ecstasy which made their act wholly passive to the Holy Ghost. It is not quite so clear how the formula can apply to the resurrection, where there is no basis of nature to supernaturalize. In general I think that supernaturalization will take us a long way and it has been remarked that St John appears to apply the transfiguration to the whole of the incarnate Life. I would suggest for further reflection the question, 'What is the relation between ecstasy and vision on the one side, and basic supernaturalization?' The virtues of the saints may be all the more supernatural for not being ecstatic or visionary.

I should say that you have been a bit casual over Isaiah 7.14. If, as seems very arguable, the traditions of virginal conception go back to semitic origins, why should anyone suppose that Isaiah 7.14 prescribed a belief in virginal conception. If the Christians (as the Jews complained) read it into the text, how can they have read it out of the text? They must have been predisposed to belief in it: though of course the predisposing influence may have been something other than a true historical memory of the fact.

I agree with you (and with Emil Brunner) that an orthodox doctrine of the Incarnate Person can be held apart from belief in the virginal conception. But I think that if I decided to go with Brunner I should content myself with the supernaturalization of Christ's humanity and should not feel that it added anything to have his parents mate in ecstasy.

I found your paper truly interesting.

[This first letter (dated 1 December 1966) was followed by one on 10 February (1967?)]

It has always seemed to me that the incarnation could have been believed in a perfectly orthodox sense if Christ had been born (or conceived, rather) by common process of nature. So, for example, Emil Brunner, writes in that very orthodox book, *The Mediator*. And, perhaps we should say that if the incarnation had taken place in our days, it would have been so, if indeed God accommodates his ways to our understandings in matters indifferent. But the mind of that age was otherwise and I doubt if the faith of the incarnation could have been taught to the world except through the physical miracle. What you say about the theophanic character of Christianity I take to be profoundly true throughout. I say that there would be an end of complaint about the aimlessness of preaching if every preacher knew that every sermon should be *theophanic*.

I found great pleasure in your generosity of attitude to St Luke in doing your best for the true values (as you see them) of his narrative. But I will make a couple of observations. First I think you overstate the influence of Isaiah 7.14 on the sub-apostolic mind. Isaiah or no Isaiah, Israel didn't expect a virginally-conceived messiah, any more than a messiah who would undergo martyrdom on the way to glory. The faith of the Church springing out of events found support and expression in the text of the Old Testament; second, however it was later, there is no evidence that either St Matthew or St Luke attached any importance to the virginal purity of Mary (as exempt from the experience of natural lust). So far from seeing Christ's birth as pure, St Matthew saw it as scandalous, putting in for parallel

243

all the scandalous mothers in the genealogy, while St Luke, with a hint of scandal about Mary's initial distress of mind, concentrates on the sheer supernaturality of cause. John Baptist's conception brings back the miracle of Isaac's. Christ's goes further. Both evangelists, and St Matthew especially, see it as a *supreme manifestation of free election* (the promise or blessing does not follow legitimacy of descent). God who had made so many irregular grafts into the chosen stock, now plants in a slip without a drop of David's blood – and this is the Son of David.

I am most happy to share with you the substance of faith.

# Notes to the Text

*

## 2 The Hidden Years: St Paul's School 1917–23

1. The Eighth Form at St Paul's corresponds to the Sixth Form at other schools.
2. A letter from Bishop C. K. Sansbury.
3. No doubt a parody of Milton's devils debating foreknowledge and predestination.

## 3 Balliol College 1923–7

1. Dorothy L. Sayers, *Murder Must Advertise*. Gollancz 1971.
2. Numbers in brackets after extracts from letters refer to the Index of Letters Quoted on p. 259.
3. In 1924 Aldous Huxley's only published works were *Limbo*, *Crome Yellow* and *Antic Hay*.
4. T. E. Bleiben, later Vicar of Headington and singing chaplain of New College.
5. Classical tutor at Balliol.
6. H. M. Burge.
7. Reprinted in *The End of Man*, pp. 48–51.
8. Professor J. N. Findlay, Professor of Metaphysics at Yale, Gifford Lecturer 1964–6.
9. The first use of this key word that I can find in his writings.
10. *The Glass of Vision*, pp. 7–8.
11. The examination for the Jenkyns Exhibition.
12. A. F. Loisy (1857–1940), French modernist biblical scholar.
13. In the *Socratic Digest*, no. 3, 1945, in an article 'Can Myth Be Fact?', Farrer takes roughly Hodges' position.
14. Later Bishop B. C. Butler.
15. A Vergilian echo.
16. Vergil on Dido's love for Aeneas.
17. Banishment to an island – a punishment used by Roman emperors such as Tiberius.

## 4 Balliol and Cuddesdon 1927–8

1. Kirby is almost certainly the 'Philip' mentioned in the sermon

'Fences and Friends', reprinted in *The End of Man*. He took his own life in 1932, to Farrer's great distress.

2. Lord Ramsey once said: 'I had just read the theology tripos at Cambridge when we met and Austin had not yet begun the theology school, so for quite three weeks I was ahead of him.'

3. K. Lake and F. J. Foakes Jackson (eds.), *The Beginnings of Christianity*. Macmillan 1938.

4. His tutor for the theology school was Dr K. E. Kirk, then a Fellow of Trinity.

5. Hugh Lister, a great friend (see chapter 6).

6. Butler had earlier urged Farrer to seek holy orders.

7. F. R. Barry, later Bishop of Southwell.

8. A. D. Lindsay, the Master of Balliol.

9. Possibly the Faculty of Theology, together with all the other clerics who congregate in Oxford.

10. Canon F. Wolde (see chapter 5).

11. His youngest sister, Eleanor.

12. Penny-dropping: the collection.


## 5   *Borealia Regna: Dewsbury 1928–31*

1. Spinning mules

2. Threads to the line.

3. E. G. Selwyn (ed.), *Essays Catholic and Critical*. SPCK 1926.

4. An inebriate he had come across in an early visit.

5. T. R. Glover, public orator at Cambridge and author of *The Jesus of History*, a monument of Liberal Protestantism.

6. Later, in *Love Almighty and Ills Unlimited*, Farrer developed this point, in denying that the Devil is the cause of evil.


## 6   *St Edmund Hall 1931–5*

1. See Appendix II, p. 240.

2. R. G. Collingwood, Fellow of Pembroke College, later Waynflete Professor of Metaphysical Philosophy.

3. F. R. Barry, at that time Vicar of St Mary's.

4. Followers of Frank Buchman, later known as Moral Rearmament.

5. Hugh Lister is described in volume 2 of Canon Roger Lloyd's *The Church of England in the Twentieth Century* (pp. 222–5). There is also an appreciation from Farrer's own pen in *The Brink of Mystery*.

6. Lady Margaret Professor of Divinity and Canon of Christ Church.

7. Paul's sermon to the Athenians in Acts 17.

## 7 Trinity College 1935–45

1. Professor Sir Cyril Hinshelwood – probably the only chemist to be also President of the Classical Association and President of the Royal Society.
2. Sir Ronald Syme OM, the distinguished historian, later Camden Professor of Ancient History.
3. Anthony Flew, *God and Philosophy*, Hutchinson 1966.

## 8 Trinity College 1945–60

1. Though there were of course notable exceptions, such as I. M. Crombie at Wadham, J. R. Lucas at Merton, Basil Mitchell at Keble, I. T. Ramsey at Oriel – not to mention Farrer himself and his friend E. L. Mascall at Christ Church.
2. This trait is even more evident in his books: in the text he argues his points with other writers ancient and modern, identifiable but unnamed because he spurned footnote references.
3. Dr Michael Goulder (see chapter 11).
4. See below, p. 145.
5. The substance of this lecture has been published posthumously in *Interpretation and Belief*.
6. The group which produced the volume of essays *Faith and Logic*, edited by Basil Mitchell and published by Allen and Unwin in 1957.
7. See Appendix I, p. 232.
8. 'The Ministry in the New Testament' (1946). His mature position on Anglicanism can be found in the sermon, 'On Being an Anglican', in *The End of Man*.
9. Father Algy Robertson SSF, described by Farrer as 'a Franciscan in a brown frock with spectacles on the end of his nose, like a fairytale dwarf'.
10. See below, pp. 144–5.
11. *A Study in St Mark*.
12. The Gifford Lectures given in the University of Edinburgh 1957.
13. Later Dean of Christ Church.
14. Then student of Christ Church.
15. Eric Abbott.

## 9 Keble College 1960–8

1. Published in *A Celebration of Faith* and in *The Brink of Mystery*.
2. Cicero's indignant address to Catiline. Here it means, how much longer do we endure certain aspects of modern theology?
3. Reprinted in *Reflective Faith*.

# Notes to the Text

4. *Love Almighty and Ills Unlimited.*
5. Published as *The Freedom of the Will.*

## 10 Farrer the Philosopher

1. Published as *The Glass of Vision.*
2. See Appendix I.
3. Letter to the author.
4. *Finite and Infinite,* p. 6.
5. Expanded and published as *Faith and Speculation.*
6. cf. F. Michael McLain, 'Austin Farrer's Revision of the Cosmological Argument' (*The Downside Review,* July 1970).
7. *Faith and Speculation,* p. 112.
8. *Faith and Speculation,* p. 116.
9. *Faith and Speculation,* ch. 7.
10. ibid., ch. 9.
11. ibid., ch. 11.
12. ibid., ch. 9.
13. ibid., ch. 10.
14. cf. 'The Prior Actuality of God' (a lecture given at Louisiana State University), reprinted in *Reflective Faith.*
15. *Faith and Speculation,* ch. 11. For a valuable review of Farrer's thought see John Glasse, 'On Doing Theology Metaphysically: Austin Farrer' (*Harvard Theological Review,* October 1966).
16. *Finite and Infinite,* p. 299.
17. *A Science of God?,* p. 127
18. Published as *The Glass of Vision.*
19. Later Ely Professor of Divinity at Cambridge.
20. Reprinted in *Reflective Faith.*
21. From an unpublished lecture.

## 11 Farrer the Biblical Scholar

1. *Interpretation and Belief,* pp. 14–22.
2. See Appendix I for Farrer's own account of his approach to the Gospels – his Hulsean Sermon, 1948.
3. M. Goulder, *Midrash and Lection in Matthew,* SPCK 1974.
4. B. W. Bacon, *Studies in Matthew,* London 1930.
5. *A Rebirth of Images,* p. 34.
6. *A Rebirth of Images,* p. 22.

## 12 The Doctor of Divinity

1. cf. p. 190.

2. *Saving Belief*, p. 80.
3. ibid., pp. 98–107.
4. ibid., p. 99.
5. ibid., pp. 112–13.
6. Published by Allen and Unwin in 1938.

## 13 Conclusion

1. In this chapter I am much indebted to the unpublished Gresham Lectures of Gordon Phillips.
2. 'An English Appreciation', in *Kerygma and Myth*, ed. H. W. Bartsch. SPCK 1953.

# Chronological List of Published Writings by Austin Farrer 1933–76

\*

## 1933

'A Return to New Testament Christological Categories', *Theology*, vol. 26, pp. 304–18.

Review of *The Life of Jesus* by Maurice Goguel, in *Theology*, pp. 229–30.

## 1936

Review of *The Doctrine of the Word of God* and *God in Action* by Karl Barth, in *Theology*, vols. 32–3, pp. 370–3 (the former is vol. i, part 1 of the 2nd edn of *Prolegomena to Church Dogmatics*).

Review of *God Transcendent* by Karl Heim, in *Church Quarterly Review*, vol. 122, pp. 334–7.

## 1937

'Eucharist and Church in the New Testament', *The Parish Communion*, ed. A. G. Hebert, SPCK, pp. 75–94.

Review of *Der christliche Glaube und die altheidnische Welt* (2 vols.) by K. Prümm, in *Journal of Theological Studies*, vol. 38, pp. 95–7.

Review of *Religion and Reality: An Essay in the Christian Co-ordination of Contraries* by Melville Chaning-Pearce, in *Church Quarterly Review*, vols, 123–4, pp. 328–30.

## 1938

'The Christian Doctrine of Man', in *The Christian Understanding of Man*, ed. T. E. Jessop, vol. ii, Oxford Conference Series, Allen & Unwin, pp. 181–213; reprinted in *Interpretation and Belief* (1976).

Review of *Die Kirche und die Schöpfung* by Eugen Gerstenmaier, in *Church Quarterly Review*, vols. 125–6, pp. 345–6.

## 1939

'"The Blood is the Life" and the Blood of Christ in the New Testament',

*Oxford Society of Historical Theology*, vol. 1933–42/43, pp. 60–7. (An abstract of a paper read 23 February 1939 on Eucharistic theology).

'The Theology of Morals', *Theology*, vol. 38, pp. 332–41; reprinted in *Interpretation and Belief* (1976).

Review of *Philosophie de la Religion* by Paul Ortegat, in *Journal of Theological Studies*, vol. 40, pp. 100–1.

## 1940

Review of *The Problem of the Future Life* by C. J. Shebbeare, in *Journal of Theological Studies*, vol. 41, pp. 343–4.

Review of *St Paul and the Church of the Gentiles* by W. L. Knox, in *Church Quarterly Review*, vol. 129, pp. 339–41.

## 1941

Review of *The Nature of the World; An Essay in Phenomenalist Metaphysics* by W. T. Stace, in *Journal of Theological Studies*, vol. 42, pp. 108–10.

Review of *The Realm of Spirit* by George Santayana, in *Theology*, vol. 42, pp. 123–5.

## 1942

Review of *The Philosophy of David Hume* by Norman Kemp Smith, in *Journal of Theological Studies*, vol. 43, pp. 229–32.

Review of *The Revelation of St John* by M. Kiddle (assisted by M. K. Ross), in *Journal of Theological Studies*, vol. 43, pp. 227–9.

## 1943

*Finite and Infinite*, Dacre Press; 2nd edn, with revised Preface, 1959 (USA: Macmillan and Humanities, 1966).

'How was Jesus Divine?', *Socratic Digest*, no. 1, pp. 25–5.

## 1944

'Can we know that God Exists?' (editor's summary of a discussion by the Rev. A. M. Farrer and Mr MacNabb), *Socratic Digest*, no. 2, pp. 12, 13.

## 1945

'Can Myth be Fact?', *Socratic Digest*, no. 3, pp. 36–44; reprinted in *Interpretation and Belief* (1976).

## 1946

'The Ministry in the New Testament', *The Apostolic Ministry*, ed. K. E. Kirk (republished 1957 with a 'New Foreword' by A. Farrer), Hodder & Stoughton, pp. 113–82.

'Epigrams' (two poems), *Theology*, vol. 49, p. 238.

Review of *Christ in the Gospels* by A. E. J. Rawlinson, in *Journal of Theological Studies*, vol. 47, pp. 77–8.

## 1947

*Catholicity: A study in the conflict of Christian traditions in the West*, Dacre Press. (A report presented to the Archbishop of Canterbury by a committee of Anglicans of which Farrer was a member.)

'The Extension of St Thomas's Doctrine of Analogy to Modern Philosophical Problems', *Downside Review*, vol. 65, pp. 21–32; reprinted as 'Knowledge by Analogy', in *Reflective Faith* (1972), pp. 69–81.

'On Credulity', *Illuminatio*, vol. 1, no. 3, pp. 3–9; reprinted in *Interpretation and Belief* (1976).

'Thought as the Basis of History', (a broadcast talk on R. G. Collingwood). *The Listener*, vol. 37 (20 March), pp. 424–5.

'Does God Exist?', *Socratic Digest*, no. 4, pp. 27–34; reprinted in *Reflective Faith* (1976).

Review of *The Authority of the Biblical Revelation* by H. Cunliffe-Jones and *The Old Testament in the New Testament* by R. V. G. Tasker, in *Theology*, pp. 351–2.

## 1948

*The Glass of Vision* (Bampton Lectures), Dacre Press.

## 1949

*A Rebirth of Images: The Making of St John's Apocalypse*, Dacre Press (USA: Beacon Press, 1963, with a new Preface by Kenneth Burke; rebound in hardcover by Smith, 1964).

Review of *The Glory of God and the Transfiguration of Christ* by A. M. Ramsey, in *Christendom*, pp. 134–5.

## 1950

Review of *Abelard's Christian Theology* by J. Ramsay McCallum, in *Journal of Theological Studies*, new series, vol. 1, p. 221.

## Farrer's Published Writings

### 1951

'A Midwinter Dream', *University: A Journal of Enquiry*, vol. 1, pp. 86–90 (reprinted as 'A Theologian's Point of View', *The Socratic*, no. 5, 1952, pp. 35–8); abridged version reprinted as 'Theology and Philosophy', in *Reflective Faith* (1972), pp. 1–4.

*A Study in St Mark*, Dacre Press.

'Editor's Introduction', *Theodicy: Essays on the Goodness of God, the Freedom of Man, and the Origin of Evil* by G. W. Leibniz, ed. A. M. Farrer, tr. E. M. Huggard, Routledge and Kegan Paul, pp. 7–47 (excerpt reprinted as 'The Physical Theology of Leibniz', in *Reflective Faith* (1972), pp. 91–113).

'Messianic Prophecy' (a sermon preached at Oxford, Hilary Term, 1951), *Theology*, vol. 54, pp. 335–42.

### 1952

*The Crown of the Year* (weekly paragraphs for the Holy Sacrament), Dacre Press (USA: Morehouse-Barlow, 1953).

'A Liturgical Theory about St Mark's Gospel' (a review of *The Primitive Christian Calendar*, vol. 1, Introduction and text by Philip Carrington, Archbishop of Quebec), *Church Quarterly Review*, vol. 153, pp. 501–8.

Review of *Holy Communion and Holy Spirit* by J. E. L. Oulton, in *Theology*, vol. 55, pp. 107–8.

Review of *The Originality of St Matthew* by B. C. Butler, in *Journal of Theological Studies*, new series, vol. 3, pp. 102–6.

### 1953

'An English Appreciation', in *Kerygma and Myth: A Theological debate*, ed. H. W Bartsch and tr. R. H. Fuller, SPCK, pp. 212–23 (paperback, 1972).

Loaves and Thousands', *Journal of Theological Studies*, new series, vol. 4, pp. 1–14.

The Trinity in Whom We Live', *Theology*, vol. 56, pp. 322–7. (Originally a broadcast talk, 'Meditation for Trinity Sunday', 8 June 1952); reprinted in *Lord I Believe* as chapter 2.

### 1954

St Matthew and St Mark (Edward Cadbury Lectures, 1953–4) Dacre Press; 2nd edn, 1966 (USA: Macmillan).

### 1955

Absolute', *Twentieth Century Encyclopedia of Religious Knowledge*, ed.

Lefferts A. Loetscher, vol. 1, Baker Book House, Grand Rapids, p. 3.
'Analogy', ibid., pp. 38–40; reprinted as 'The Concept of Analogy', in *Reflective Faith* (1972), pp. 64–8.
'Being', ibid., pp. 120–1.
'On Dispensing with Q', in *Studies in the Gospels*, ed. D. E. Nineham, Blackwell, pp. 55–88.
'The Queen of Sciences', *Twentieth Century*, vol. 157, pp. 489–94.

## 1956

'An Examination of Mark 13.10', a reply to G. D. Kilpatrick, *Journal of Theological Studies*, new series, vol. 7, pp. 75–9.
'The Dies Irae: A New Translation', *Theology*, vol. 59, pp. 155–7 (published separately in card-form by SPCK, no. 3218, 1957).
'How Do We Know We Have Found Him?' (one in a course of sermons on 'Evangelism in the Church', preached in the chapel of Pusey House, Oxford), in *Christ and the Christian*, Mowbray, pp. 21–7; reprinted as 'Assurance' in *Said or Sung*, 1960, pp. 83–8.
'Important Hypotheses Reconsidered; viii: Typology', *Expository Times*, vol. 67, pp. 228–31.
*A Short Bible*, ed. with general introduction, Fontana, pp. 5–15 (published in the USA as *Core of the Bible*, Harper, 1957).

## 1957

'The Everyday Use of the Bible' (one in a course of sermons preached in the chapel of Pusey House, Oxford), in *The Bible and the Christian*, Mowbray, pp. 55–60; reprinted as 'The Doctor of Divinity', in *Said or Sung*, pp. 147–52.
'New Foreword', *The Apostolic Ministry* (republished from 1946), pp. v–xviii.
*The New Testament*, ed. with a general introduction and note to each book, Collins, pp. 7–19.
'Revelation', in *Faith and Logic*, ed. B. G. Mitchell, Allen & Unwin, pp 84–107.
'A Starting Point for the Philosophical Examination of Theologica Belief', in *Faith and Logic*, ed. B. G. Mitchell, Allen & Unwin, pp 9–30; (reprinted as 'A Moral Argument for the Existence of God', ir *Reflective Faith* (1972), pp. 114–33.

## 1958

*The Freedom of the Will* (Gifford Lectures, 1957), A. and C. Black; 2n edn, 1963 (USA: Scribners, 1960; Greenwood Press, 1982).
*Lord I Believe: Suggestions for Turning the Creed into Prayer*, Faith Press

2nd edn, revised and enlarged, reissued by SPCK in paperback, 1962 (USA: Morehouse-Barlow, 1959; Seabury, 1962).

## 1959

Introduction to *The Easter Enigma: An Essay on the Resurrection with Special Reference to the Data of Psychical Research* by Michael C. Perry, Faber & Faber, pp. 11–16.

'On Looking Below the Surface' (a Presidential Address, 22 October 1959, replying to Miss Helen Gardner's Riddell Lectures in *The Business of Criticism*, OUP, 1959), *Oxford Society of Historical Theology*, vol. 1959–60, pp. 3–18; reprinted in *Interpretation and Belief* (1976).

'Predestination' (one in a course of sermons preached in the chapel of Pusey House, Oxford), *Christianity According to St Paul*, Mowbray, pp. 37–44; reprinted in *The Brink of Mystery* (1976).

## 1960

'In the Conscience of Man' (one in a course of sermons on 'Signs of God' preached in the chapel of Pusey House, Oxford), *God and the Universe*, Mowbray, pp. 30–7; reprinted in *The Brink of Mystery* (1976).

*Said or Sung* (an arrangement of homily and verse), Faith Press (published in the USA as *A Faith of Our Own*, with a preface by C. S. Lewis, World Publishing Company, 1960).

## 1961

'The Gate of Heaven' (a pamphlet–sermon preached at the patronal festival of St Edward's House, Westminster); reprinted in *The Brink of Mystery* (1976).

*Love Almighty and Ills Unlimited* (Nathaniel Taylor Lectures, 1961), Doubleday, New York (published in England by Collins, 1962; Fontana, 1966).

'Messianic Prophecy and Preparation for Christ', *The Communication of the Gospel in New Testament Times*, Theological Collections, 2, SPCK, pp. 1–9. (Originally a sermon given at Oxford, 1958.)

## 1962

'Continence', in *Lenten Counsellors: A Catena of Lent Sermons*, Mowbray, pp. 83–90 (published in the USA by Morehouse-Barlow as *These Forty Days: Lenten Counsels by Twenty-one Anglicans*). reprinted in *The Brink of Mystery* (1976).

'The Descent into Hell and the Ascent into Life' (one in a course of

sermons preached in the chapel of Pusey House, Oxford), The
Gospel of the Resurrection, Mowbray, pp. 13–18; reprinted as
'Gates to the City', in *A Celebration of Faith*, Hodder & Stoughton, pp.
95–9).

## 1963

*Bible Sermons* by C. F. Evans and A. M. Farrer (a course of sermons
preached in the chapel of Pusey House, Oxford, to which each
contributed four sermons), Mowbray, pp. 32–57; reprinted in *The
Brink of Mystery* (1976).
'Inspiration: Poetical and Divine', in *Promise and Fulfilment*, ed. F. F.
Bruce, T. & T. Clark, pp. 91–105; reprinted in *Interpretation and
Belief* (1976).
'Mary, Scripture, and Tradition', *The Blessed Virgin Mary: Essays by
Anglican Writers*, eds. E. L. Mascall and H. S Box, Darton Longman &
Todd, pp. 27–52; reprinted in *Interpretation and Belief* (1976).
'Objections to Christianity' (a poem), *Theology*, vol. 66, pp. 317–18.
An untitled sermon on Psalm 26.11–12 at St Margaret's, East
Grinstead, on St Margaret's Day, 1962, *St Margaret's Half-Yearly
Chronicle*, vol. xvi, pp. 2–6; reprinted in *The Brink of Mystery*
(1976).

## 1964

'The Datum in Divine Revelation', (abstract of a paper read on 19
November 1964; related to chapter 6 of *Faith and Speculation*),
*Oxford Society of Historical Theology*, vol. 1964–6, pp. 10–11.
Matriculation Sermon in the Chapel of the Good Shepherd (Friday, 30
October at Evensong), *The Bulletin* (of the General Theological
Seminary, New York), pp. 15–17.
*The Revelation of St John the Divine: Commentary on the English Text*,
OUP.
Review of *Models and Mystery* by Ian T. Ramsey, in *Journal of
Theological Studies*, new series, vol. 15, pp. 489–90.
*Saving Belief*, Hodder & Stoughton; paperback edn 1967 (USA:
Morehouse-Barlow, 1965).

## 1965

*The Triple Victory* (Christ's temptations according to St Matthew),
Faith Press (paperback) (USA: Morehouse-Barlow).

## 1966

'The Christian Apologist', *Light on C. S. Lewis*, ed. J. Gibb, Harcourt
Brace and World, New York, pp. 23–43.
*A Science of God?*, G. Bles, (published in the USA as *God Is Not Dead*,
Morehouse-Barlow, 1966).

Reply to 'Review Discussion of "A Science of God?"' by Dorothy
Emmet, Ted Bastin, Margaret Masterman, *Theoria to Theory*, vol. 1,
pp. 55–75.
Review of *Philosophie du fait chrétien* by Henk Van Luijk, in *Journal of
Theological Studies*, new series, vol. 17, p. 553.
Review of *St Anselm's Proslogion* by M. J. Charlesworth, in *Journal of
Theological Studies*, new series, vol. 17, p. 502.

## 1967

*Faith and Speculation* (Deems Lectures, 1964), A. and C. Black
(paperback).

## 1968

'The Eucharist in 1 Corinthians', *Eucharistic Theology Then and Now*,
Theological Collections 9, SPCK, pp. 15–33.
'Infallibility and Historical Revelation', *Infallibility in the Church: An
Anglican-Catholic Dialogue*, Darton Longman & Todd, pp. 9–23;
reprinted in *Interpretation and Belief* (1976).
Review of *The Bounds of Sense: An Essay on Kant's Critique of Pure
Reason* by P. F. Strawson, in *Journal of Theological Studies*, new series,
vol. 19, pp. 420–1.

## 1969

Review of *The Cambridge History of Latin, Greek and Early Mediaeval
Philosophy*, ed. A. H. Armstrong, in *Religious Studies*, vols. 3–4, pp.
287–8.

## 1970

*A Celebration of Faith*, ed. L. Houlden, Hodder & Stoughton; paperback
edn, 1972.

## 1972

*Reflective Faith: Essays in Philosophical Theology*, ed. Charles C. Conti,
SPCK.

## 1973

'Free Will in Theology', *Dictionary of the History of Ideas*, Scribner's,
New York; reprinted in *Interpretation and Belief* (1976).
*The End of Man*, SPCK.

## 1976

*Interpretation and Belief*, ed. Charles C. Conti, SPCK.
*The Brink of Mystery*, ed. Charles C. Conti, SPCK.

# Index of Letters Quoted

*

The letters begin with chapter 3 when Farrer went up to Balliol. Wherever possible the date of the letter is given, but some undated letters have been included because of the illumination they throw on Farrer's ideas. Where the correspondence is undated, it can sometimes be dated by context.

I am most grateful to those who allowed me to use their letters and to those whose letters, though not directly quoted, I have plundered.

# Index of Letters Quoted

# Index of Letters Quoted

# General Index

*

# General Index